Men
D0452874
262.142

Men Women and God

edited by Kathy Keay

Marshall Pickering

Marshall Morgan and Scott
Marshall Pickering
3 Beggarwood Lane, Basingstoke, Hants RG23 7LP, UK

Copyright © 1987 Kathy Keay
First published in 1987 by Marshall Morgan and Scott
Publications Ltd
Part of the Marshall Pickering Holdings Group
A subsidiary of the Zondervan Corporation

All rights reserved. No part of this publication may be reproduced, stored in a retrieval system, or transmitted, in any form or by any means, electronic, mechanical, photocopying, recording or otherwise, without the prior permission in writing, of the publisher

ISBN 0-551-01501-2 20015350

Text set in Linotron Ehrhardt by Input Typesetting Ltd., London
SW19 8DR
Printed in Great Britain by The Guernsey Press Co. Ltd.,
Guernsey, Channel Islands

Contents

Part III: Is Biology Destiny?

Preface

On 28th September 1985, some 400 people gathered at Kensington Temple in London to listen to 'the feminist case against God', and to examine ways in which feminist issues affect our lives at home, in church and in the world in which we live. Under the title *Men Women and God*, the day's events were planned by a group of women from different denominational backgrounds, and sponsored by the Evangelical Alliance and the London Institute for Contemporary Christianity.

The Revd John Stott, then Director of the London Institute, stressed the need to understand contemporary issues like feminism from a biblical perspective. 'We must engage in a double listening,' he said, 'both to the voice of feminists and to the voice of God.' This double listening remains at the heart of Men Women and God, which is now a charitable trust based in London, and run corporately by a group building upon the original aims of the conference.

The contents of this book include material which formed the basis of the conference addresses and workshops. Other chapters have since been added, in the light of growing interest and commitment to the issues over the last two years.

Although the book has been compiled under the auspices of Men Women and God, not all the authors are formally associated with the MWG Trust. There is therefore material in the book which does not necessarily express MWG's view on the subject, but which we believe is an important emphasis which needs to be heard.

Evangelicals have always rightly focused on the liberating gospel of Jesus as the central aspect of the Christian faith.

Men Women and God is concerned within this tradition to free men as well as women, helping to liberate us all from limitations which Church and society wrongly impose upon us because of our sex. Though evangelicals were often among the leading supporters of earlier forms of feminism and during the evangelical revivals saw women as well as men within the forefront of action within the Church, half a century has put us far behind. Many evangelicals now ardently resist change.

Men Women and God takes the biblical view that regardless of sex, women and men are called to discover and exercise their gifts in order to be more responsible servants in the Church and in the world. As R T Kendall, Minister of Westminster Chapel, has said, it remains clear that 'if the sleeping giant of the laity (in most churches women) were to be awakened and mobilised, the effects would be as great as during the Reformation'. It is the aim of this book to help each of us examine our individual and corporate lives, to rid ourselves of sexism in every form, to move beyond rhetoric and to work with greater commitment towards a more biblical partnership between men and women in our churches and world today.

I would like to thank everyone who has made this book possible. In particular Maurice and Margaret Smith, in whose home most of the hard work was done and whose lives and Christian commitment remain a rare challenge and inspiration. I am grateful too, for all who have honestly shared their experiences and struggles through letters, in workshops and seminars, and for the insights gained from both Christians and feminists. A special thank you to Kate Montagnon and Elaine Storkey for their invaluable personal support; to David and Pat Ward whose photocopier and friendship sustained me throughout; to Ruth Etchells, Mary Evans, David Lyon, Roy McCloughry and Tim Dean (Trustees of Men Women and God); John Stott and Martyn Eden of the London Institute, and Marlene and David Cohen, whose encouragement in the later stages helped more than they realise. Thanks too to Iain McKillop, Tony Walter and Mike LeRoy for their comments on early drafts, and to Gill Goodliffe, Linda Caldicott, June Osborne and to Lindsey

Passenger for typing the manuscript the week before her first baby was due. Lastly, thanks to all the contributors, many of whom continue to work out these issues often painfully within their own lives.

Kathy Keay
March 1987

For details of the MWG Trust contact:
Men Women and God
c/o LICC
St Peters Church
Vere Street
London
W1M 9HP

Introduction

In many parts of the world today traditional values are being questioned. In response to the influence of contemporary feminism, people are being faced with questions which challenge traditional relationships and roles and attitudes towards men and women. Many Christians are confused by this, feeling that to question traditional values is to strike at the very heart of our faith. But sometimes traditional values have developed from cultural mores of a previous generation, within or even outside of the Church, and they are not necessarily to be identified with biblical teaching. We must not be afraid of seeking biblical answers to modern questions, remembering that raising a question is not the same thing as presupposing an answer!

How do women and men relate to God? What separates men and women from God? How can sinful men and women be saved from the consequences of their sin? How should women and men relate to one another? How do parents relate to their children? How do men and women relate to governing authorities? How should wives and husbands relate? The Bible has much to say about these and many other questions. The vast majority of biblical teaching of course deals with humankind – men and women together – or with individuals, whether women or men. The material that does deal with the relationship between the sexes, or with roles or functions particularly appropriate to one sex or the other, must be seen in this overall context.

This is an emotive area about which people express strong views. All of us must be aware of the way in which our own prejudices and preconceptions can influence our understanding and prevent us from listening to what the Bible itself is saying. Those who begin with the question, 'How does the Bible teach us to deal with the problem of women?' are likely to come to very different conclusions from those who begin with the question, 'How can the Bible help women to fight for their rights?' But surely both of these approaches are wrong. The first because unlike Freud, Scripture does not present women or femininity as being a 'problem', and the second because the Bible as a whole seems more interested in the voluntary giving up of rights than in the insistence upon them.

Perhaps a better starting point is, that in his 'very good' Creation, God deliberately and consciously chose to make humankind as male and female. The question then is how in today's world and in today's Church can men and women live and work together in a way which reflects their creation in the image of God? How can Christians give a positive expression to their perfect complementarity – expressing both difference and equality? How should men and women together be working out God's purpose as managing directors of his Creation? Any approach, if it is to be biblical, must recognise the complementarity and interdependence of the sexes. Thus we must reject both the extreme patriarchal view, which sees the real world as composed primarily of men, with women as irrelevant except for child-bearing and child-rearing, and the radical feminist view which sees it as possible, acceptable and even desirable that a society should be composed entirely of women.

This book seeks to outline some of the issues facing men and women today, to raise some of the questions and to provide a biblical and practical response to these questions, working through the implications chapter by chapter in different areas of church, social and personal life.

Part I explores a number of problems and inconsistencies within the Church, particularly in relation to the question of women in leadership and ministry roles. It brings out into the open some of the accusations of contemporary feminist thinkers against God, and Elaine Storkey concludes that though their case against God does not stand up at all, their case against the Church sometimes does. Christians are challenged to admit that there are problems here, in the hope that increased awareness will bring about an incentive to change.

Part II picks up some of the issues facing men and women in society. Where does discrimination exist? How are attitudes and images shaped? Is Creation complementarity being worked out in our society and if not, what should Christians be doing about it?

Part III asks the question, Is biology destiny? To what extent is lifestyle within the family and within society determined by personal status and by gender, and to what extent should it be so determined? This section recognises the growing problem of sexual abuse and violence against women and aims to help the Church take this problem more seriously. It also raises the question as to whether lesbianism can ever be seen as a legitimate Christian option. The concluding chapter asks, in the light of all this, whether wholeness is possible? What does it mean to be made in the image of God and what are the implications for women and men in personal and public life today?

Asking questions and tackling issues can be a painful process, but it is vital that Christians do take up the challenge. It is the hope of all the contributors that this book will be a help to those who wish to live in God's world in God's way and to reflect Christ in a society which largely does not recognise him.

Mary Evans

Part I:

Women and the Church

Elaine Storkey

Elaine Storkey has taught philosophy at Manchester College, Oxford and Sociology at Stirling University. She has also taught women's courses in the USA and lectured in sociology and philosophy at Oak Hill College, London. On the Faculty of the London Institute for Contemporary Christianity, and a trustee of Men Women and God, she is married with three sons, has been a tutor with the Open University for ten years and is author of *What's Right With Feminism* (SPCK/Third Way).

1. The Feminist Case Against God

Elaine Storkey

During my student years I became a close friend of a Jugoslavian woman. Her name was Boba. At a fundamental level we had little in common. She was a Freudian psychologist, an atheist and a Marxist. She had never known any evangelical Christian before and my own commitment to Jesus Christ was a source of some amusement and amazement to her. It's curious, I suppose, that our friendship ever got off the ground. But it did, and I loved her. She was a person without cant or guile, and her harsh analysis of our society was often close to the truth.

Our relationship grew, deep and warm. We shared much of ourselves and each found in the other a humanness always ready to respond. There were some interesting repercussions too, for although she disliked the Church intensely and saw it as a symbol of institutional hypocrisy and oppression, her affection for me meant that she was willing to come with me and watch the worship. She would listen patiently to the gospel being presented and subject all that was said, to her usual careful, analytic scrutiny. She always commented on the fact that every church we visited was populated largely by women, but inevitably led by men. 'What's in it for the women?' was her constant query, and she would build up theories to account for the anomaly. Her conclusion was often that the Church – and by implication, Christianity – was for women who needed male props, father figures, male authority. It was for women who needed to be subservient, to be told what to do. It was for women who were pleased for men to do their thinking for them, and cheerful to be excluded from decision-making. It was for women who had no social conscience and were happy to close their eyes to inequality and injustice. The problem was that her theory had some exceptions. Women out there might be like that, but the only one she knew well wouldn't accept her analysis. She gave her affectionately taunting laugh: 'So, OK Elaine, why have you swallowed the God system?' We would talk for hours about why I believed and why she couldn't. When I watched her struggling with that deep sense of cosmic meaninglessness I longed for her to know the peace and joy that Jesus Christ had brought for me.

Some time later she returned to Jugoslavia. We corresponded for three years. Then, one day, one of my letters was returned to me by the local psychiatric hospital where she had worked. I never saw or heard from her again.

Many years later all those arguments were to become very familiar. They were to become part of the massive rejection of Christianity by feminists. The external situation today is the same. The Church still gains most of its grass-roots support from women. Women still provide the unpaid but powerful back-up services of the Church and ensure that the next generation is acquainted with the Christian gospel. Yet outside Christian circles, and increasingly inside them, the gospel is under attack because of what it seems to be saying about women. The allegation is being made that although women have supported the Christian faith, the faith has not supported women. What is more, this allegation is receiving ever wider acceptance. And this could have quite alarming consequences. For if women, who have traditionally been so loyal, should heed the arguments and begin to turn their backs on Christianity, it would present the Church with a grave crisis. There is much more at risk, too, than losing workers for the church bazaar. Truth itself is at stake. For what is the gospel if it is not Good News for women? What are we as Christians if we are not salt and light in the world? If what most feminists say is correct, we Christians have not been concerned for justice, motivated by love and looking after other people's interests rather than our own. We have not brought liberty to the captives, recovery of sight to the blind, freedom for the oppressed, binding for the brokenhearted and proclaimed the year of the Lord. If they are right, we have not in fact been living as the people of God.

But this is the irony of the situation, because radical feminists come up with a different conclusion – the very opposite conclusion, in fact. It is, they say, precisely because Christians do live as people of 'God' that injustice, oppression and inequality towards women persist. This is because indeed, our God, as they see him, is nothing other than a tyrannical male deity, erected by a patriarchal society with the aim of giving injustice to women a divine seal of approval. In other words, we are the people of 'God', but this god is woman-denying and evil.

With either response it would seem that Christians have a case to answer, and it is time to unravel that case in more detail. Why has the Christian gospel attracted so much anger from women who a generation ago might have been found in our church pews? Reasons lie on every level. Christianity in its structures, its attitudes, its social implications and its theology has been weighed and found wanting, for, it is claimed, where the Christian faith does not actively condemn women, it keeps silence. Like those pious plantation owners in the Southern States who read their Bibles whilst cruel employees beat their slaves senseless, Christians pray and worship and turn a deaf ear to those injustices and inequalities that are carried out in God's name.

At this point we need to pause and mention that the term 'feminist' is too broad for the discussion we are about to engage in. I have spent much energy elsewhere[1] showing how many different kinds of feminist exist and would not want now to spoil that with generalisations. But for those familiar with the categories, most of what I will now argue would be found amongst radical, Marxist and 'post-Christian' feminists, although on very many points there would be assent among a much wider grouping than that.

The male as norm

One of the strongest arguments levelled at the Christian Church is that we accept without question the idea that the male is norm in our society. We do this in many ways. In family life it is almost always the man's career, the man's interests, the man's vocation, the man's concerns which are followed through. Without even reflecting on this, Christians have taken it as somehow a Creation ordinance. The results have often been sad and destructive. I did a sociological study of policemen's families some years ago in Scotland. What interested me particularly was the way in which men in one police force were constantly moved around, from area to area and house to house. It was this aspect of police life, more than any other, that their wives commented upon negatively. It left them feeling insecure, unable to put down roots, and constantly lonely as they would be separated from their own families and lose their local friends.

This situation is not, of course, peculiar to the police forces. Indeed, that particular force has now abandoned the practice – I hope because it was willing to listen to the results. But in almost all walks of life the requirements of the father's job might mean disruption and sacrifice for many others in the family. The interests of employers and firms and the career interests of the man so often take precedence over what a wife might feel to be her own needs, or those of her family.

The same practice is very evident in the Christian Church. In many denominations even today it is assumed that only men have any vocation from God, whether this be in a lay or ordained capacity. A woman's 'vocation' is to be his domestic and emotional support. Yet women also have concerns which need to be heard. Real mutuality of support is a very recent practice, and has not caught on in a big way in some circles! Single women are allowed some other kinds of vocation, but almost invariably still in a supporting role, and indeed are always somewhat 'suspect' for not being wives and mothers. It is generally true that women who feel called by God to exercise their gifts so often have to sit and watch.

There are other aspects of the male-being-the-norm syndrome which also have strong repercussions. Studies which have been carried out on expectations of men and women whilst at school or college have shown that whilst men make independent choices about their future work, women rarely feel able to make such choices without reference to whether they will marry, and whom they will marry. Many choose jobs or training which hold less interest for them than other areas, but which are compatible with getting married and being prepared to give this up for husband and family. No boy in any study I have looked at has suggested that this might be a constraint on his future.

It is not the preparedness to make sacrifices that worries me here. I feel that there is enough in Christ's teaching that suggests that this is how we all should live. In the New Testament Epistles also there are constant reminders that we should be putting the interests of other people before our own. Women have often learned this well, and accepted it as part of their commitment to marriage and family life. But it is the one-sidedness of the sacrifice which needs to be examined. For the teaching is not only for women. It is for all who are prepared to bear the name of Christ. And as Christian communities we have been very slow to recognise this.

Another point follows quickly from this one. When it comes to interpreting the way women should live, or what they should feel, who decides? Most feminists point out that until very recently it has inevitably been men. Because male experience is the norm, most of the books on women, the sermons about women and the psychology of women have been done by men. When I was expecting my first baby, three books on childbirth were my constant reading. They were all by men. When I was actually in labour I realised how little they really knew! When my husband and I worked hard to look after our first two children, *Baby and Child Care* was our reference guide. It was of course written by a man.[2] The classic text on 'maternal deprivation' was for many years a book by a male writer, John Bowlby.[3] It was some time before the fact that he was a man awoke people to the enormous male bias in his work. Women have had themselves and their lives interpreted by men for centuries, and within the Church and Christian organisations it is still largely men who tell women what to do, how to live and what to feel.

It is not surprising, then, that many women feel a sense of 'anomie', feel that they do not know really who they are as women. Their own experiences seem so readily disregarded and their own talents so underused whilst they are stereotyped in a hundred inaccurate ways by those who do not listen. These stereotypes have not merely been accepted, but have been fostered by the Christian Church for a long time. It is 'normal' for a man to be aggressive, a good leader, logical, unemotional, decision-making, abstract, active, and non-domesticated. It is 'normal' for a woman to be docile, passive, domestic, submissive, irrational, emotional, illogical, nurturant, soft, gentle and good with her fingers. (This last point has often been given to me as a reason why women are best suited to do the knitting, typing, sewing, etc. When I ask why there aren't therefore women brain surgeons – since that requires enormous dexterity – there is usually no reply!) It is dubious, anyway, that as Christians we have the right to see these stereotypes as 'normal'. Where do we get these ideas from? To be 'normal' in a sin-ridden society is not necessarily a state we should aim at. From a biblical standpoint there is just one set of characteristics given for both men and women – that is, the fruit of the Spirit: love, joy, peace, faithfulness, gentleness, self-control and so on.

Some of the examples I have given so far will not be seen as particularly problematic by some women. But there is one which most would find disturbing. There is an argument that much of the violence and abuse of women in our society stems from the fact that the male is accepted as the norm. This will be taken up in a later chapter, but here it is worth saying that until recently domestic violence was not taken seriously and even rape was not seen as a particularly horrific crime. Before the most recent legislation (and even after, of course), distinctly light sentences could be given for some quite vicious attacks on women. The police, too, were known to be not always sympathetic to an alleged rape victim, and rape crisis centres have always reported higher numbers of women coming to them than those who go to the police. Why has this been the case? The argument has been that because the male has been norm in our society, this is represented in the laws about rape, in the judiciary, the legal profession and the police force. Male behaviour is understandable, even when it involves sexual attacks on women. Therefore, although it cannot be condoned, it can be seen in proper (male) perspective. Women who bring rape charges, on the other hand, cannot so easily be understood. Why would they be alone at night? Why would they be walking down dark alleys? Why would they allow a colleague to buy them a drink? Why indeed, if they weren't prepared to see what might result? Why indeed, if they weren't actually prepared to be raped? Even in cut-and-dried cases where the rape takes place in a home and the rapists plead guilty, a male judge has been known to comment that the woman has not really 'suffered' all that much.[4]

The implication of all this is, of course, worrying. Women are invited to see themselves through male eyes, to assess all their behaviour through male eyes and then to behave in a way that puts them beyond any danger from men. But as long as to be male is to be normal, there is no place of safety for some women.

The notion of patriarchy

We may now be in a position to understand the central focus of the feminist attack on Christianity. For what is behind this fact that the male is norm in our society? Is it part of the inevitable structure of human relationships, or is it a distortion of them? Most of the feminists we have been talking about are in no doubt. What is behind this situation is a ruthless demonstration of power. But the demonstration is not limited to individual men. It is embedded into all aspects of our society; it is part of patriarchy. For patriarchy – the dominance of men over women – is structured into all social relationships. It is there in work, marriage, family life, business, the professions, the law, education. It is there in male violence and sexual abuse. It is strong in the Two-Thirds World as well as in the industrial West. With the possible exception of a few small communities, patriarchy exists everywhere. We find it in the White House, the Kremlin, the Politburo, the Broederbond, the Vatican. It is present in our financial empires, our universities, our political parties, our trade unions, our legal structures, our economies and our churches. It undergirds all human systems, whether capitalist, Marxist, tribalist, Hindu, Islamic or Christian. Mary Daly, herself a former Catholic theologian turned radical feminist, sums up their case: 'Patriarchy is the prevailing religion of the entire planet.'[5]

This point is the important one. For if it is true, what does that say about the distinctiveness of the Christian faith? Is Christianity at root no different from any other religion or human system?

Is Christianity patriarchal?

There can be little doubt that within Christianity there is a legacy of strong negative views about women. The early Church Fathers wrote some things for which even *Christian* feminists find it hard to forgive them. Tertullian, Chrysostom, Augustine, Aquinas, Clement of Alexandria and so many others all taught that not only were women more or less to blame for all the sin in humankind, but they were here as 'defective men', or 'not in God's image', or simply as agents in procreation.

Nor were these views limited to the early Church Fathers. They have reappeared in different guises within the Church throughout the centuries and in some quarters are with us still. Maybe the language is a little less enthusiastic than John Knox's *First blast of the Trumpet against the Monstrous Regiment of Women*, but under contemporary sophistication and gentlemanly manners the same kind of attitudes still lurk in many a male Christian breast!

But it is not merely the traditions of Christianity which the attack is focused upon, nor even the attitudes we have looked at earlier. The very structures of the Church – male hierarchies and dignitaries, male 'shepherds', papal edicts, houses of bishops – all echo the male centrality and open us up to the allegation of patriarchy. So, of course, do our liturgy, our language, our practices. But it is at Christian theology that some feminists want to launch their strongest attack.

For their claim is that our very theology is sexist. The view apparently held and undoubtedly propagated by people in the Church is that God is male. The Trinity is male. Christ, the male Son of a male Father, comes to earth to die for men. Then, of course, the Jewish patriarchs were male, the twelve apostles were male. The Bible writers were male. For many women this is the final statement of the irrelevance of the Christian faith for them. The Christian faith proclaims, endorses and affirms a male-centred universe. It accepts patriarchy wholesale, and in doing so goes along with all other ideologies and religions. In the words of one sympathiser, 'If God is seen as simply and exclusively male, then the very cosmos seems sexist.'[6]

Another writer puts it differently. She points not to the current life of the Christian faith, for she believes it to be non-existent, but to the legacy which Christianity has left 'behind'. Wryly, she suggests that 'even the god we no longer believe in is still envisaged as male.'[7]

The weight of this position must hit us all. For if the Church is in the business of worshipping a male god there is no way out of patriarchy. For here, in the very focus of our commitment, in the author of all reality, the sustainer and upholder of the universe, the principle of male power is upheld and justified. Inequality for women, subservience, and lack of full humanness is structured into Creation itself. If this is true, then to be a Christian must mean accepting it as a fact of life.

Agreements and disagreements amongst Christian feminists

Not all Christian feminists do accept this as true, however. What I have been saying here is deliberately introductory and general, but these allegations have been around for many years now and have been discussed in considerable depth by a large number of feminist Christians from many different theological and cultural traditions. There is probably considerable assent among us that Christianity, as it is practised and preached, is a patriarchal religion, and that although women are large in number in the Church, they are small in visibility within the Church's leadership. The assent would go beyond the kind of traditional approach which looks at 'the role of women in the Church' and thereby suggests, as Elizabeth Fiorenza points out, that 'women and not an institutionalised male Church [are] the problem'.[8] There is considerable agreement with Catherina Halkes, a prominent Dutch theologian, who sounds a resounding echo when she talks about the need for *shalom* – for peaceful and just relationships between men and women. Her emphasis on justice, and her vision of the new heaven and new earth of 2 Peter 3:13 are widely shared.[9]

In a similar vein, few would dispute the suggestion that women are not the Wholly Innocents and free from sin. Rosemary Radford Reuther speaks for many of us when she says: 'Women need to acknowledge that they share the same drives and temptations as men, not just sins of dependency, of which they have been guilty, but also the sins of dominance of which they have been less guilty, not for want of capacity, but for want of opportunity.'[10]

There is not much dispute either on the reading of some post-biblical history. Most of us recognise and bewail the fact that the misogyny of the early Church Fathers comes out of a particular philosophical stance known as Dualism. In fact, although it was introduced so early into Christian theology, there is still evidence of it today, particularly in the Catholic tradition, and it has had enormous implications for women. In this philosophy the body was degraded, and along with it an everyday, normal, working existence, and the 'soul' was elevated, and along with it all the 'supernatural' area. Women were then either to be seen as temptresses or reflections of the Holy Virgin. Most feminists, and indeed most other biblical scholars, agree that such a dualism is not an emphasis in the Bible itself, but that bodily life is there given a high priority.[11]

Moreover, the suggestion that we might revise our liturgies and our language to include women would not find much opposition amongst Christian feminists. Nor would the plea that the traditional interpretations of many biblical passages should be looked at again, from a standpoint which assumed the fundamental equality of women, as in Galatians 3:28.

Yet as well as these areas of agreement, there are some important differences between Christian feminists. Interestingly, these are not necessarily along traditional denominational lines. Catholic and Protestant women will be found together in each grouping. Instead, the areas of distance reflect more the differences of starting point and of biblical hermeneutics.

One of the ways in which those of us who want to be called biblical feminists find ourselves at odds with liberal Christian feminists is over how we approach Scripture. Although we might all agree with Elizabeth Fiorenza's suggestion that 'feminist theology begins with the experience of women struggling against trivialisation and oppression as well as for liberation and human dignity', the issue of where we go from there is the important one. For what interprets the 'experience' of women? Many feminist theologians outside an evangelical tradition would want to maintain in some way that experience provides its own framework of interpretation. The whole Christian tradition, even Scripture itself, must be subject to the experiences women have of themselves and of their lives. Where there is dissonance between our experience and any of the biblical writings, then it would be inauthentic – even hypocritical – to hold on to 'dogma' over what we know to be true inside us. The idea of the Bible having some kind of authority over against our real experiences would not be tenable. So say many non-evangelical feminists.

This is already several stages removed from the kind of hermeneutic which wants to re-read or reappraise traditional interpretations of certain biblical texts. It is removed also from the kind of argument we see in Fiorenza, who *can* say that ecclesial exclusion of women is 'not the will of God or the intention of Jesus Christ'.[12] She sees the legitimation of feminist theology in the eschatological view of freedom and salvation in the Bible. For the approach we are looking at would ask, Why do we need to focus so strongly on the Bible anyway? It is a human document, culture-bound, born into a patriarchal culture, and written by men. In what possible sense can God be said to be the author? It makes much more sense, in fact, to read the Bible as a piece of propagandist polemic, written to vindicate the activities of a certain group of people. Interestingly, the New Testament often fares rather more badly than the Old in this approach, for the writers of the Gospels and the Epistles are seen by these feminists as highly partisan, narrow, sectarian and anti-semitic.

The conclusion drawn by liberal-Christian feminists, then, is that we must lie loosely with Scripture, and at times reject it altogether, if we are to understand our world and ourselves in a coherent and meaningful way. We can only start from what we know to be true, and that means from what we experience ourselves day by day.

What then, does it mean to these women to be called 'Christian' feminists? Certainly, it does not suggest anything distinctive or unique about Jesus Christ. Being Christian involves being religiously open, open to all other cultures and religious traditions where freedom for women is being sought, and open above all to the possibility that Christianity might be wrong. It means being prepared to allow experience to sift through the traditions into which we have previously seen ourselves and to work out a new hermeneutic which will make sense of this. In some cases it means being prepared to embrace a new paganism which will begin to incorporate the old female earth religions with a new non-patriarchal Christianity. Some liberal Christian approaches to feminism start from a similar position.

When this point is arrived at, it is only a short step from Christian feminism to post-Christian feminism. For some years this movement had only one main exponent, Mary Daly. But increasingly over the last decade others have begun to accept the same label. In some senses, of course, the label is misleading. The return to paganism and the ancient polytheistic goddesses are far more a symbol of pre-Christianity. But Mary Daly's own position is not replacing God by the goddess in any reified sense. Her aim is to go beyond God the Father, Son and Holy Spirit but not to anything else: 'A patriarchal divinity and his son are not able to save us from a patriarchal world.'[13] But nor are there any other saviours outside ourselves; no powers, no spirits, no forces. There is nothing we can call 'God'. So her 'god' is not the name of anything at all, but a verb. 'God' is the Verb To Be, and will replace woman's present state of non-being or becoming with full Being. In one sense her feminism is an attempted total repudiation of Christianity, in another it is nothing more than a series of linguistic and literary devices.[14]

This, then, is the feminist cast against God. And there are none who have formulated it as strongly as those who were once within the Church but have moved right outside. For them, the conflict between their own experience as women and the demands of a male-centred religion has become a total one. But for many the exit has not been a painless one. For all the hurt and anger, the disappointment and loss at this resolution of the struggle is thrust upon the departing God and on the Church which would enshrine him. Among the most powerful and vociferous opponents of the Christian faith are those post-Christian feminists who have tried and failed to accommodate the need for affirmation as women with a belief in God.

Some ways of responding

Have we then lost the case against God? I think not. Much of the rest of this book will be given to showing how we do not need to go in that direction. It simply remains for me to give some pointers as to how we might redirect our thinking.

We might start by looking very briefly at those feminists with whom we have already identified many points of agreement. Does being a Christian feminist entail that we must go in their direction and reject anything which cannot be validated by our own experience? The answer to this is much more complex than it seems. I have difficulties, in fact, in knowing what it means to allow experience to be its own interpreter. I do not think that those who hold this position operate on self-explanatory experience either. Behind liberal-Christian feminism lies a very specific theological stance which is usually unexamined, and it is this theological stance rather than undefined 'experience' which provides the framework of interpretation and evaluation. Post-Christian feminism is similarly not neutral, but starts from philosophical ideas derived from the Enlightenment two centuries ago. Even the idea that we must start from experience as our interpreter is itself an Enlightenment concept.

But what is this 'experience' of myself? What is a 'self'?

We need to presuppose some answer to the basic and deepest question, 'Who am I?' and that is indeed the problem. For if all I am is the sum total of all that I experience, what is the 'self' that is doing the experiencing? It is in order to discover who this self is and what these experiences mean that we need to look beyond our raw experience for some clue to our identity.

The post-Christian feminists have already done this, despite any insistence to the contrary. They have found the principle of human autonomy which they now impose on experience, and say that fundamentally we are on our own, responsible to no higher authority. Biblical Christians have the opposite response. For us, the principle of dependency is the one with which we interpret our experience. The need for a framework of interpretation leads us *back* to Scripture, not away from it. But it is not to a few isolated passages taken out of context; we need rather the full biblical disclosure of who we are and what is our purpose in living. It is the disclosure that we are the creation of a personal, loving God which begins to make sense of our experiences of ourselves and shows us where we find our true identity.

Once we have established that, there are of course many other questions to answer, for the feminist case against this God still stands, unless we can meet it point by point. We need still to ask how we are to understand Scripture, for nothing has been solved by rejecting the extreme liberal position unless we can put something in its place. The next chapter, by Andrew Kirk, will be taking up this theme, but it is worth noting here that even amongst biblical feminists there are different emphases. Although they would all accept the Bible as the Word of God, there are several different approaches to the 'difficult' passages for women. This arises particularly with respect to Paul's letters. Some (see Virginia Mollenkott[15]) resolve the difficulty by pointing to a discrepancy between Paul and Jesus, and suggesting that although most of Paul's teachings can be accepted at face value there are times when he lapses into a rabbinic position. These times are obvious from the text, when weighed up with other aspects of his teachings (1 Tim chapter 2, especially verse

15). Therefore we need not place the same kind of importance on these passages.

Other biblical feminists would feel less than happy with this argument, and would seek to show that although some teaching is specific it is also culturally relative. In other words, to concentrate still upon Paul, there are many passages in his letters which really apply only to the people to whom he was writing, and are not relevant in the same sense for us today. We already distinguish many passages in this way (the covering of head, eating of strangled meat, braiding of hair) and we need only to recognise that the list is far longer (see Paul Jewett[16], Nancy Hardesty[17]).

Then a third, more conservative approach would want to maintain that we need to concentrate on a more accurate exegesis, which takes into consideration local practices and local heresies, but also is more faithful to the Greek text than we have often been before, looking at classical as well as New Testament Greek scholarship. When we begin to do this faithfully we will begin to realise that we have come to Paul through centuries of inaccurate interpretations and mistranslations (Catharine Clark Kroeger has done some excellent work here[18]).

Finally there are those who would want to stress that the Scriptures were never intended to be interpreted in an 'academic' way, and that the Holy Spirit will bring to us a fuller understanding of the Bible if we sit under it with humility and reverence. Even the Old Testament underwent considerable reinterpretation when the Spirit interpreted it in the New Testament.

With the exception of the first possibility, I feel that each of these approaches enriches our understanding of Scripture, and each can open up the Bible for women in a living and worshipping way. They are important in looking at any passage, not just those which have traditionally been problematic for women.

There are, of course, other fundamental issues which we have to face. One of them involves asking if it is true that we are actually worshipping a male deity. The experience of isolation and alienation which many women feel in a church which appears to worship a male God still needs to be considered. How do we interpret *this* experience by Scripture? A biblical answer would have to be that if we are really worshipping the God disclosed by revelation, then we are not worshipping a male God. The fact that we call God our Father is no indication that God has any human gender. We are simply doing as Christ has bidden us. And what he was inviting us to do was address the sovereign Creator of the universe as *Abba* or 'Daddy'. There can be no doubt that the point Jesus has in mind is that we can approach this God as little children. We can come to God in trust and dependence, in love and peace. We do not need to be afraid. God is not a God who is distant, threatening or patriarchal. This no more implies a male God than talking of God as having wings implies that God is a bird. God, indeed, is the author of sexuality, and as such is beyond the things which have been created. God is not to be explained or identified by the things within Creation. The first commandment goes to great pains to warn us of the dangers of that.

A similar point can be made about Jesus himself. Although it is undoubtedly true that Christ came to earth as a man, the important point about him is that he was the Word made Flesh, not indeed the Word made Male. He came as *anthropos* (human being), not primarily as *aner* (male human being). The Church, of course, makes this so hard for us to experience. Jesus is so often shrouded in male mystery, served up by male popes and archbishops with male pomp and circumstance. Yet this is such a far cry from the Jesus of the Gospels. In that Jesus we see a man who derides hierarchy, warns his disciples against ambition and wanting to be in positions of prominence. We see a Jesus who, though he was God, made himself of no reputation. We see a Jesus who was a friend to women, the poor, the discarded, the rejected; a Jesus who washed the dirty feet of his disciples; a Jesus who died for people even whilst they were yet sinners.

What can we say, then, about the case against God? I think we can say that it *is* a case against the *people* of God. We *are* guilty of living as children of a sexist god. We have not been obedient to the Scriptures in the way that other contributors in this book will shortly open up for us. We have allowed a patriarchal religion to be erected and to flourish in God's name. Above all we have put stumbling blocks in the way of those who would believe. When women have come to us and said, 'We would see Jesus,' we have offered them a counterfeit, and then have been horrified when they have rejected this.

There are women who will not bow the knee, whose feminism has idolatrous roots, and an apostate direction. But God knows who they are, and we are not any woman's judge. There are many others who are searching for God but who only find a Church which they cannot stomach. If we are to be God-carriers in our age and generation, we need both to call the Church – ourselves – to repentance, and to help people past the barriers we erect, so that they can begin to get a glimpse of the living God, in whom there is no male and female, but in whom there is liberty and reconciliation and fullness of life.

Questions for discussion

1. Which parts of the feminist case do you identify with most? Which do you identify with least?
2. 'The reason so many women become feminists is because men don't listen to them.' Do you think this is true?
3. How would you introduce a feminist friend to church?
4. Have any of the issues in this chapter ever been raised in your own religious or church group? What have been the reactions if they have?
5. What do you think are the deepest needs of women? Of men?
6. Try to think through what it would be like to be a member of the opposite sex for a day! What do you learn from this?
7. How do you understand the importance of Jesus Christ for women?

References

1. Elaine Storkey, *What's Right with Feminism* (SPCK/Third Way Books, 1985).
2. Benjamin Spock, *Baby and Child Care*.

3. John Bowlby, *Maternal Deprivation.*
4. Judgement given in the 'Vicarage' case, February 1986.
5. Mary Daly, *Gyn-Ecology: The Metaethics of Radical Feminism*, p. 39.
6. Paul Moore, *Take a Bishop like me* (New York, 1979), p.8.
7. Wendy Collins et al., *The Directory of Social Change* (Wildwood House, 1978), p.13.
8. Elizabeth Fiorenza, *Concilium*, 'Religion in the 80s' (T & T Clark 1985), p.xi.
9. See Jane Burns, *Catholic Herald*, November 1984.
10. Rosemary Radford Reuther.
11. The supreme statement of the importance of the body was of course in the *bodily* resurrection of Christ.
12. Elizabeth Fiorenza, ibid, Editorial, p.x.
13. Mary Daly, *Beyond God the Father.*
14. See a fuller account of Mary Daly's position in Elaine Storkey, *What's Right With Feminism*, chap. 11.
15. Virginia Mollenkott, *Women, Men and the Bible* (Nashville, Abingdon Press, 1977). 'A Challenge to Male Interpretation: Women and the Bible' in *The Sojourners*, February 1976.
16. Paul Jewett, *Man as Male and Female* (Eerdmans 1975).
17. Nancy Hardesty, 'Women: Second Class Citizens?', *Eternity* 1971; (with Letha Scanzoni) *All we're meant to be* (Word Books 1974).
18. Catherine Clark Kroeger, *Women Authority and the Bible* (Marshall Pickering 1987).

Andrew Kirk

Andrew Kirk has been involved in theological education for twelve years in Latin America, based in Buenos Aires. He is currently Theologian Missioner with the Church Missionary Society and senior Faculty Member of The London Institute for Contemporary Christianity. He is married with three children. Among books he has published are *Liberation Theology*, *A New World Coming* and *God's Word for a Complex World*.

2. Theology From a Feminist Perspective

Andrew Kirk

Introduction

A suspicious person with a somewhat conservative view of life might consider that a deliberate conspiracy was launched in the early 1960s to undermine traditional Christian thinking about a number of subjects, for at that time the opening salvos of the liberation, black and feminist theologies were fired. A person with radical convictions, on the other hand, would reply that the conspiracy had already been launched centuries ago in that the Church has been (and largely still is) successfully controlled by wealthy white males. From the 1960s onwards, however, this hegemony has been constantly and severely attacked by those who feel oppressed by their inferior position: the poor, black people and women. Not least, they have demanded the right to do their own theological reflection from their own standpoint.

Each type of reflection has, in its own way, raised crucial questions about the meaning, purpose, content and basis of theology. In particular, each has caused Christians of all persuasions to be aware of the subtle influences of Church tradition, culture and ideology on their handling of Scripture and the formation of their opinions. The major debate in theology today, therefore, is about *hermeneutics* – not an abstract science of interpretation, but the complex process of relating a text from the past, which uniquely reveals God, to a contemporary reality which in many instances seems historically and culturally remote.

In attempting to focus on feminist theology (whether

radical, liberal or conservative), I want to concentrate on the hermeneutical issues which are being raised. Some of the excessively blunt rhetoric and the extreme positions may so offend us that we fail to see that feminist theology is posing major questions about how we interpret and apply the Bible today. It offers us, therefore, an excellent case study in hermeneutical procedure, challenging us to re-examine the methods we use to discern how God's Word, spoken through prophet and apostle, speaks to us today.

The place of context in reading the text

Obviously feminist theology has, to differing degrees, been influenced by the feminist movement. There are different types of feminism, but all are strongly egalitarian. The first stage was marked by a clamour for women's liberation: to secure equal rights before the law (such as the ownership of property) and equal access to job opportunities with men. Basically, it was demanding for women what men already had. For this reason, some saw it as no more than a preliminary skirmish, for it aimed no higher than the attainment for women of a greater status, but at the cost of leaving the world still dominated by male values, interests and decisions.

Feminism, by contrast, is a movement which allows no compromise with the present ordering of society along patriarchal lines. In order for society to become a place where women genuinely have an equal voice in the shaping of the future, a number of far-reaching changes of attitude, customs and institutions will have to take place. Women must not be defined any longer in relation to men – the bearers of *their* children, the keepers of *their* houses, the supporters of *their* professional ambitions. They must recover the integrity of their personhood, which throughout the ages has been arbitrarily defined by men in categories which disintegrate the unity of their being. They are, for example, stereotyped as either a seductress or a faithful mother: either the provider of passion or the provider of love, warmth and security. As Daniel Schipani, a Christian psychiatrist, says, 'Only rarely are women accepted as emotional, intellectual and sexual beings at the same time.'[1]

One of the chief causes of anger and protest is that a woman's role in society should be defined by her biological functionings. Because of her part in bringing a child into the world, the woman is expected to give up her career opportunities and leisure activities in order to dedicate herself to caring for the needs of the children and the home. Only rarely do men take part-time jobs in order to shoulder the major responsibility for the family, whilst the woman works full-time in her chosen profession.

As a result of what they see as an essential injustice, therefore, some radical feminists have totally rejected the traditional family. They view it as a system used by men to subordinate and exploit women. The really free woman, according to this outlook, is the lesbian, for she can live without men altogether. Indeed, with the advent of AID a woman can now have children without any physical contact with a man. Traditional heterosexual relationships are no longer considered to be the norm. Women are free to state their own personal sexual preference. To cohabit with a person of either sex is a matter of legitimate individual choice and should not be censored in any form by society.

Whilst in the 1970s radical feminism tended to emphasise the undifferentiated and symmetrical nature of both sexes, it now seeks to contrast the positive characteristics of being feminine (as they define these) with the negative, *macho* elements in the male psyche (aggression, lust, the will to possess and control, the competitive spirit, etc.). The belittling view of women held by many men – that they are passive, gullible, dependent, less rational and more emotional than men – is no longer seen as something necessarily to reject when compared with the typical qualities of men, which many women see as directly contributing to the chaos of the modern world.

The feminist movement has set an agenda which forms part of the backdrop against which the Bible has to be interpreted. The degree to which we accept the feminist critique or reject parts of it as exaggerated, extreme and destructive will affect the way we understand the biblical teaching about God, humanity, sin and authority. In the following quotation, for example, Rene Padilla demonstrates a basic sympathy with some of the issues raised by feminist theologians and uses their 'language' in some of the things he says about the relationship between men and women:

> . . . Women are not defined biblically on the basis of marriage and child-bearing, only by God's mandate to have dominion over nature in collaboration with man. More important than her femininity is her humanity. This is a matter of calling, not of biology. Therefore, to fight for the vindication of women is not necessarily to deny their differences in relation to men . . .
>
> As a result of the fall woman ceases to be *'ishah* (bone of his bone, flesh of his flesh) and becomes *Eva* (living). Now Adam sees her not as a companion who shares his life, but as the 'mother of all living' (Gen 3:20), a means of reaching a goal linked to feminine biology.[2]

Attitudes to the authority of the biblical text

It is not surprising that diverse attitudes to feminism have led to different views about the place of the biblical message in forming one's opinion about the place of men and women in society. There are those who have moved to a position of uncompromising opposition to the whole of biblical revelation. We might call these *post-Christian feminists* (though, because of the religious symbols they use to replace the Christian ones, we might just as well call them pre-Christian feminists). The best known representative of this group is probably Mary Daly.

There are others who believe that the biblical tradition has elements within it which are truly liberating for women. Therefore, the biblical interpreter needs to distinguish ruthlessly between patriarchal and non-patriarchal emphases, rejecting the first and using the second as the core of a non-sexist, Christian theology. We might call this group, represented by people like Rosemary Radford Reuther and Elizabeth Fiorenza, *Christian feminists.*

A final group, while still accepting many of the concerns of the feminist movement, is characterised by its acceptance of the authority of the whole Bible as God's written Word. Within this third group, however, there are at least three further groups, each characterised by a different approach to those passages which appear at first sight to place women in a subordinate and inferior position. Some accept the texts at face-value, stressing that the subordination of women and the headship of husbands, though one facet of the way God has ordered human relationships, in no way implies either inferiority of being or status nor sexually-defined roles in society. Others maintain that, by careful and patient exegesis, it is possible to demonstrate that the texts in question strengthen rather than question the equality of the sexes. Yet others argue that there is a large degree of ambiguity in the texts, due mainly to cultural factors which were important at the time of writing, but are irrelevant to our situation today.

Amongst this latter group of *biblical feminists* more attention has perhaps been given to the role and status of women within the Church than to an ideal situation within the family and society. There is a vigorous debate about the meaning and significance of texts which say that women should keep silent in church, not teach or have authority and learn from their husbands. On the other hand, few have ventured to say explicitly what the notions of 'headship' and 'subordination' actually mean in practice.

Universal and culturally specific biblical injunctions

From the variety of general pre-understandings which shape basic approaches to the authority of Scripture, we turn to specific questions of interpretive method. One crucial question concerns the contextual shaping of the biblical text.

Few interpreters of Scripture today would claim that God's Word is spoken as a set of timeless propositions, valid irrespective of the specific historical circumstances in which they came. God's Word was always communicated with reference to particular events. At the same time it transcends those events, otherwise it could not meet us as an authoritative Word now. The hermeneutical problem, then, is to know how to relate the Word given in one historical period to another period. There are a number of interlocking questions to face. We will try to show how the way we answer them affects our attitude to the issues raised by feminist theology.

1. The priority of texts

Differences of opinion may arise because interpreters, in the application of biblical principles to contemporary life, give unequal weight to particular texts. In seeking to discern the significance of different parts of the Bible can we find criteria by which to judge which text should be understood in the light of which other text? Do certain texts have a controlling influence, perhaps because of the transparency of their message or because they are foundational texts?

(i) Creation

Most feminist theologians give a high priority to the Creation narratives of Genesis chapters 1 and 2. The Genesis 1 account of human creation uses an economy of words. It records both the fact of two sexes and that God's image is enjoyed equally by both. Man, generically speaking, is male and female – the terms 'man' and 'woman' are not used in Gen 1:27. The story stresses the unity of the two sexes. Humanity alone, of all Creation, is in the image of God. It is a reality only as male/female. Neither sex reflects the *imago Dei* on its own. Therefore, to seek to live in sexual isolation signifies a denial of God's image. Jesus establishes the priority of the Genesis 1 account in answering the Pharisees' question about divorce – 'he who made them from the beginning made them male and female' (Mt 19:4).

The priority of Genesis 1 has important consequences when we come to interpret the second Creation story. Sexuality is not something we possess, but something we are. Our sex is our humanity. In Genesis 1 the two mandates 'to multiply' and 'to subdue the earth' are given equally to the male and the female of the human species. Neither mandate is sex-specific. Hence, as Rene Padilla says, 'their fulfilment as human beings depends not on the opposite sex, but on their calling as the image of God . . . More important than her feminity is her humanity, which is a matter of calling, not of biology.'[3] In other words, Genesis 1 makes absolutely no distinction between man and woman. Their equal humanity is based on their equal relationship to the one who made them. When they relate to one another, they do so as full bearers of the divine image. It follows that the loss of humanity in the one will negatively affect the other.

When we come to Genesis chapter 2 it seems to me that *prima facie* we should, unless there is convincing evidence in Scripture indicating the reverse, read it in the light of chapter 1. Let us notice the main features of this second account of Creation:

First, man's relationship to the animals is one of domination. But this does not satisfy him. He is made for a relationship of self-giving love with an equal. Man's problem was not that he had more work than he could cope with, nor that he lacked someone to give orders to, but that he was *alone*. He lacked a companion, someone to share his life with.

Secondly, the woman is to be an *ezer* – often and unhelpfully translated 'helper' (e.g. RSV and Jerusalem). The *ezer* is the counterpart, expected to engage fully in the same activities. Literally it means someone who 'stands opposite to' or 'corresponding to' in the same work (like two people at each end of a two-handled saw). So, the word stresses both distinctness and mutuality or complementarity of work. There is no suggestion, either in the context or in the etymology of the word, that the term connotes subordinate status. Indeed, the story rules out such an interpretation.

Thirdly, the woman belongs to the same level of Creation as man, not only in a physical sense, but at every level. He is *'ish*, she is *'isha* (verse 23). God decided to create the female sex by taking her out of man, not to stress subordination, even less inferiority, but rather sameness. The man's joy is reflected in the first (love) poem ever composed: 'this at last is bone of my bones and flesh of my flesh.'

Fourthly, the relationship between the two is expressed in the act of marriage. God himself brings her to the man (verse 22). She now becomes 'wife' (verse 24). The relationship is harmonious, for fear had not yet destroyed the perfect love between them (Gen 2:25; 3:10; 1 Jn 4:18).

Fifthly, the account speaks of the union between them without speaking of procreation. This fact is crucially important, for it helps to dispel a deeply distorted view of sexual intercourse. Rene Padilla states the biblical position with great clarity:

> . . . Sexuality is rooted in creation as something that orients the mutual complementarity of man and woman. Bodily union, therefore, is an act in which husband and wife give expression to the fact of having been created for each other and experience the intimate union that defines the reason for their sexuality. Sexual desire is not oriented around the fruit of the conjugal union, but around the union itself.[4]

From a careful, detailed interpretation of these two primary texts it is hard to avoid the conclusion that they are wholly egalitarian in the picture they present of the two sexes. Those who want to find the roots of a hierarchical relationship in chapter 2 can only do so by reading into the passage what they want to find.

In summary, we may say that the worth of a woman is not in her relationship to man, but in her womanness. She is not a possession of her husband. The same is true of the man. However, the Fall drastically altered the perfect balance of Creation.

(ii) The Fall

As a result of the first disobedience, human beings became separated from one another. Henceforth, their relationship would be built on distrust, selfishness and manipulation. Often they would find personal satisfaction in exploiting, humiliating or dominating other people. They have found subtle, and not so subtle, ways of making others into a means to satisfy their own ends. Violence is an integral part of sinful existence. Therefore it characterises every part of human life. The first ever division of humankind was between man and woman. It exemplifies the total experience of human alienation.

This particular consequence is stated forcefully in a celebrated passage: 'your desire shall be for your husband, and he shall rule over you' (Gen 3:16). The woman is torn between her desire to give herself to her husband and her fear of losing her liberty.

It has been suggested that Eve was the real cause of original sin, and that her subordination is the result of God's punishment upon her for falling so easily prey to Satan's temptation. This belief is said to spring from a natural interpretation of 1 Timothy 2:14: 'and Adam was not the one deceived; it was the woman who was deceived and became a sinner.' One or two comments on this view are in order here:

First, the passage in 1 Timothy is a valid interpretation of the story of the eating of the fruit in the garden, as far as it goes. Eve was the one in direct contact with the serpent. Adam received the fruit from her and ate. One might argue, however, that Eve was less culpable: she was deceived by Satan's cunning, whilst Adam flagrantly disobeyed God's command and then blamed his wife. Paul is not making the point that Adam was less of a sinner, because of the way he came to eat; rather that, chronologically, he sinned second.

Secondly, elsewhere in the Pauline corpus Adam is held accountable for the original disobedience: 'sin came into the world through one man . . . many died through one man's trespass . . . by one man's disobedience many were made sinners.' 'As in Adam all die . . .' Eve is held out as a warning not only to women, but also to men (2 Cor 11:3).

Thirdly, punishment for sin is not distinguished according to sex, except in the case of child-bearing. Both Adam and Eve are given the maximum sentence of banishment, although Adam alone is accused for what he did (Gen 3:17).

Fourthly, in terms of exegetical methodology, it is correct procedure to interpret the 1 Timothy passage in the light of treatments of the Fall elsewhere. One crucial passage, Romans 1:18–25, makes no suggestion that Eve was more gullible than Adam, or that original sin was in some way due to the greater weakness of woman. Paul speaks of man generically, presenting the Fall as an act of rebellion in which the creature desired to change the nature of the universe (*hybris*): 'they exchanged the truth about God for a lie . . . they did not see fit to acknowledge God' (Rom 1:25, 28).

Fifthly, one of the main results of the Fall has been the drive by humans to dominate one another. Setting themselves free from the lordship of God, they have arrogated to themselves the position of 'lord' over others. The statement in Genesis 3:16 that 'he shall rule over you' is descriptive, not prescriptive. We can agree with John Stott that 'this primeval sexual equality was . . . distorted by the fall . . . Men have exploited this judgement of God, and have brutally oppressed and subjugated women in ways God never intended.'[5]

(iii) The Pauline passages (1 Cor 11:2–16; 14:34–36; 1 Tim 2:8–15)

The texts which deal with the Creation and the Fall are clearly intended to reflect universally valid truths. All human beings are the way they are because of the significance of being made in God's image and because of the consequences of sin. It is not so clear, however, whether a cluster of texts from Paul's pen are designed to be universally valid principles or culturally conditioned injunctions, elaborated to meet a specific set of circumstances.

The controversy which has erupted over these three texts in particular is heated. Biblical exegetes do not agree about what Paul intended to convey. There are two main reasons for this, one objective and the other subjective. Objectively, the meaning of all three passages is obscure. Neither the context for which they are written nor some of the language used can be clarified with certainty. Subjectively, a lot is at stake in their interpretation because of the way in which people on either side of the debate about women's ministry in the Church today want to use these texts. In the space available I cannot do much more than try to elucidate some of the issues before rounding off the debate about men and women with a look at some of the main hermeneutical considerations.

1 Corinthians 11:12–16

Obviously the primary question concerns the actual meaning of the texts. What did Paul really intend to convey? What would the original hearers of these words have done as a result of Paul's instructions? The answer to these questions is by no means simple. Part of the reason for this is that we have to reconstruct the situation which Paul is addressing. It is not clear. Unlike other parts of 1 Corinthians, there is no introductory *peri de* or 'now concerning'. Instead of beginning with a particular issue like litigation between believers or food sacrificed to idols, Paul begins his directive with an apparent theological principle (verse 3), before going on to talk about head coverings. However, the exact nature of the problem in the Corinthian church is not apparent. It has to be deduced from what we know about the practice of head covering in Greek culture. It also has to be assumed that Paul is giving these particular instructions for the sake of not giving unnecessary offence.

There are further exegetical problems. What is the relationship between the overtly theological statements and the practice which Paul is laying down? What are the theological principles which Paul is appealing to? In what way is he using the Genesis chapter 2 account of Creation? Where does the idea of woman being the glory of man come from? Paul seems to be suggesting that only the male sex is in the image of God (verse 7), but this would expressly contradict Genesis chapter 1.

At another level, it has been suggested that many of the passage's apparent contradictions would be resolved if one assumed that Paul was debating with an interlocutor. On this understanding, most of the argument of verses 4–10 is put forward by a Jewish Christian with a very imprecise grasp of the liberation of sex roles which Christ has achieved. According to this view, verse 11 marks a transition. Paul now puts the true Christian case: 'in the Lord, however . . .' (the adversative, *plēn*, is very strong). He then continues the argument by agreeing that it is right (*prepon*) for a woman to pray with her hair covered, not because of any reason directly deducible from the gospel, but because of custom and the general practice of the churches. Nevertheless, in order to safeguard Christian freedom, it is a matter of corporate decision, not an issue of theological truth (verse 13, 'judge for yourselves').

Finally, there are a series of lexicographical problems. Several of the key words used in the discussion are not transparently clear in their meaning. We mention two. For the word *kephale*, 'head', 'chief', 'first', 'source', 'eminent', 'honoured' are some of the possible translations which have been suggested. The situation is made more complex by the difficulty of knowing how to interpret the phrase *kephale tou Christou ho Theos* – 'the head of Christ is God' (clearly it is not a proof-text for subordinationism). The other word is *exousia* (verse 10), mistranslated by the RSV as 'veil'. What is the authority on a woman's head? Her own or someone else's? There is no reference in Greek literature which has so far come to light to a husband having power over a woman's head.

1 Corinthians 14:34–36

The passage about women keeping silent in church is much shorter. It begins where the other passage leaves off: the practice in all the churches. This statement plunges us at once into a major difficulty. The churches of God recognise no other practice but that women should pray and prophesy with their heads covered (their long hair arranged neatly on the top of their heads?); and yet, women should keep silent in all the churches.

At first sight Paul seems to contradict himself. The apparent discrepancy has been resolved to the satisfaction of some in one of two ways. *First*, it has been assumed that two different kinds of worship service are envisaged: in 1 Corinthians chapter 11 it is an informal gathering of church members, in chapter 14 it is the formal gathering of the whole church (cf 1 Cor 14:23). However, in response to this idea, there is no evidence elsewhere of such a distinction being made; it has been necessary to invent it to avoid a problem. The gathering for worship in chapter 14 also includes prophesying. There is no suggestion that only men are allowed to prophesy. Indeed, Paul envisages the possibility that all are prophesying at the same time (1 Cor 14:24), or better one by one (14:31). *Secondly*, it has been suggested that the keeping silent refers either to an authoritative teaching role – women are not permitted to teach – or to a discussion of the significance of the prophecy. However, making a tight distinction between teaching and prophecy is not without problems. Although they are listed as different gifts of the Spirit, teaching is not distinguished from prophecy as a sex-specific gift. Moreover, prophecy has a clear teaching function. Its purpose is to build up, encourage, edify and teach (1 Cor 14:3–4, 31). Moreover, in the priority of the gifts prophecy comes before teaching. Unlike glossalalia, it is not an ecstatic gift: 'the spirits of the prophets are subject to prophets' (1 Cor 14:32).

Another suggestion made is that *lalein* means to 'chatter'. Women, according to this conjecture, were in the habit of whispering among themselves either because they did not understand what was going on or because they had been separated from men (as in Jewish synagogue custom) and were not taking a full part in the service. This would seem to account for the injunction that they should ask their husbands at home about anything they did not understand. (They might not have been as well instructed in the Scriptures as men – but cf 2 Tim 1:5; 3:14–15).

Because of the difficulty of making sense of Paul's command within the wider context without making him contradict himself, some exegetes have suggested a solution of a different order. The opinion expressed here about women is not held by Paul at all, but is one he wants to refute. As in 1 Corinthians 10:23 and possibly in chapter 11, he is quoting a position held by some in the Corinthian church. The words, 'they are not permitted', 'they should be subordinate' are not spoken by Paul but by an unspecified group in the church who are seeking to impose their views. It is uncharacteristic of Paul to leave 'subordinate' without an indirect object (with 1 Tim 2:11 it would be the only case) – subordinate to whom or what? The reference to the Law (1 Cor 14:34) fits much better in a Jewish Christian context than as an argument used by Paul himself. Or, it might conceivably refer to a civil law which restricts the participation of women in public concourse. That Paul is refuting an opinion with which he does not agree is underlined by the abrupt contrast of verse 36. This is introduced by the strong exclamation, *ē*, or 'what?' It is best to interpret it as the introduction to a rebuke. Paul is forcefully questioning the opinion held. Whereas in verses 34–35 women are referred to in the third person, Paul now speaks to his audience in the second person – 'you only' is in the masculine form, suggesting that Paul is addressing men who silence women, not the women themselves. His tone is ironical, because these 'puffed up' men (1 Cor 8:1) imagine that they have a monopoly on God's Word.

1 Timothy 2:8–15

The final passage (from 1 Timothy) is the most obscure of the three, though it is interesting to note that some of the same problems of interpretation are present. For example, what is the specific situation in the church at Ephesus which occasions these injunctions? Are they intended to be universally valid or directed to a specific, geographically and temporally circumscribed set of circumstances? What is the exact relation between the commands and the theological reasoning which follows? What do certain words like *didaskein* and *authentein* mean? Why does *hupotage* (submission) appear again without an indirect object?

In discussions about the role of women in the Church, verses 11–14 tend to be isolated from the rest of the passage. It has been argued, however, that the instructions on a woman's dress and adornment are as unqualified as those about not teaching and keeping silent. Therefore, so the reasoning goes, if the second set of commands are universally valid ('I do not permit'), the first set (introduced by 'I desire', verse 8) must be considered in the same light. Otherwise the principle of interpreting according to the natural sense is made void. Others reply by saying that the second set of injunctions is explicitly based on a Creation ordinance, whereas no theological rationale is adduced for the wearing of certain kinds of clothing only or not wearing jewelry.

A further problem is created by the probable reference to female deacons in the next chapter (1 Tim 3:11), for this clearly constituted a position of leadership in the Early Church (cf Phil 1:1). It may be, therefore, that the reference to not teaching or having authority is not a general command applicable to all women in the Church, but specifically to wives in relationship to their husbands. This would account both for the change from plural to singular in verse 11 and for the reference to the priority of man in the Creation narrative.

In this section we have tried to lay out some of the more important exegetical issues which crop up in each of these complex passages. There are no easy solutions. No exegete can confidently claim any degree of certainty as to the real meaning of Paul's statements or commands. Every interpreter is bound to resort to conjecture to fill in the gaps in our knowledge. This necessity is not sufficiently recognised by those people who want to make exaggerated claims on the basis of their particular understanding of the texts in question. These texts in my opinion provide a flimsy basis for insisting on wide restrictions on the ministries which women can exercise in the congregation of God's people.

2. Hermeneutical considerations

We want to try and draw some of the threads together by pinpointing some of the most important hermeneutical issues which are raised by this debate about the place of women in Church and world.

(i) The interpretation of individual texts

There are a cluster of questions thrown up by trying to understand specific texts relevant to the theme. *First*, there is the problem of identifying the situation to which Paul is responding. Yet, one of the cardinal principles of biblical exegesis is to deal with the text within its historical context. God's Word is always spoken within a concrete reality, with the purpose of commanding obedience by God's people in that situation. Paul's practical teaching aims to promote faithfulness to the gospel in circumstances where it might be compromised and its effectiveness blunted. For the text to be God's Word to us in a way which demands our obedience we have to deduce principles from the context which are applicable in our circumstances. We can only do that if we can discern the author's original intention. Achieving this depends upon our ability to reconstruct the original scene of the recipients. This is particularly crucial in the case of the 1 Timothy passage. Some exegetes, for example, have suggested that the restriction on women teaching is perfectly comprehensible if the context was the influx into the Church of heretical doctrine from the mystery religions or gnosticism via women. Radical though the suggestion may seem at first sight, I think we may have to face the possibility that these passages simply are not directly applicable to the Church today, at least along the lines of the controversy we have been outlining. It just could be that we are engaged in debating a non-issue!

Secondly, there are a number of notoriously difficult problems of translation to solve. Before we can apply texts to our context we have to be sure we know the meaning of crucial terms. Words like *ezer* ('companion'), 'head', 'subordination' and 'have authority' do not have unequivocal meanings. And yet, in the present debate, they are made to bear a lot of weight. It is also widely recognised that two of the main texts have some of the most obscure sayings in the whole of Scripture – for example, 'because of the angels' and 'women will be saved through bearing children/the birth of the child'. Methodologically it is not permissible to build up a case for one particular interpretation if we are, in all honesty, still having to resort to conjecture to make sense of the text. Another question in the same area concerns grammatical nuance. A slightly different and yet perfectly legitimate translation into another language can substantially alter the sense. Thus in 1 Timothy 2:12, if we translate *ouk epitrepo* ('I do not permit' Greek simple present) by the English periphrastic present (using the verb, to be), rather than by the English simple present, we achieve a remarkably different meaning: 'I am not at present permitting a woman to teach or have authority . . .' C F D Moule comments that 'the Greek Present Indicative normally denotes "linear" action in present time, and it is therefore wise, in any given instance, to start by seeing whether it can be translated by the English periphrastic Present'.[6] By contrast the Greek Periphrastic Present is rare in the New Testament.

Thirdly, there is the important principle of comparative exegesis: no passage should be so interpreted that it appears to contradict other passages. It has always been a principle of sound evangelical interpretation to attempt to reconcile texts. Where this remains difficult without resort to fanciful reconstruction, evangelicals have generally preferred to remain agnostic than to sacrifice their commitment to a wholly truthful Scripture. This principle, however, raises some thorny issues in the discussion about women. It is not easy, for example, to see how one can make texts on headship and subordination harmonise with the clearly egalitarian texts of Genesis chapter 1 and Galatians 3:28, or the revolutionary reciprocity in marriage relations between the sexes introduced by Jesus into divorce proceedings and endorsed by Paul in 1 Corinthians chapter 7.

There are two subtle variations of this question. In the first place, we have to decide which texts we are going to use as fundamental hermeneutical keys and which as secondary commentaries on these. This is an indispensable interpretative process, if we want to avoid a head-on collision between texts which seemingly contradict one another. The danger to avoid is the 'mirror game' in which key texts are used to reflect one another, whilst others which do not easily fit into a particular pattern of interpretation are suppressed or interpreted too narrowly. There is no option but to choose an interpretative centre. But it is precisely this choice which lies at the heart of the disagreement about the relationship between men and women. Biblical feminists choose egalitarianism (starting from Genesis chapter 1, appealing to the teaching and practice of Jesus, the freedom charter of Galatians 3:28 and the practice of the Early Church). Subordinationists begin with Paul's statements about headship and his apparent interpretation of Genesis chapter 2. Both groups of exegetes, of course, have to be able to give an adequate account of the other's interpretative centre, using their own.

In the second place, we have to judge how we handle the relationship between description and prescription. The reconciliation of texts demands that we compare Paul's teaching with his practice. The latter seems to indicate that he accepted women into leadership and teaching roles in the Church. Phoebe in the Cenchrean Church is called a *diakonos* and *prostasis*. In the first case, it has been argued that just as the generic terms 'saints', 'elect' and 'sons' include women, so should also 'apostles', 'prophets', 'teachers', 'elders' and 'deacons'. Philippians 1:1, then, would naturally refer to both men and women: 'to all the saints . . . with the overseers and deacons'. It is hard to see why *diakonos* should be given a different meaning in Romans 16:1 to that in 1 Timothy chapter 3, without incurring the accusation of arbitrary exegesis. In the second case, it has been observed that *prostasis* (or *proistemi*) is often given a strong, heightened meaning when presumed to refer to men (e.g. 1 Thess 5:12, 'those who are over you in the Lord . . .'; 1 Tim 5:17, 'let the elders who rule well . . .') and a lesser, weaker meaning for the feminine form (Rom 16:1, 'she has been a helper of many and of myself as well'). The question of meaning is neatly begged. Whatever the exact significance of the terminology, Phoebe clearly exercised a leadership role in the church at Cenchreae and was presumably an official representative of that church in a mission to Rome. This is only one example of many where women are clearly prominent in the Early Church. This has led some exegetes to conclude that in 1 Corinthians chapters 11 and 14, and 1 Timothy chapter 2, Paul is regulating particular local situations rather than mandating principles for all time.

(ii) The universal and the particular

The discussion has been beset by an unresolved tension between texts which are universally valid and applicable, therefore, to all circumstances and those which refer to a temporary situation, where no principle deriving directly from the heart of the gospel is at stake. There are different ways of trying to resolve this distinction.

First, there is the argument from analogy. Are the injunctions concerning the subordination and silence of women wholly *sui generis*, or can they be compared to those regarding slavery, meat offered to idols and kosher food? Though in former years biblical Christians have argued strenuously in favour of the institution of slavery, it is now universally accepted that Paul did not support the practice, but regulated its exercise in the Church by setting it in a new context, that of submission by master as well as slave to the controlling lordship of Jesus Christ. By analogy, it is stated that the same consideration applies to women. Given the culturally universal custom of women's subordination, it would not have been expedient for women obtrusively to exercise their undoubted freedom in Christ either by adopting a different attitude to their husbands, or by teaching groups comprising both men and women. This might have caused an unnecessary barrier in the way of the gospel, a scandal not immediately to do with Christ crucified. Two arguments are used to support this deduction by analogy. In the first place, Christ's freedom does not apply only to an internal state, but to an external one as well. The principle of equality does not refer to an individual's state before God alone, but extends to human relationships in society. 'Neither male nor female' is of the same order as 'neither Jew nor Greek', 'neither slave nor free'. The abolishing of disparity between each pair has corporate as well as individual implications. In the second place, Paul seems to make a distinction between issues which are fundamental to the integrity of the gospel and ones which refer to codes of discipline in the churches. Thus, he distinguishes between a command of the Lord, his own opinion and his 'rule in all the churches'. Against the deduction from analogy some exegetes point out that, unlike slavery, the man/woman relationship is given a fundamental theological undergirding in passages like Ephesians chapter 5 and 1 Corinthians chapter 11. Moreover, Paul would never have compromised the principle of freedom in Christ for the sake of relative cultural conventions (yet, cf Acts 16:3; Gal 2:3; Rom 14:1ff).

Secondly, there is the approach from the framework of God's purposes in human history – Creation, Fall, redemption, consummation. What light do each of these great events throw on the male/female relationship? Two main questions have to be faced here. In the first place, does Paul deduce headship and subordination from the Genesis chapter 2 account of Creation? Are they built into the warp and woof of the way God ordered the world (in which case as Nicholas Wolterstorff has pointed out he could have ordered the reverse relationship)? Or are they to be interpreted in the light of the Fall, in terms of the husband's protective role towards the 'weaker' sex (1 Pet 3:7) in a world characterised by exploitation and violence (in which case they do not seem to be relevant to questions of women's ministry in the community of redemption)? In the second place, how does redemption in Christ affect the relationship? Here we need to consider in detail Jesus' own attitude to women, in particular the non-sexually-specific nature of discipleship – the absolute call to follow is incumbent equally on both sexes.

There are further questions raised by the nature of the Resurrection age of the Spirit inaugurated by Jesus: does the 'headship' of the husband in the context of marriage have any bearing on the Church community? It has been pointed out that the Church is the new family already living in the dawn of the age to come, and in the fulness of that age marriage relationships will be abolished. Meanwhile, at the point of tension between the present world and the future redeemed world, in the community called to be the first fruit of the kingdom, mutual subordination is the principle which operates (Eph 5:21). In the new order in Christ neither the headship of the husband nor the subordination of the wife is applicable. They are germane only to marriage, which is an ordinance for this present age (Mk 12:25).

Are not the gifts of the Spirit poured out equally on men and women? 'On my servants, both men and women, I will pour out my Spirit in those days . . .' (Acts 2:18; cf Acts 1:14 with 2:1). This seems to suggest that God's Spirit equips men and women equally for tasks in relationship to the Church's growth into maturity. Neither in 1 Corinthians chapter 12 nor in Ephesians chapter 4 is there the least hint that particular gifts are reserved to only one sex: 'to each one grace has been given as Christ apportioned it . . . some to be apostles . . . prophets . . . evangelists . . . pastors and teachers' (Eph 4:7–11). Just as the gifts of prophet and evangelist were (and are) exercised in the Church by women as well as men, so likewise the others must be open in the same way. Incidentally, this text also contradicts the false distinction which arose at a later stage (and which bedevils much contemporary discussion about the issue of ordination) between gift and office.

If these arguments from salvation-history are sound, then we can interpret Paul quite consistently in terms of the tension between freedom in Christ and good order in public. Women are not to abuse the undoubted freedom which they have in the community of the redeemed in ways that might undermine the continuing stability of relationships within the family.

(iii) The burden of proof
One final point remains in this rather lengthy discussion. It will have to remain an open question as far as this paper is concerned, though one that merits careful consideration. Where there are quite major disagreements as to the meaning and contemporary significance of texts, is either side of the debate required to prove their case rather than the other? If we imagine the case as a suit in law, which of the parties is innocent until proved guilty? Those who presume that the coming of Christ has already brought into existence full equality of vocation and calling to both sexes, or those who maintain that Creation itself dictates a certain biblically mandated restriction of roles on one of the sexes? Here, perhaps, is the real nub of the question.

Questions for discussion

1. Why do you think Christians draw different conclusions from the Bible about a woman's place in Church and society?
2. What kind of relationship does God intend man and woman to enjoy? In what ways has that relationship been spoilt by sin?
3. Do you think it is right to suggest that Paul did not fully follow Jesus' radical attitude to the freedom of women?

References

1. Paper presented to a Consultation on the Family (Quito, Ecuador, 1979).
2. 'The Human Couple: A Biblical Perspective' (*Theological Fraternity Bulletin*, Nos. 2–3, 1983), p.21.
3. Ibid, p.21.
4. Ibid, p.23.
5. *Issues Facing Christians Today* (Basingstoke, Marshalls, 1984), p.239.

6. *An Idiom-Book of New Testament Greek* (Cambridge, CUP, 1960), p.7.

Bibliography

Atkins, Anne, *Split Image* (Hodder and Stoughton, 1987).
Clark, Stephen, *Man and Woman in Christ* (Servant Books, 1980).
Cook, David, *Are Women People Too?* (Grove Ethics No. 21).
Evans, Mary, *Woman in the Bible* (Paternoster, 1983).
Hurley, James, *Man and Woman in Biblical Perspective* (IVP, 1981).
Langley, Myrtle, *Equal Women – A Christian Feminist Perspective* (Marshalls 1983).
Swartley, Willard, *Slavery, Sabbath, War and Women: Case Issues in Biblical Interpretation* (Herald Press, 1983).
Swidler, Leonard, *Biblical Affirmations of Woman.*

Faith and Roger Forster

Faith and Roger Forster are founders and leaders of the Ichthus Fellowship, South London. Both have an extensive ministry in teaching, training, counselling, church planting and evangelism, all of which are hallmarks of Ichthus. They have taken a lead in involving women in Church leadership and speak extensively on the subject. They are married and have three children.

3. Women's Spiritual Gifts in The Church

Faith and Roger Forster

'In the last days, God says, I will pour out my Spirit on all people. Your sons and daughters will prophesy . . . Even on all my servants, both men and women, I will pour out my Spirit . . . and they will prophesy . . .'[1] Peter ushered in the Church age by quoting Joel's prophecy that the Holy Spirit would be outpoured on both men and women and that they would proclaim God's message (prophesy). The Church age is marked by an outpouring of the Holy Spirit with the result that both men and women exercise spiritual gifts.

There can be little doubt that this was true in the first century or so after Pentecost. Early Church history is littered with references to women who preached and taught and often laid down their lives in the cause of Jesus Christ. Eusebius, the historian, refers to the daughters of Philip as 'mighty luminaries' in the Early Church. Tertullian, another historian, acknowledged that Priscilla (whom he called 'the holy Prisca') preached the gospel. Justin Martyr, who lived until about 150 AD says, in his dialogue with Trypho, that 'both men and women were seen among them who had the extraordinary gifts of the Spirit of God . . .'[2]

Yet there are many churches today who seem to be unaware of both biblical teaching and of Church history. It is entirely possible to enter a church today and find:

* that the steward who greets you at the door is male
* the leader of the service is male
* a man opens in prayer
* the Bible passage is read by a man
* a man gives the talk to the children

* another man reads out the notices
* the teaching is given by a man
* enquiries and enquirers are attended to by a man.

This state of affairs is not made less oppressive to women by their entering the back hall of the church and finding women busy making tea or minding children. It seems a curious way to fulfil Joel's prophecy.

Male and female with the Godhead

Some readers, at this point, are undoubtedly saying to themselves, 'Yes, this is all very well, but the Bible plainly teaches that whilst a woman may *serve* in the church (in back hall duties, presumably) she may not *lead* or *represent* the church in any way.' Many hold this view and, while they may allow women to engage in some public functions (e.g. reading the Scriptures or praying), they restrict her in any sphere which seems to give her a leadership role. Some base this on Bible passages such as 1 Corinthians 14:34–35 and 1 Timothy 2:11–15, which we will look at later. Others have their objections rooted in the nature of God himself.

> Dear God,
> Are boys better than girls?
> love,
> Sylvia
> P.S. I know you are one, but try to be fair.[3]

We may smile at this childish letter penned to God, but it does, in fact, represent the thinking of many people, particularly religious people. The assumption that God is male inevitably raises questions. In addition to the implication of male superiority ('if God is male then the male is God'), there is the problem of whether a woman can represent a male God. This is a serious issue to many in their consideration of whether women may exercise spiritual gifts in the Church, particularly public or leadership gifts. (It seems not to have occurred to those who hold this view that an even deeper 'problem' to some is whether a woman can be fully indwelt by the Spirit of a 'male God', and if so what difference this makes to her femininity.)

Of course, to any serious student of the Bible the above is all nonsense. In the first chapter of the Bible we are told that God made both male and female 'in his image'.[4] Therefore masculinity and feminity must both be in his nature, as in ours. Moreover, God frequently alludes to himself in feminine terms, including describing himself as a mother: 'As one whom his mother comforts, so will I comfort you' (Is 66:13; see also Is 49:15). In the New Testament, the writers choose the Greek word *anthropos* ('human being') to describe Jesus, rather than the word *aner* which specifically means 'male' (see Rom 5:15, 17). Moreover, 'the Word' (Jesus) of John chapter 1 is a development of 'Wisdom' (represented as feminine) from Proverbs chapter 8 (cf 1 Cor 1:30). Even more interestingly, in the book of Revelation the glorified Lord Jesus is described as having female breasts (see Rev 1:13; modern versions unfortunately obscure the specifically feminine word for 'breast' used here).

Similarly, the Holy Spirit is represented as a *dove* – a feminine word and symbol. The word 'spirit' is itself of feminine gender in Hebrew and neuter in Greek. Moreover, the Holy Spirit is pictured as giving birth like a mother in John 3:8. All these facts, and there are many more we could highlight, point to God as one who embraces masculinity and femininity in his nature and who is the source of both. Even the Old Testament name for God, *El Shaddai*, contains the Hebrew word for the female breast (*shad*) at its root.

The nature of God is a deep subject with many philosophical implications which are not in the scope of this chapter. However, it is evident that woman, as well as man, is made in the image of God. There is no reason therefore why a woman may not speak and act on God's behalf if she is moved by the Holy Spirit. In fact, the pages of the Bible frequently highlight women who did so, and with divine approval.

Women and spiritual gifts

The New Testament contains two lists of spiritual gifts, in Romans 12:6–8 and 1 Corinthians 12:7–11, and the Bible gives us examples of women exercising many of them. For example, the list of gifts in Romans mentions prophecy, serving, teaching, encouraging, giving, leadership and showing mercy. These are gifts given to the Church in order to build it up. They are the manifestation of the Holy Spirit in individual believers and are meant to benefit others as we use them in the Holy Spirit. Each of the gifts mentioned in Romans has biblical examples of women as well as men using them.

1. Prophecy

The Good News Bible describes prophecy as 'speaking God's message', which is a succinct definition of this sometimes misunderstood word. We are told in 1 Corinthians 14:31 that prophecy is for instruction and encouragement; here, it is a public gift for church meetings. In other places, we see prophecy used privately. There are a number of women mentioned in the Bible as prophetesses, including Miriam, Deborah, Huldah and Isaiah's wife in the Old Testament, and Anna and Philip's four daughters in the New Testament.[2] In most cases, it is evident when you read the accounts of these women and their prophesying that they spoke with authority and expected their message to be heard and received. When the king of Judah sent the high priest to Huldah to enquire from her the will of God, referring to the book of the Law which they had found in the house of the Lord, she answered authoritatively as the prophet of the Lord. In the words of Catherine Booth, one of the founders of the Salvation Army, 'the authority and dignity of Huldah's message to the king betrays none of that trembling diffidence or abject servility which some persons seem to think should characterise the religious exercises of woman.'[5]

Today, many churches are more familiar with the 'preaching' aspect of the prophetic gift than with the more direct, 'supernatural' aspect of it, but in either situation the authority of the Holy Spirit is required. When Jesus told Mary to go and tell the disciples that he had risen from the dead, he was commissioning her to proclaim to a mixed company the glorious truth of his Resurrection, which is at the heart of the gospel message for all time.

2. Service

This gift, as its name implies, refers to a variety of practical labours for the Lord, including hospitality. The apostle Peter says, 'If anyone serves, he [or she] should do it with the strength God provides, so that in all things God may be praised through Jesus Christ' (1 Pet 3:11). Many women excel at serving and love to do it, though they would probably acknowledge that they need to draw on 'the strength God provides'. Romans chapter 16 contains a list of people to whom the apostle Paul wishes to send greetings. One third of the people mentioned are women. Four women (Mary, Tryphena, Tryphosa and Persis) are described as those who had 'worked very hard in the Lord'.[6] They probably had the gift of serving. Another, the mother of Rufus, Paul describes as having been a mother to him also. She probably gave him hospitality and cared for his physical needs. Paul publicly expresses appreciation for this kind of ministry and describes one of these women as 'my dear friend'. Lydia is another woman who gave hospitality to Paul and later hosted a church in her house.[7]

3. Teaching

Another woman friend of Paul's undoubtedly had the gift of teaching. Priscilla, the wife of Aquila, gave Paul hospitality and the three of them worked together in secular work (they were tent-makers by trade) and spiritual work. Priscilla's is another name mentioned by Paul in Romans chapter 16. He refers to her and her husband as 'fellow-workers in Christ Jesus' who risked their lives for Paul, and to whom both he and 'all the churches of the Gentiles' owe gratitude. He also refers to the church that met in their house. Priscilla and Aquila are mentioned six times in the New Testament, and on four of those occasions Priscilla's name is first in the Greek text – an unusual practice in the first century, suggesting she was better known or more prominent than her husband. In Acts chapter 18, Priscilla and Aquila are seen instructing Apollos in the faith. This is the only biblical record of Priscilla teaching, but we know from references to her in Church history that she had a wide ministry. There is even a school of thought today suggesting that Priscilla was the author of the book of Hebrews. Such a suggestion cannot be conclusively proved, of course, although the argument for it is well reasoned. At any rate, even Tertullian, who at one time did not approve of women in ministry, acknowledged that Priscilla preached the gospel. Would Priscilla, a close friend and fellow-worker of Paul, have done so if Paul forbade such a thing, as some assert he did?

4. Encouraging

The gift of encouragement is a ministry which gives courage and strength to others to go on when they are perhaps under pressure. It can be used publicly as an aspect of preaching, or privately in a personal interaction with another Christian. Elizabeth is a beautiful example of the gift in Luke 1:39–45. When Mary finds herself pregnant with the Christ-child, she travels across the hills to visit her relative Elizabeth. Mary must have been pressured by fear and doubt as to how she would cope with the enormous responsibility being given to her. How encouraging it must have been to her to receive the spontaneous prophetic utterance from Elizabeth as she greeted her! It awakened in Mary the response that we have today as the prophetic song, the Magnificat. Mary then stayed on with Elizabeth, presumably until the birth of John the Baptist – another event which was surrounded by supernatural happenings and which must have encouraged Mary in her own situation. Encouragement is in some people a gift closely associated with prophecy and in others with the pastoral gift.

5. Giving

The gift of giving enables people to gladly share their money or property with others, over and above the giving which we would expect from every Christian. Some Christians love to give and have counted it an adventure with God to trust him to prosper them financially, not for their own sakes, but in order that they might share their blessing with others. They use their gifts to support the Church and Christian work in general. In New Testament times not many women had independent means, but there are several examples of women giving generously to Jesus. Mary of Bethany is a striking example. She took a very costly jar of perfumed oil – possibly it was her dowry, saved for her marriage – and poured it out as a prophetic act of extravagant love toward a Saviour who was about to pour out his costly love through death.

Another woman is recorded as having given to God, out of her poverty, all the living that she had (Lk 21:1–4). Jesus reserves his highest praise for these two women who exercised the gift of giving. It is also recorded in Luke 8:1–3 that some women travelled with Jesus in his team and they helped to support the ministry out of their own means.

6. Leadership

Some Christians today assert that it is contrary to the will of God that women should exercise leadership. However, the Bible records several examples of women who did so and who appear to have been approved by God. We read first of Miriam, sister of Moses, in Exodus 2:1–10. She comes to the fore again after the Israelites have come out of Egypt, in Exodus 15:20, when she leads the women in prophetic dance. When God speaks about this period of Israel's history he says, in Micah 6:4, 'I sent Moses to lead you, also Aaron and Miriam.' God plainly includes Miriam in the leadership team with Aaron and Moses. However, some might argue that Miriam's leadership was strictly confined to the women and cannot be used as an argument for women to lead men.

Whether or not Miriam's leadership was restricted to the women's work, this certainly could not be said of Deborah

(Judg 4:4). She was plainly a leader of the Israelite people as a whole and exercised authority over Barak, commander of the army. God used her leadership and prophetic insight to deliver Israel from their enemies.

In the New Testament, Paul refers to Phoebe in Romans 16:2 in leadership terms. First of all he describes her as a *deacon* of the church at Cenchreae. The word 'deacon' is in the masculine form here, emphasising the nature of the office rather than the gender of the person. It is the same word that Paul uses to describe himself and other apostles and is usually translated 'minister'. Paul requests the believers in Rome to receive her in a fitting way and to help her in any way she requires. He then describes her as a 'helper' of many. The word translated 'helper' here is a word literally meaning 'to stand before' (*prostrates*). The usual translations of the word are 'front rank person', 'chief', 'leader of a party', 'protector or champion'. None of these definitions give the impression that Phoebe was merely a kind of messenger-girl, as some have suggested. History reveals that Phoebe travelled widely, presumably for the gospel's sake. Theodoret, the Early Church historian, notes that 'the fame of Phoebe was spoken of throughout the world'. Considering the restricted life most women led in the first century, this is truly remarkable.

7. Showing mercy

This gift is an expression of the love and concern God has for the poor and oppressed. It is usually exercised in practical forms of caring. A good example is Dorcas in Acts 9:36. We are told she was 'always doing good and helping the poor'. Although the expression 'doing good' has the rather negative connotation of the 'do-gooder' these days, it conveys the fact that her caring had a practical expression. She evidently made clothes for the poor and probably helped them in other financial ways. That her love and concern was deeply appreciated is evidenced by the widows who wept for her when she died and the fact that her church summoned the apostle Peter to bring her back from death! Her gift of mercy was obviously too valuable to lose.

Besides the gifts already described, we know that women also engaged in evangelism and pastoring. For example, Paul mentions Euodias and Syntyche in Philippians 4:2 who 'laboured side by side with him in the gospel'. In fact, the prophecy (in the original Hebrew) of Psalm 68:11, 'The Lord gives the word; the women who proclaim the good tidings are a great host', has certainly been fulfilled in the various missionary movements over the centuries, even if less so in the home churches. The gift and office of pastor is obviously needed also among women. In the first century in particular it is unlikely that men could have effectively pastored women (which would have included visiting them in their homes) without offending the proprieties of the day. Women were needed to pastor women, and Church history informs us that women did indeed visit the sick, prepare women for baptism and generally instruct and encourage other women in the Lord. These women pastoral workers are probably the ones addressed by Paul in Titus 2:3–5 and 1 Timothy 3:11. At some point in the first three centuries of the Christian Church there were also women elders, since this office was disbanded by the Council of Laodicea in 363 AD, which proves it was in existence prior to that time.

With so much evidence for the ministry of women in Bible times, it may seem strange that churches today are often slow to acknowledge women in any area of ministry. This is usually attributed to two statements of the apostle Paul where he apppears to silence women in church and not permit them any authority. The first statement is in 1 Corinthians 14:34: 'Let the women keep silence in the churches; for they are not permitted to speak, but let them subject themselves [literally 'put themselves in order'], just as the Law says.' This passage might seem at first glance in a modern translation of the Bible to prohibit women preaching in church. However, an examination of the context and the Greek words reveals that Paul is talking about *order* in the church (verses 32, 34, 40) and is forbidding women – as well as men in certain situations (verses 28, 30) – to chatter noisily in church. (The word 'speak' is the most general word for oral utterance, including 'babble', 'chatter' and 'sing', and its meaning is determined by the context. It is not a formal word for 'teach'.) Instead, he exhorts them to be orderly (i.e. self-disciplined), which is something the Old Testament Law required in worship and which Paul commends to the Colossian Christians also (Col 2:5).

The second passage widely quoted as barring women from any public ministry in the Church is 1 Timothy 2:11–15: 'Let a woman quietly receive instruction with entire submissiveness. But I do not allow a woman to teach or exercise authority over a man, but to remain quiet. For Adam was first created and then Eve. And Adam was not deceived but the woman being quite deceived fell into transgression. But she shall be saved through the birth of the child, if the women continue in faith and love and sactity, with self-restraint.'

This passage is far too complex for an in-depth analysis here. However, if we construe this passage as barring women from public ministry and leadership, then we have to charge Priscilla and Phoebe and others with disobeying Paul. If that were the case, it would seem strange that Paul does not publicly rebuke them, but rather specifically commends them and their ministry in his writings. If we allow that Paul did approve of women in ministry – and there is a weight of evidence that he did – then we must conclude that the 'traditional' interpretation of this text (silencing women in ministry) is inaccurate. What is the alternative interpretation?

First, we should note the context. Paul is urging that women be encouraged to learn. (This was unusual in the first century, when women were not generally taught the Scriptures nor expected to learn anything.) They were to receive instruction in the meetings in an orderly way, without talking to each other. Furthermore, they were not allowed to argue or disagree while they were being taught. The words 'exercise authority' are a translation of an unusual Greek word (*authentein*) which is unique in the New Testament. It is a strong word, made of of two words, 'self' and 'weapons'. Perhaps the word 'self-assertion' is the nearest to it. However, in society it could even be used for fratricide (i.e. murder within the family), although it could also have a less violent meaning like 'taking authority over'. Paul may have been forbidding *wives* to contradict their *husbands* in public (the Greek words for 'woman' and 'wife', 'man' and 'husband' are the same, as in German and other languages). Equally, he may have been forbidding domestic strife in private, caused by the wives learning as well as the husbands. The added phrase, 'but to remain quiet' (1 Tim 2:12, NASV) is evidence that Paul is not referring to a woman being invited to preach, but a woman in the congregation who is supposed to be learning. Paul was concerned that women should not continue in ignorance, as they had been forced to do until that time by the dictates of society and religious leaders. Ignorance breeds deception, which is probably why Paul refers to Eve at this time. It was the deception of Satan that led her into sin. The only way to guard against deception is to know and keep in the truth. In 2 Corinthians 11:3 Paul uses a similar reference when he says, 'I am afraid lest, as the serpent deceived Eve by his craftiness, your minds should be led astray from the simplicity and purity of devotion to Christ.' It is not necessary to ban women from public ministry because some women (and some men) have been deceived by Satan and led away from the truth.

There is much more that could be written about women's gifts in the Church, but space does not permit.[8] Hopefully, this condensed account will encourage women to grow and mature in the faith of Jesus Christ and to find the areas of gifting God wants to release them in. We hope also that male Church leaders will help the women in their midst to find their true callings and ministries and to demonstrate that 'in Christ there is neither Jew nor Greek, there is neither slave nor free man, there is no "male and female"; for you are all one in Christ Jesus' (Gal 3:28).

Questions for discussion

1 What value is placed on single women in your church? (see 1 Cor 7:34–35). How could their gifts and service be encouraged?
2 How may women more effectively pastor women? (see Titus 2:4–5).
3 In what ways do you think a church with an all-male leadership misses out on the fullness of Christian living?

4 What problems may arise when women are placed in leadership over men? How could these problems be dispelled or minimised?
5 Many married women who see homemaking and motherhood as their prime calling feel devalued in today's world. How can we ensure that they are honoured and valued in the Church?
6 How can we in our churches aim at fulfilling Galatians 3:26–28 without falling into the trap of 'tokenism'?

References

1 *Children's Letters to God* (Fontana).
2 See Exodus chapter 14; Judges chapter 4; 2 Chronicles 34:22–28; Isaiah 8:3; Luke 2:36–38 and Acts 21:9.
3 For a fuller discussion of these and other verses see *The New Humanity*, obtainable from Ichthus Christian Fellowship, 116 Perry Vale, Forest Hill, London SE23 2LQ.

Valerie Griffiths

Valerie Griffiths read Theology at Oxford in order to teach Religious Education. After marrying Michael, she spent ten years in Japan with the Overseas Missionary Fellowship, working with women in evangelism. After a further thirteen years in Singapore they returned to Britain. Valerie is now a visiting lecturer on the Old Testament at London Bible College and Michael is Principal. Valerie has travelled widely, mainly in East Asia, and has four children.

4. Women in Mission

Valerie Griffiths

'The Lord gave the command, and many women carried the news' (Ps 68:11).

Pale, serious faces gaze back from old photographs. The dark dresses, high collars and hairstyles with centre partings reveal women who were typical mid-Victorians. They were probably unaware that they were standing on the threshold of a new era, and that thousands of women would follow where they led.

The secular world in the early nineteenth century had provided a dead end for many women. The poor were sucked into the long hours, gruelling conditions and minimal wages caused by the Industrial Revolution. Middle class girls without private incomes became humble governesses for the wealthy. All were brought up for marriage and motherhood. The more fortunate did marry and spent the rest of their lives at home, waited on by servants, passing their days with painting, music and social visits. Their education had been minimal, and when in their narrow world their minds stagnated and their health crumbled, it all seemed to confirm to the men how frail they were. They had few legal rights and little control over their own lives. The 1851 census revealed a million surplus unmarried women between twenty and forty years of age, many of whom were forced to spend their lives dependent on relatives for all their needs.

As the decades passed, boredom led to mounting pressure as women found their traditional role unrealistic and frustrating. New ideas were spreading in society, emphasising the basic equality and human rights of all people. Women became more bold, asking for their own rights and freedom as equal human beings made in God's image. The furore over their ability to contribute to public life lasted for the next fifty years until the First World War proved them right.

There were new winds blowing through the Christian world too. The clergy were no longer experts who could not be challenged. Their congregations were being educated and were no longer passive. In the mid eighteenth century John Wesley had abandoned the respectable middle and upper classes to take the Christian message to all people and those who took responsibility for their own sin and repented developed a deep concern for others in society, taking action on behalf of the poor, morally vulnerable, exploited and oppressed. They were critical of the conservative clergy who were no longer in touch with a changing world. The Christian faith these people embraced affected not only their own lives, but those of their neighbours too.

The Early Church – women liberated

A thoughtful reading of the New Testament shows how the Christian gospel transformed the lives of women in the first century AD, setting them free to serve God as full, participating members of the local church, working alongside men in witnessing to the Christian faith. Romans chapter 16 refers to a surprising number – including Junia, a woman apostle – who worked with Paul and were appreciated by him and affirmed by him. Jesus himself defied the cultural patterns of his time and counted women as well as men among his closest friends. Women continued to serve until restrictions were imposed in the Middle Ages. With the increase in travel and communication in the seventeenth century, Roman Catholic nuns became more active again. Quaker women helped to take the gospel to North America, the West Indies, Greece and Turkey. On the Continent single women found a vocation through service in the deaconness movements. In 1706 the first Christian couple left Saxony as missionaries to India.[1]

But it was another hundred years before the Protestant missionary movement began to gather momentum, and even then most societies insisted that anyone going overseas must first be trained as a minister in his own country, a training designed to mould him for British middle class churches. A few wives accompanied their husbands, but the clergy/laity gulf was great and jealously guarded. A doctor who went out to India for medical work was forbidden to evangelise and thereby trespass on clergy preserves. There were no openings for the laity or skilled artisans. Single women could not even live alone in their own country, let alone overseas.

Women who broke the mould

Yet those who did go overseas, whether for Christian or secular work, became deeply concerned with the ignorance, poverty and hardship of women and girls in those countries. The first single woman to go to India to try and start schools for girls was probably Miss Cooke in 1821, but the local opposition made it impossible. In 1827 the newly formed Society for Promoting Female Education in the Far East sent Miss Newell to Malacca, where she started five schools for girls. Miss Aldersley joined her in 1832 and in 1844 managed to reach Ningpo, just as China was beginning to admit foreigners. She began a girls' school there and in the 1850s accepted help from two sisters in their late teens. One of them, Maria Dyer, was married to Hudson Taylor just after her 21st birthday.[1] Meanwhile in 1852 Mrs Elizabeth Sale began village work in India and in the same year the Calcutta Normal School was opened. This last event is regarded as the founding of the Zenana Bible and Medical Mission, which functioned as a women's mission for over a hundred years before admitting men as members in 1952 and becoming the Bible and Medical Missionary Fellowship.[2]

The achievements of these women may be better understood if we remember Florence Nightingale defying society to nurse the wounded of the Crimean War in 1855–56: 'I would have given the Church my head, my heart, my hand. She would not have them. She told me to go back to do crochet in my mother's drawing room; or marry and look well at the head of my husband's table. "You may go to Sunday School if you like it," she said, but gave me no training even for that. She gave me neither work to do for her nor education for it.' Her words epitomise the dilemma of her contemporaries, and like many of them she had to by-pass the Church to use her gifts of admistration and caring elsewhere. This included organising health and sanitation for the British Army and adjacent villages throughout India, briefing several viceroys before they left for India, planning the development of district nursing in Lancashire and the first training school for nurses in Britain. Florence Nightingale was an invalid for the rest of her life but she had demonstrated the vital part women could fulfil in public life.

Meanwhile Hudson Taylor had returned from China burdened with the needs of 400 million Chinese, especially for those in the nine inland provinces where there was no Protestant witness at all. He had no time for the decades of Church structures and traditions. In his view evangelism was the responsibility of every believer who received the gifts and calling for such work (Eph 4:11–13). The need was so vast that he was ready to accept all men and women, married or single, called by God to serve him there. At that time there were only fourteen single women from the West living in the whole of China and Hong Kong. All had to receive basic Bible training for the work, all would be full members of the mission and all finance would be shared equally. It was very simple but revolutionary. Just ten years after Florence Nightingale's return from the Crimea, the first group of the China Inland Mission embarked on their four-month journey by boat. There were two married couples, five single men, and nine single women.

No-one knew how these women would serve in China. There were no safely structured communities based on hospitals and schools where they could go. No western woman had ever travelled inland. No-one knew what reception they would have. Distances were vast, travel was rough and dangerous and expatriates on the coast were outraged that western women should don Chinese teachers' gowns and be exposed to the rigours and dangers of local life. As the group began language study the future was uncertain.

The breakthrough finally came eleven years later, in 1877. There was an appalling famine in Shansi province when an estimated nine to thirteen million people died, disease was rife, and women and children were being sold into slavery. In such circumstances there were open doors to minister to women and children, but there was no experienced woman to lead. Finally Maria Taylor felt the Lord calling her to help. Leaving her husband in London convalescing with their six children, she made the long journey back to China and then travelled on to the famine area (a further three weeks) with two younger women. They were the first women to go so far inland, demonstrating that it was safe, and they were able to start an orphanage.

Here we should pay tribute to another unsung heroine, Amelia Broomhall, Hudson Taylor's sister, who would get 'depressed, contrasting myself with some clever women', was conscious of making mistakes and felt very inadequate, but with her husband poured out her life, receiving and caring for missionaries passing through London. She made it possible for Jenny Taylor to go to China, by adding Jenny's six children to her own ten. The neighbours thought she had started a school![3] 1877 marked the turning point for women missionaries in China.

A hundred years later those pale Victorian faces still gaze out of yellowing pages. They were indeed women of their time, but women prepared to defy society and obey God, women with a passionate desire to proclaim the name of Jesus to millions who had never heard it before, almost literally going to the ends of the earth.[4]

Women in mission today

An examination of British missionary societies with more than fifty members today[5] shows that women still play a significant part. Only four societies have a predominance of men. They are the Seventh Day Adventists, the United Society for the Propagation of the Gospel (which has a strongly male celibate tradition), Operation Mobilisation and Youth with a Mission, both of which use large numbers of young people. Denominational societies have an average of 55% women and interdenominational societies average 62%. The figures are remarkably consistent for all. Since administration is usually in the hands of men, this leaves a great deal of the day-to-day work with women.

In 1985 the Evangelical Alliance sponsored a survey of single women missionaries by Gill College.[6] It covered 818 women from forty-one societies listed in the 1981 *UK Christian Handbook*. One of the basic issues which emerged was the definition of a missionary today. Increasingly churches are having to decide whether they have an obligation to support any member who goes overseas for Christian work, even for short periods. Journeys which once took four months now take less than twenty-four hours, and where people went overseas for seven years they can now go for weeks. Can people be missionaries in their own countries, so often more pagan than those overseas? Is any Christian working overseas a missionary?

Dr Ralph Winter's analysis[7] of evangelism is helpful here in distinguishing the issues involved:

E0 evangelism means evangelising nominal Christians in one's own language and culture. This should be the easiest form of communication.

E1 evangelism entails sharing the gospel with non-Christians of one's own language and culture. Here the Christian/non-Christian gulf must be crossed.

E2 evangelism involves sharing the gospel with those whose language and culture are different, yet similar to one's own – Europe, for example.

E3 evangelism means communicating in a totally different language and culture, as in Asia.

Communication with each of these groups needs different gifts and skills. E0 and E1 usually take place in one's home country and are the responsibility of every Christian. E2 and E3 usually involve going overseas or at least crossing frontiers or borders, adjusting to and understanding another culture and learning a language well in order to communicate in it. This is surely missionary work. It is a long-term commitment to God's call to proclaim the gospel throughout the world. Those who are called should face up to their inadequacy and ignorance and recognise the need for specialised help and training in preparation. However, in some less homogeneous societies, where people of different languages and races and cultures live together, there may also be a need for E3 evangelism within one's own country, but it must then be recognised that those who are called still need to face the challenge of understanding a new language and culture in order to share the Good News. In Britain the need for E3 evangelism has increased in the last thirty years because of immigration, and Christians are not finding it easy to cross the barriers of race and language without special help and commitment. The early churches could move comparatively easily from Jerusalem to Samaria to the world because they all lived in the Roman Empire and used Greek at least as a trade language. As soon as Paul and Barnabas were confronted with another language in Lystra, they were in trouble (Acts 14: 11ff).

What makes a missionary?

The basic command in Matthew 28:19–20 is to make disciples of all nations, baptising and teaching them. Missionaries are those who make this their primary aim, leaving their own culture and language to live and communicate in another, working to support the local church in that place. We spend years preparing for secular work. We should not expect to spend less time preparing to serve God. Many national churches still welcome such help and partnership. In some countries visas can only be obtained for secular work, and Christians must use this route to get in. But whatever a missionary may be doing, the primary purpose should be to share the Christian message and assist the local church.

When such freedom allows a woman's gifts to develop, what happens? When the work of these modern missionaries was analysed[8] it fell into seven main categories, and these are broken down further in the attached analysis which follows. It reveals what a wide variety of work is being done by women. Some of this is predictably in traditional areas such as medicine, teaching and secretarial work. However, 'church ministries' includes a wide variety of work not always found in this country, and certainly not usually done by women. Church planting can involve moving into a town of up to 40,000 people where there are no Christians. It means making friends, sharing the Christian message as there is opportunity, teaching those who show interest, nurturing and teaching those who become Christians, training new Christians to study the Bible for themselves, training people to take responsibility in the Church and lead meetings and so on. In tribal work one would add Bible translation and adult literacy to the list of jobs. As soon as the group is large enough to support their own pastor (when they have twenty or so members) the missionary can move on to the next place.

In some areas churches are growing at an exciting rate, in others it is much slower. In areas of booming population it is possible to have a church of one hundred members before they get their first married couple. In these situations no-one has grown up absorbing the things we take for granted in our churches. In Sunday school, the big ones may grab the front seats and the smallest be left at the back where they can see nothing. Families need biblical teaching as they work out what God's will is for husbands and wives, parents and children. Committees and church leaders need to understand biblical principles and disentangle themselves from their own culture where it clashes with biblical truth. The missionaries must also be disentangling themselves from their own culture where that is not necessarily biblical. The teaching on pastoral problems should be given by national pastors who know their culture, but very often they are too few to cope. Potential leaders who cannot go to Bible school can be taught in their villages 'by extension' if someone is available to teach them. Women are involved in all of this work. Some are working with national women preparing materials for the women's meetings and training the Sunday school teachers of whole denominations. There is an enormous hunger for teaching and help in the churches overseas and a great awareness of how much they still have to learn. By comparison churches in the West are inert and complacent.

Comprehensive list of missionary job descriptions

1. Medical
2. Teaching

3. Church Ministries
4. Translation
5. Administration
6. Institutional
7. Other work

Categories of job descriptions

Medical
Nurse in Institution
Nurse in Community
Nurse Tutor
Midwife
Doctor
Para-Medic. e.g. Physiotherapist

Teaching
Secular Teaching
Teaching missionary children
Church School Teaching
University Lecturer
Educational Adviser
College Principal

Church Ministries
Lay Church Worker
Church Planter
Evangelist
Bible Teacher
Women's Worker
Pastoral Ministries
Theological College Lecturer
Bible College Lecturer
Leadership Training
Theological Education by Extension
Preparation of Bible teaching materials
Minister/Pastor

Translation
Translator
Literacy Worker
Literature promotion

Administration
Accounts and Finance
Administration in the Church
Administration in the Society
Secretarial

Institutional work
Care of: Guest houses
Orphanage
Hostels
School Dormitories

Miscellaneous job descriptions
Vet, Librarian, Student work, Language Supervisor, Social worker, Cassette Ministry, Radio work, Editor, Agricultural worker, Refugee work, etc.

From: *Single Women in Mission*, Gill College/E.M.A. 1985

It seems that when women are freed from cultural restrictions and allowed to follow the leading of the Holy Spirit, using the gifts he has given them, they can develop a rich and effective ministry.

The gifts of the Holy Spirit are given to the whole Church, regardless of sex,[9] so it should not be surprising that women are working alongside men as fellow human beings. This does not mean they are identical, for they were created different, but while it may sometimes be possible to feel in retrospect that certain work has been done in a certain way because that person was male or female, it is not usually possible to predict such a distinction beforehand and we must beware of stereotyping people and trying to fit them into roles. We shall only end up trying to jam square pegs into round holes.

Single women in mission

One of the greatest assets for the single woman is her time. She is not limited by the demands of family as married people are and can give herself wherever she is needed. The people surveyed did not feel there were any particular types of work they did best, but recognised this gift of freedom. Both married and single women sometimes found they were accepted by groups which feared men, especially in tribal areas, and sometimes men were only accepted through their wives. Moreover single women have been able to work alongside national leaders without complications of authority and hierarchy. They are less threatening to the emergence of national leadership. This accounted for the growth of the work under women and Chinese pastors in the Kwangsin River area in China in the nineteenth century. Most women have found that the national churches treated them with respect, and in some cases they have been given positions of great responsibility. At the same time they need great flexibility as situations are constantly changing, and they must be prepared to move from one kind of work to another and hand over to others when the time comes.

However, there are also aspects of their work that they find hard, and ironically it sometimes happens in the areas where they are most valuable. In tribal work they find travelling alone difficult and they have less physical stamina than men for gruelling travel and living conditions. And yet they do it. They also find it hard living in Moslem societies where men are dominant and women have no recognition at all, and in some countries cannot even be seen in the market, which is the men's area. But they work there, to reach women. Pioneer church work is hard for many women, starting from scratch in a strange town. But they do that too, because if they do not, no-one else will. Missionary work has never been easy (2 Corinthians 11:23–29). Paul talks of fighting not 'against human beings, but against the wicked spiritual forces in the heavenly world, the rulers, authorities, and cosmic powers of this dark age' (Eph 6:12). It is a spiritual battle. Churches need to understand this when their members go overseas, and provide the emotional and spiritual support they are going to need.

When the personal problems of single women were listed in the survey, 67% proved to be common to all missionaries of both sexes living abroad in a strange culture and language. For example, all would experience cultural loneliness, physical loneliness (being away from close friends), and spiritual loneliness. Only 16% of their problems involved their being women, married or single, in cultures where women were restricted. Travelling alone, fending off sexual advances and avoiding giving offence were mentioned. One nurse who had to visit remote villages, travelling by motor bike through lonely rice paddies in a lawless area commented, 'Yes, we are afraid. But we have to go on.' One of the single person's main problems comes in cultures where singleness is not understood. If all responsible parents arrange marriages for their daughters, whatever is wrong with this woman if her parents have been unable to find anyone? Gill College comments, 'There is obviously a very thin dividing line between not causing an offence by the Gospel, and being single for the Kingdom of God's sake.'[10]

Married women in mission

Where married women are concerned, the circumstances vary. One well-known mission in the nineteenth century declined to train wives and fiancées on the grounds that 'their role was in the home, and no ministry was contemplated for them which could not be taught them by their husbands.'[11] In fact, the vast majority of churches in Britain today still take the same view of their minister's wives. A few missions still do not bother to interview wives or include them as mission members. Wives should beware of such. If a woman does not have a personal calling and commitment to serve God overseas, she may be very unhappy there and make it impossible for her husband to remain. This is why most societies expect her to have the same call and include her as a full member alongside her husband. One of Britain's leading Bible colleges will not accept married men for training for overseas service unless their wives are trained with them. Sometimes a man's job does not include his wife (e.g. a doctor) but missionary work is usually so diverse that she will find a niche somewhere, even though professional work passes are often refused to wives.

A mother's first responsibility must be to her children when they are small, for the Lord has entrusted them to her, but he has also put her where she is, and if she is one of a few Christians in an area she cannot shut her door on the people among whom she lives. To make a happy, secure home for her children in another culture, she must herself be at home in it, competent in the language and able to be at ease with her neighbours and in the local church if there is one. Therefore she must find time daily in the early years for several hours of serious language study, and young couples need to take this into account if they feel the Lord is calling them overseas.

A married couple also have their own particular contribution which single people cannot fulfil, for they may be the only Christian family in a church and new Christians will be using them as a pattern of a Christian home and marriage. The couple must then try to live as Christians in that society, not necessarily as they would in their own society. Becoming a Christian must not mean becoming 'English' or 'American'. That would put a stumbling block in the way of others. Missionary children may suffer deprivations, but they are usually far outweighed by the benefits and privileges of living overseas, and they have a great gift for opening doors and crossing cultural gulfs. Where foreigners are feared, shunned and ignored for their height, fair skin and blue eyes, children break barriers and demonstrate that we are all human beings underneath. Also, married women often find it easier to cross the cultural gulf and get alongside other mothers as mothers and so share the Christian message.

It is strange that controversy still rages over the ministry of women. Their commissioning is clear from the commissioning of the whole Church at Pentecost. The Lord had taught his followers from the Old Testament for five weeks before he left them, and promised they would receive power to be his witnesses to the ends of the earth, when the Holy Spirit came upon them (Acts 1:8). Both men and women waited in Jerusalem and ten days later, when they were all together, the Holy Spirit fell on all of them (Acts 2:1–4). Peter, surely on the basis of what Jesus had taught him, clearly identified this event with the prophecy of Joel 2:28–32, which speaks of the Holy Spirit being given to all people, sons and daughters, men and women, so that they could proclaim the word of God. This is the charter for women's service, as well as men's, and all other Biblical verses must be interpreted in the light of it.

Vocation not fulfilment

The women who went overseas in the nineteenth century were not concerned for their own self-fulfilment or fame. They were responding to the call of their Lord to follow him and were prepared to pour out their lives in serving him, even when it involved the possibility of danger and death. Their overwhelming concern was to share their knowledge of Jesus Christ with men and women – and especially with the women – who were 'separated from Christ, having no hope, and without God in the world' (Eph 2:12). If the description sounds old-fashioned and remote from us today, we need to search our own hearts and ask why. For if we call ourselves Christians such a conviction lies at the heart of our faith, and our calling must be to share that with others.

So we come back to evangelism – sharing the Good News of Jesus with those around us who do not know him, and the numbers are very great. Recent estimates indicate that neighbourhood evangelism is not enough. If Christians simply witness to those they meet, many separated from them by language, race, culture, class, education and work will never hear the message. In Britain we cannot be complacent about evangelism when churches tend to concentrate on the middle classes and few are prepared to develop the skills, understanding and maybe language to communicate with other groups in our society. Few are concerned to help those trying to build churches in the inner cities. In Pakistan the Christians have Hindu origins and cannot communicate with Moslems. The great Batak Church of Sumatra cannot readily communicate with the Moslems in the next province. In India 95% of the Christians come from only five out of a hundred castes. The rest do not meet Christians. Of the non-Christians in today's world, 80% have no Christian neighbours and will not hear the message unless people learn how to cross barriers of race, culture and language to establish local churches in those areas which can continue to witness. The neighbourhood evangelism of the local church in their own language and culture is the most effective. But for the moment cross-cultural evangelism (E2 and E3) is still desperately needed.

> *God be merciful to us and bless us;*
> *look on us with kindness,*
> *so that the whole world may know your will,*
> *so that all nations may know your salvation.*
> (Ps 68: 1–2, GNB)

Israel knew she worshipped the living God of the whole earth, but she never worked out the implications of that faith for the rest of the world. Have we?

Questions for discussion

1. Study Romans chapter 16 and list all the men and women who are said to be involved in ministry of some kind (Junia is feminine). In what different ways does Paul describe their ministry and who is said to do what? You should have more women than men!
2. The majority of missionary societies send an average of two women overseas for each man. Why do you think this is so? Here are some possible reasons:
   a) the churches do not use them properly here
   b) there are more women than men in the churches
   c) the women are more obedient to God's call
   d) they respond more easily to emotional appeals
   e) men are more disobedient or responsible for families
   f) God chooses to work this way and use the 'weak' for his work
   g) other.
3. Women are involved in a variety of church ministries overseas (see p. 62). How many of these are open to women in this country? If not, why not?
4. What do you consider are women's special gifts, and what are men's? Consider some people you know and see how far these apply. In a group, how far can you agree on male and female qualities?

References

1. M Broomhall, *The Jubilee Story of the China Inland Mission* (London, Marshall, 1915), p.122.
2. J C Pollock, *Shadows Fall Apart* (London, Hodder & Stoughton, 1958), chapters 1 and 16.
3. Phyllis Thompson, *Each to her post* (London, Hodder and Stoughton, 1982) chapter 1.
4. Dr and Mrs Howard Taylor, *Hudson Taylor and the China Inland Mission* (London, CIM, 1949), chapters 21, 22, 23.
5. Peter Brierly, *UK Christian Handbook* (Bromley, MARC Europe, 1986), pp.344–368.
6. Gill College, *Single Women in Mission* (London, Evangelical Missionary Alliance, 1985).
7. J D Douglas, (ed.) *Let the Earth Hear His Voice* (World Wide Publications, 1975), p.213.
8. Gill College, ibid, pp.10, 52.
9. M C Griffiths, *Serving Grace* (Bromley, MARC Europe, 1986), chapter 5.
10. Gill College, ibid, p.40.
11. Peter Williams, *Recruitment and Training of Overseas Missionaries in England Between 1850 and 1900* (Unpublished dissertation, Bristol University).

Myrtle Langley

Myrtle Langley has lectured in Missiology at Trinity College Bristol and is currently a Diocesan Missioner in Liverpool. She is author of *Equal Woman* and is a leading member of MOW (the Movement for the Ordination of Women.)

5. The Ordination of Women

Myrtle S Langley

For two kinds of Christians, women's ordination is not an issue of immediate or paramount concern: for those whose denomination already admits women to its official ministry and for those who believe that ordination and the nature of ministry itself should be re-examined. This is not to say that all the members of churches which do ordain women are in favour of women's ordination nor that all women ministers find it easy to obtain full-time pastoral appointments. Many Christians still balk at having a women minister.

In Britain the Salvation Army and the Society of Friends have for a very long time welcomed women to positions of leadership in the fellowship on an equal footing with men, and more recently several denominations such as the Baptist, Congregationalist, Lutheran, Methodist, Pentecostal, Presbyterian and United Reformed Churches have ordained women to official ministry. Groups like the Christian Brethren and the House Churches, however, do not have an official full-time ministry. Rather, they have developed new, largely innovative and often experimental forms of ministry which they claim to be biblical and relevant for the times. Moreover a number of Christians of all complexions are increasingly critical of an 'official' ministry. They believe it to be bound by tradition, ridden with clericalism, shot through with anomalies, out of touch with reality and consequently irrelevant and of limited use in an increasingly post-Christian society. For example, on more than one occasion down-to-earth Roman Catholics, enthusiastic House Church members, evangelicals, charismatics and radical Anglicans have asked me questions such as, 'Why ordain women to a suspect institution?' 'Why lumber women with a questionable role?' 'Why not first reform the ministry itself?'

There is much force in these arguments and I would be the last to deny that the churches are in need of constant renewal of their ministries. Yet over two millennia the Church Universal has developed certain accepted doctrines and practices relating to its ministry which cannot and must not be ignored. It is the churches which claim to lay great store by the authority of Scripture or tradition or both which challenge the admissibility of women to the ordained ministry – an office which until recently has been the prerogative of men and even now remains so among seventy-five per cent of the world's Christians.

The two great branches of Christianity, the Eastern Orthodox and the largest branch of Western Christianity, Roman Catholicism, do not ordain women and at present have no intention of doing so, although the Roman Catholic Church worldwide contains many women's pressure groups and continues to produce the foremost among feminist theologians. In addition, many evangelicals and catholics with a concomitant appeal to Scripture and tradition reject the ordination of women. Catholics and evangelicals of this kind are to be found amongst the members of the Anglican Communion, a church which looks for guidance in matters of faith and doctrine to Scripture, tradition and reason, although in the last analysis appealing to the authority of Scripture.

It is no accident then that it is within the worldwide arena of the Anglican Communion that we are at present witnessing the great debate on women's ordination. In 1944, due to war-time need, Bishop R O Hall of Hong Kong ordained Deaconess Florence Li Tim Oi. In 1971 his successor, Bishop Gilbert Baker, priested an Englishwoman, Miss Joyce Bennett of the Church Missionary Society, and Chinese-born Miss Jane Hwang. Since 1976, when the irregular Philadelphia ordinations of eleven women in 1974 were regularised and the ordination of women became official practice in the Episcopal Church of the USA, many of the Anglican Communion's autonomous provinces have admitted women to the ministerial priesthood of the Church; but not the

Church of England, although that Church has been seen as 'the mother Church' and therefore pivotal in the debate.

In 1975 the Church of England's General Synod expressed the view that there are 'no fundamental objections to the ordination of women to the priesthood' but since then has been unable to pass the necessary enabling legislation. In 1986 the issue became a crisis one with three matters before the July Synod: the permission for women ordained abroad to exercise their ministry when on visits to England; the admission of women to the diaconate; and the scope of enabling legislation for the priesting of women. Led by certain of the small minority of bishops opposed at any cost to the admission of women to the priesthood, many expressed fears of schism and the setting up of a 'continuing' or 'parallel' Church of England. In the midst of the fray all the arguments pro and con were once again rehearsed, this time in both the secular and religious press. Eventually Synod voted against permitting women ordained abroad to exercise their ministry while visiting England but gave approval to the admission of women to the diaconate and to long-term preparations for the priesting of women. And in 1987 the first women were admitted to the diaconate and thus for the first time to Holy Orders in the Church of England.

Ministry in the Church of England

Before we state and examine those arguments, however, I propose to look at the official ministry of the Church as understood by the Church of England in the light of its appeal to Scripture, tradition and reason. It is widely accepted today that the New Testament itself contains no blue-print for ministry. But it is also believed by the mainline historic churches that since early times the Church has possessed an official ministry. Churches in the Reformed tradition recognise one order: that of 'presbyters'. Churches in the Catholic and Orthodox traditions recognise three orders: of bishops, priests (presbyters) and deacons. Anglicans recognise all three orders, although through the centuries opinion has been divided on the nature and meaning of 'priesthood'. The issue may be focused in asking whether or not by ordination the 'priest' is separated from rather than just distinguished from the 'laity'. If the former, then his priesthood is of a different nature; if the latter, then his priesthood is of a different order, gathering up and focusing the 'priesthood of all believers' and representing 'Christ the one High Priest' as he celebrates and presides at the Holy Eucharist. In so doing he exercises a representative priesthood. A recent Anglican statement on the matter may be usefully summarised at relevant points in order to serve as a basis for later discussion.

The report, entitled *The Priesthood of the Ordained Ministry*, traces the understanding of the idea of priesthood from the New Testament, through the patristic period to the present, paying particular attention to Anglican tradition and to the emerging ecumenical convergence on the priestly character of the ordained ministry set out in the Lima document of the World Council of Churches, and the official reports of bilateral dialogues with Roman Catholics, Lutherans and Reformed Christians. It concludes by offering a contemporary expression of priesthood. Christian tradition uses the terminology of priesthood in three distinct but related ways to refer to: the unique priesthood of Christ; the priesthood of the whole Church (the 'priesthood of all believers'); and the ministerial priesthood of bishops and presbyters. Christ is unique. He is our one High Priest. The priesthood of the Church and the priesthood of its ministers are derived from the priesthood of Christ and may thus be called priestly only in a secondary sense; they are priestly only by grace and only by participation in his unique priesthood. The ordained ministry has a representative function, both in relation to Christ and in relation to the whole community of faith. It has a particular relationship to Christ, which is not simply derived from the common ministry of all Christians, both in representing Christ to his people and also, in union with him, in representing the people to the Father. Bishops and presbyters represent both Christ and his people in their leadership of the Church and its mission, in the proclamation of the gospel, in the articulation of faith, and in the celebration of the sacraments. Because of their particular relationship to Christ as Lord of the Church, those who are called to this ministry receive a particular vocation to holiness and consecration of life. They are to share in the priestly ministry of Christ by lives of consecrated love and service for the sake of the whole Body.

By means of this summary it becomes possible to identify and appreciate the significance of the two major areas of argument against the admission of women to the order of priests or presbyters: leadership and priesthood respectively. Leadership is the main stumbling block for evangelicals who take literally the biblical injunction that man is the head of woman, and make it normative for all time and in all cultures. Priesthood is the main stumbling-block for catholics who take as literally, historically and ontologically relevant the maleness of Christ in the Incarnation and make the maleness of the priest who is the icon ('image') of Christ a necessary prerequisite for all time and in all cultures. This leads, as I have often remarked, to catholics protecting the altar and evangelicals the pulpit from John Knox's 'monstrous regiment of women'. Common to both is the view that 'in the nature of things', intrinsically, it is unfitting – indeed impossible – for a woman to be a ministerial priest; that is to say, either to be a leader of men or the representative of God to men. Somehow, merely being of the female sex precludes women from being able to exercise authority in the Church or from receiving the grace of orders. A woman *per se* cannot be a priest in the Church of God. To put it basically and bluntly, the female must always be subservient to or presumed to be represented by the male. Consequently the main arguments adduced both from Scripture and tradition against the ordination of women centre on the differences between the sexes rather than on their similarities and complementarities as created each alone and both together in the image and likeness of God.

Arguments against the ordination of women

The main arguments against the ordination of women to the ordained ministry of the churches are as follows:

* For almost two thousand years the ordained ministry of the Church has been male.
* Jesus chose twelve male apostles.
* The New Testament, particularly St Paul, enjoins women to keep silence in the churches, forbids women to teach men and, on the analogy of Christ and the Church, exhorts the wife to submit to her husband.
* Nature itself teaches that man is head of woman, the female is created *from*, *for* and *after* the male.
* If the priest represents Christ to the Church, is the icon or image of Christ – an *alter Christus* (a 'second Christ'), then it follows that because God became incarnate in Christ as male, then a male and only a male can take on this priestly role.
* If a woman were allowed to be an *alter Christus*, then the very concept of God himself would be threatened.
* If the two great Christian churches of East and West, the Orthodox and Roman Communions – representing as they do the continuity of the faith throughout the ages – do not ordain women, then the ongoing talks on the unity of the churches are gravely threatened and the eventual reconciliation of all Christians seriously delayed if not altogether jeopardised.
* Moreover, for Anglicans who are at a delicate stage in negotiations with Rome on the validity of Anglican orders, the ordination of women constitutes a grave threat to eventual recognition and intercommunion between the two churches.
* Traditionally, for instance as enunciated by Calvin, vocation alone was never considered reason enough for admitting a person to orders, but rather personal vocation and the confirmation of the Church.
* In view of all the many evils besetting the human race, such as world hunger, war and the nuclear threat, increasing poverty, racism and many other injustices, then the ordination of women pales into insignificance. It is just not a priority.
* As a consequence of the lack of consensus and the threat to unity it is not expedient – the time is not ripe – to ordain women priests *now*.

Arguments for the ordination of women

The main counter arguments, mounted in response to the above, run somewhat as follows:

* Against the claim that the universal practice during two thousand years of tradition militates against the admission of women to the ordained ministry it is pointed out justifiably by Anglicans that their concept of tradition is dynamic and not static – the Holy Spirit, it is affirmed, continues to lead into all truth.
* Whether or not Jesus chose all males as apostles, it is equally true that many of his most intimate followers were women, that he treated women with a dignity and integrity of personhood unusual if not unique for a Jewish man in Palestine of the time, that all four Evangelists record women as the first witnesses of the Resurrection, and that many of the prominent leaders of the New Testament churches were women. Moreover, in order to communicate the better both in relation to his person and to his mission Jesus (either historically or as interpreted by the Early Church) allowed himself in many respects both to be bound by the culture of his time and to act in conscious fulfilment of Old Testament prophecy regarding the Messiah and God's New Israel, the Church.
* On the basis of New Testament evidence generally it must be said that when taken at face value two contradictory positions must be admitted: Jesus himself went out of his way to accord women a dignity and integrity of personhood which on any reckoning recognised them as equal with men, and Paul, in his letter to the Galatians, set forth his great manifesto of Christian liberty which at baptism and therefore in the eyes of God and humankind declared there to be no difference between Jew and Greek, slave and free, male and female. In so doing he abolishes inherent inequalities of race, class and sex. In contrast, on other occasions Paul and his disciples exhort women – I would claim on the basis of a missionary strategy of accommodation to patriarchal structures – to play a subservient role to men in the churches.
* It is not at all proven that 'in the nature of things' men

must take the lead, always being the initiators, while women must follow. There is ample evidence to suggest that in part at least such reasoning is due to nurture, not nature; to role stereotyping rather than to natural inclination.

* The argument deriving from the priest as icon of Christ raises interesting questions in at least two respects: the universal reference of salvation and the nature of symbolism itself. If God became incarnate in Christ so as to represent all humankind, then it is his humanity and not his maleness which is operative for salvation, or else the female sex is excluded from the scope of redemption. If the priest represents Christ and Christ's body, the Church, then again it is not the literal historical male referent of the symbol which is significant but rather its humanness. God created man (humankind) in the image of himself, in the image of God he created him, male and female he created them (Gen 1:27, JB). Moreover, it can be argued that for by far the greatest part of Christian history the presence of Christ in the sacrament has been seen to be located not in the person of the priest but in the elements of bread and wine.
* Similarly, if God is transcender of gender, then our concept of God can in no way suffer impoverishment but rather enrichment when women and men respectively and equally perform the role of *alter Christus*.
* On the unity of the churches it can be said that already not only the churches of the great Reformed traditions but also some provinces of the Anglican Communion ordain women, and many Roman Catholics request the Church of England to give the lead and pave the way for them. And although some Anglican provinces ordain women (this poses a problem for Anglican-Roman Catholic dialogue), both sides are agreed that talks should go on, with joint study on the subject of women's ordination now firmly on the agenda.
* With regard to the validity of Anglican orders in the eyes of the Roman Catholic Church, it must be countered that even male orders have not yet been recognised.
* Of course the confirmation of the Church must be sought

for even a woman's felt vocation to priesthood. All that is being requested is an opportunity to test vocation.

* The ordination of women is a priority: women 'hold up more than half the sky'. To deny them priesthood is to oppress and diminish women and at the same time spiritually impoverishes the human race. Moreover, a church that can vote overwhelmingly for the abolition of apartheid in South Africa and deny its own women justice is deluding no one but itself.
* As for the expediency of the move to ordain women, then, it can always be argued that truth always has prior claim, particularly when some churches have already made a move and others expect a lead.

Profound arguments for the ordination of women

Now that we are fully aware of the positions taken up by antagonists and protagonists in the debate, we might reasonably conclude that there is nothing more to be done other than make up our own minds on the basis of the evidence as it appears to us. Such conclusions, however, would be premature. Those who advocate the ordination of women to the full ministry of the Church do so for more deeply held and widely applicable reasons.

On good biblical authority it is claimed that both male and female constitute the image of God in humankind, and until this image in its totality and wholeness is reflected in the ministerial priesthood of the Church neither God's intention for the wholeness of Creation nor the nature of God's character is being mediated through the Church. This has serious implications both for our understanding of the nature of God and for the functioning of human sexuality. God must be seen to transcend gender, to embrace motherly as well as fatherly characteristics. Sexuality must be seen to involve mutual relatedness, equality and complementarity rather than subservience of the female to the male, inequality and separateness.

On good theological grounds it is believed that the Holy Spirit continues to guide the Church into all truth. In consonance

ance with Scripture there is good reason to believe that the ordination of women is the will of God for the contemporary Church.

Historical and sociological evidence suggest that the exclusion of women from the ordained ministry in the past was to a great extent due to the rule of patriarchy and role-stereotyping both in Church and society, and to the undue influence on Christian thought and practice of philosophical and ethical dualism. Today psychology, sociology and philosophy affirm the desirability of breaking away from such stereotyping, so as to allow men and women to develop their respective and collective futures on the basis of equality, mutuality and a complementarity which denies superiority but does not exclude difference.

When reporting on the recent crisis in the Church of England, the secular press did not always appreciate the churchly issues but understood only too well the issue of justice. It is neither immediately obvious nor self-evidently logical for the opponents of women's ordination to argue that theology operates on a different plane and that what applies in the world does not apply to the Church. How can the heralds of a message which is primarily a gospel of justice and peace deny to more than half humankind and seventy per cent of its own membership an equal place 'in the sun'? I fully realise that for many in the churches as well as for those on the political right in the late 1980s 'egalitarianism' has become a dirty word. However, to experience the abuse of Enlightenment values need not necessarily lead to the abandonment of the values themselves. I for one see the equality and complementarity of the sexes as one such value, albeit rooted not only in the Enlightenment but in the biblical concepts of justice and peace – the *shalom* or wholeness intended by the Creator for all of Creation. Until women take their place beside men, as race beside race and slave beside master, not only in society but also in the Church, there will be no *shalom* and the world may be pardoned its unbelief.

Questions for discussion

1. In your opinion what is the main scriptural objection to the ordination of women?
2. In your opinion what is the main traditional objection to the ordination of women?
3. Bearing these objections in mind how would you argue for the ordination of women?
4. What bearing has Paul's 'freedom manifesto' in Galatians chapter 3 on this subject?
5. What might God the Holy Spirit be 'saying to the churches' through this debate in the latter part of the twentieth century?

Bibliography

Against the ordination of women

Beckwith, Roger, 'The Bearing of Holy Scripture' in Peter Moore (ed.), *Man, Women and Priethood* (SPCK, London, 1978).

Leonard, Graham, 'The Ordination of Women; Theological and Biblical Issues' in *Epworth Review*, Vol. XI, No. 1, January 1984.

Oddie, William, *What Will Happen to God? Feminism and the Reconstruction of Christian Belief* (SPCK, London, 1984).

For the Ordination of Women

Carey, George, 'Women and the Authority in the Scriptures' in Monica Furlong (ed.), *Feminine in the Church* (SPCK, London, 1984).

Dyson, Anthony, 'Dr Leonard on the Ordination of Women: A Response' in *Theology*, Vol. LXXXVII, No. 716, March 1984.

Jewett, Paul K, *The Ordination of Women: An Essay on the Office of Christian Ministry* (Eerdmans, Grand Rapids, 1980).

Langley, Myrtle S, *Equal Woman: A Christian Feminist Perspective* (Marshalls, Basingstoke, 1983) chapters 3 and 10.

Norris, R A, Jr, 'The Ordination of Women and the "Maleness" of Christ' in Furlong (ed.), op. cit.

Wigngaards, John, *Did Christ Rule Out Women Priests?* (McCrimmon's, Great Wakening, revised edition 1986).

On Women's Ministry
Hall, Stuart G, 'Historical Light on Women's Ministry' and Raynor, Keith, 'By What Authority? A Reply' in *Theology*, Vol. XC, No. 733, January 1987.

On the position of women in Britain today
Langley, Myrtle S, 'Extended Data Sheet on the Position of Women in Church and Society' in *Epworth Review*, Vol. XIV, No. 1, January 1987.

Dave Tomlinson

Dave Tomlinson has been a leader in the British House-church Movement for over twelve years and is Director of Teamwork, based in Brixton. Teamwork aims to pioneer and pastor churches especially within inner city areas, promoting Kingdom teaching and action in a secular society. Dave has a wide teaching and preaching ministry and is married with three children.

6. Fear and Forgiveness: A Masculine Confession

Dave Tomlinson

Being asked to write a confession on behalf of the male population is a dubious honour. First, because it seems to imply that one is the embodiment of all masculine sins and secondly because one fears being rejected by all male friends for life! However, I do consider it an honour and a necessity, and I'd like to begin by mentioning how my views about men and women have developed.

I was born and grew up in a northern working class community where 'men were men' and women did the washing up. At the same time I was indoctrinated with the 'women should be silent and wear hats in church' sort of teaching from my local Brethren Assembly. Although I created consternation among my elders by asking why they even bothered to give women hymn books if they were supposed to be silent, the underlying attitudes of Brethrenism prevailed in my thinking well on into my life among charismatic house churches. The early years of my marriage to Pat were blighted by my chauvinism, dressed up in misapplied Bible texts and notions of a 'divine order' (the belief in an authoritative hierarchy where man is 'over' woman). Like so many men, I have been guilty of underestimating the vast degree to which I have been dependent upon my wife whilst at the same time believing that women are the weaker sex. In short, whilst there have been worse examples of the sexist male, I have had to do my share of repenting, and doubtless there's still more to come.

As I look at the Church in Britain today I have no question in my mind about the fact that we are guilty of large-scale sexism, which is far more deeply inbred than most of us men will yet admit. Once we lift the lid on this issue we will discover a great sea of anger, frustration and hurt within the Christian female population. If all the theological issues were finally cleared up and disposed of tomorrow, the pastoral task before us would still be enormous. And it's not just among the women; vast numbers of men need releasing from the crippling, intolerable and unbiblical expectations which society has placed upon them.

This poem by Nancy R Smith illustrates this well:

For every woman who is tired of acting weak when she knows she is strong,
there is a man who is tired of appearing strong when he feels vulnerable;
For every woman who is tired of acting dumb,
there is a man who is burdened by the constant expectation of 'knowing everything';
For every woman who is tired of being called 'an emotional female',
there is a man who is denied the right to weep and be gentle;
For every woman who is called unfeminine when she competes,
there is a man for whom competition is the only way to prove his masculinity;
For every woman who is tired of being a sex object,
there is a man who must worry about his potency;
For every woman who feels 'tied down' by her children,
there is a man who is denied the full pleasure of shared parenthood;
For every woman who is denied meaningful employment or equal pay,
there is a man who must bear the full responsibility for another human being;
For every woman who was not taught the intricacies of an automobile,
there is a man who was not taught the satisfaction of cooking;
For every woman who takes a step toward her own liberation,
there is a man who finds the way to freedom has been made a little easier.

In the second part of this chapter I shall dwell a little on the developing place of women in the House Churches, where I have spent the past twenty-one years of my Christian experience. But first we must look further afield.

Vested interests – it's a man's world!

Very few disagreements among Christians are on purely academic issues. Usually there are deeper, emotional issues at stake – for example, feelings of fear, jealousy or rejection – but they are seldom talked about or faced up to. The agenda usually stays on the safe level of intellectual disagreements which conceal the real issues. I believe that the subject of women and their rights and roles falls perfectly into this category. We men have argued over passages of Scripture for years, contending self-righteously for the 'truth', but underneath the debating the motives haven't always been so pure. I'm not for one moment suggesting that the theological issues concerning sexual role distinctions are non-existent, but society, culture and our fallen nature have planted fears deep in our subconscious which are far more significant factors than we usually recognise. We have been pitted in ancient conflict with each other and, in large measure, the male ego is dependent on its own superiority over the female.

The fact is, we men have always held the trump card. It's been very convenient to stick to an interpretation of 'divine order' which gives us the last word. All too often we've frustrated women in our churches through repressive attitudes and then turned around and hammered them for holding unChrist-like attitudes. Women with gifts which are traditionally limited to the male spheres of activity are the ones who've suffered most. But who is to blame for the fact that they have such abilities? Why should they be dubbed 'rebellious' or 'women's libbers' simply because men feel threatened or insecure? If God gave them talents in public speaking, management or decision making, our real problem is with God, not the women concerned.

We men have enjoyed having it our way; we have had 'divine' sanction for avoiding many of the tedious and mundane tasks of life. We've been philosophical about younger women being attracted to us when we're in positions of prominence, yet felt betrayed if another man shows interest in our wife. We've so often had the opportunities of stimulating business trips away from home or going on courses to broaden our horizons, but if our women have expressed interest in such things they've been asked accusingly why 'bringing up the children' wasn't a high enough calling for them to fulfil. Make no mistake – it's been a man's world, and still is to a large extent.

Not fair shares

I want to mention two topics under this heading: division of labour and money. I would argue that when men promise 'to love and to cherish' and 'on thee all my earthly goods bestow', we actually have some small print conditions tucked away in our inside pockets. Not that we are any more devious than the next guy – it's just that there are certain unspoken presuppositions on the part of both men and women which form the backdrop of our wedding vows and these are the products of our cultural expectations.

When God made Man he created them 'male and female', and he commissioned them together to take dominion over the world and to rule it in his name. The task of domesticating Creation was clearly a joint one; there was no mention of any set roles, and one can only assume that they were to do it using whatever gifts and abilities they each discovered that they possessed. Nothing was said about Adam going to the office and Eve having his slippers and a nice meal waiting for him when he returned; about Eve putting the kids to bed while Adam watched the news; about Adam going down to the pub with his mates while Eve sewed the buttons on his shirt or prepared his supper.

We've created such clear-cut expectations that it is thought abnormal for anyone to behave differently. Women themselves are often the most vehement defenders of such unbiblical values. I was telling a couple about some friends of ours whose circumstances had demanded a complete role reversal. Due to the man's inability to find work, his wife had decided to look for a job and came up with a terrific post carrying a fairly high level of responsibility. She would come home from work hoping to find a warm meal and some stimulating conversation. Her husband related how he'd taken the kids to school, had a conversation with the milkman and gone shopping! Our friends laughed at the irony of the situation and got on with life. But the wife of the couple to whom I was relating this story was furious. 'How demeaning for the man!' she cried. This kind of response is not uncommon. We're locked into traditional expectations which are nowhere prescribed in Scripture but which do provide us with a certain level of security.

I confess with shame the demands I have placed on my own wife. I have thought that she should have the super-energy to cook meals, make coffees, have the lounge dusted for visitors, get up to attend to children in the night, do the washing-up and still have the wherewithal to comfort my drooping ego if I've had a bad day. As I have repented of such expectations and learned to take my fair share of domestic duties, I can't say that I have discovered some deep fulfilment in wielding a vacuum cleaner, but at least I've stopped thinking that Pat should get excited by it. Life is full of mundane activities – it's time we shared them out more evenly.

This leads quite naturally to the matter of money. 'What's yours is mine and what's mine's my own' has usually been chuckled at as a joke, but for lots of women it's not funny. In the home of a church leader recently I was horrified to hear the husband tell his wife, 'I earn the money around here and you spend it!' It was said with some tongue in cheek, but it reveals a very basic misconception. The 'job-equals-work' mentality is a by-product of the Protestant work ethic. This perpetuates much agony in people, especially in this age of high unemployment. However, this mentality is not rooted in Scripture. We don't earn our keep in the world by drawing a wage packet, and it's high time men in particular realised this.

The vast workforce of housewives in this country is by and large unappreciated in economic terms. This is, of course, a major political issue and is highlighted by feminist sociologist Ann Oakley in her book, *Housewife*. However, for the moment I am concentrating on men's immediate response as husbands. We must repent of our mean and unappreciative attitudes. Work done at home is every bit as important as work done in a 'place of employment'. Our society in most cases gives us husbands the wage packet, but it belongs to our wives just as much as it belongs to us, and we must treat it that way. We must find ways of sharing financial decision making, sharing the right to spend casually if we're in a position to and sharing the responsibility of earning our keep.

In the case of my own family, I am glad we were able to resist the stereotyped roles concerning money which were being propagated under the banner of 'Christian family' teaching ten or so years ago.[1] I gladly confess that Pat's ability to manage finance is far better than my own and I regret that so many husbands labour under the misapprehension that they must bear the responsibility for these matters.

Different perspectives

The world has been dominated far too much by male perspectives. I don't believe that men and women are exactly alike or that God intended us to be alike. However, what I now strongly object to is the stereotyping of differences and the hard and fast roles which are generated and maintained by those stereotypes.

Take for example the way in which men and women perceive things. Now, I doubt that all-male or all-female creatures actually exist; we all possess a mixture of the traits which we normally associate with each of the sexes. But I am sure that it is valid to make broad distinctions in the way men and women see reality. I wonder how different the world might be if feminine perceptions were on a par with male ones.

To bring this down to earth, I should say that I have been guilty of bulldozing my wife's perspectives on issues, and in most cases I have paid a price. Pat is far more intuitive than I am and repeatedly I have brushed these perceptions aside because they haven't stood up to my more analytical approach. (I have also done this with the insights of certain intuitive men that I work with.) I have demanded that her contributions be 'packaged' in a male-type form or be seen as invalid. Very often women have been patronisingly thanked for their suggestions and ideas, only to be told that they are not practical in the 'real' world. In other words, we're not willing to ask radical questions about the goals, objectives and means of reaching such goals which we cherish in our very male world. Women are viewed as simplistic and better suited to dealing with domestic issues than 'important' matters of the wider community.

I realise that this picture is changing and women are moving into all kinds of areas of involvement, competing with men and showing that they are every bit as capable. In many respects I welcome such developments, but my greatest fear is that women will simply became female men, perceiving and behaving like them and denying the worlds of business, politics and other previously male-dominated spheres the distinctive female contribution. What I am suggesting demands a more radical look at the world than many of us wish to give.

Women in the House Churches

I will now comment on women in the context of the Church and the House Church scene in particular, where I have worked in various leadership roles since 1970.

The term 'house church' is vague, in most cases inaccurate and covers such a wide variety of groupings that it is impossible to say, 'House churches believe . . .' Groupings loosely termed 'Restoration churches' (which includes several quite distinct streams) would be by far the largest constituency. Most of these churches would give women the freedom to 'pray and prophesy' or make some contributions to their meetings, but very few would have women teaching or preaching in mixed gatherings and virtually none would give a woman any authority or appoint them into eldership.

This approach to women has been closely tied in to Restoration teaching on authority and 'covering'. This teaching emphasises that the kingdom of God is about the rule of God expressed through various 'governmental' roles in the Church, such as apostles and elders. A straightforward acceptance of passages like 1 Corinthians 11:3 makes it clear to Restorationists that governmental positions should be held by men, and whilst they would be at pains to show their liberated attitudes toward women, they would clearly bar them from holding any position of authority over men. This would, of course, apply to the home as well, where the 'headship' of the man is emphasised and women are exhorted to submit to their husbands in all aspects of life. In certain types of Restoration churches, women would also be encouraged to cover their heads during meetings in accordance with their leader's interpretation of Paul's teaching in 1 Corinthians chapter 11. Apart from the headcovering issue (which I refused to accept as a proper biblical requirement long ago) the above would have been a fair description of my own position.

Over the past few years some house church leaders, including myself, have been going through some radical rethinking on the subject. For myself, the theological problems have centred on 1 Timothy chapter 2, which seemed to state clearly that women should not teach or hold positions of authority over men; and on the subject of 'headship' as taught by Paul. These matters are dealt with adequately elsewhere in the book, but I'd like to comment on how my interpretation of such passages has changed.

It has been most helpful to go back to Genesis and rediscover God's original purpose for men and women to 'rule' *together;* to understand that his statement to Eve, 'Your desire shall be to your husband and he shall rule over you', was *not* his declared will but rather his predicting the consequences of the Fall. I now accept that the key to 1 Timothy chapter 2 is Paul's statement, 'Allow the women to learn', and that such learning was to be the key to women not being deceived. Now that women by and large have access to the same opportunities of learning and education as men, they should be allowed to function according to their qualifications, both in gift and character, just like the men. In practice, this means that women who have the appropriate gifts and callings should be encouraged to preach and teach, lead home groups, pastor mixed groups of men and women and participate in leadership roles.

The issue of the role of women in the Church has raised far more radical questions than are at first obvious. Many

Anglicans would contend that the real questions are about priesthood, not about the ordination of women. In house churches eldership has been seen in the context of headship, which has been perceived as a 'governmental' term applied in the home, the Church and the wider community. In my view, we won't properly resolve the problem until we have understood biblical teaching, reinterpreted headship and redefined leadership, both in its nature and its legitimate styles of operation. Leadership has been constructed around 'male' values. Simply adding women to the existing picture, will either lead to those women feeling frustrated and dropping out, or to women being forced to operate in a male style, in which case we are all the losers. Moving forward in proper partnership may lead us to eradicate some of the competitiveness and aggression which we experience and take on board more of the gentleness and servanthood which is consistently Christlike and rightly belongs in the leadership context. This should in turn broaden our whole understanding of who is suitable for leadership and open up opportunities, not only for women but also for certain types of men who have previously been excluded. The worldly image of the 'macho-man'-type leader should be supplanted by more biblical models.

Forward together

Changes in our behaviour usually begin with changes in our thinking, and in the case of the Church, with changes in our theology. The thing to avoid amid all our rethinking is ending up with a lot of talk about change with little happening in practice. This inevitably leads to a lot more frustration and perhaps, particularly for some women, to disillusionment and bitterness.

We men must make real and radical changes, both in our personal lives and attitudes and in our approach to Church life and structure. Here are my humble suggestions:

1. Repent of sexism in our attitudes and turn away from all verbal, emotional and behavioural ploys which basically put down women or give us an unfair advantage.
2. If we are married, we should repent of dumping the

'dirty' work on our wives and take on our fair share of responsibilities for the menial as well as the important issues in our life together. This sharing out should be the product of joint negotiations rather than taking the form of 'a new regime' worked out by husbands and passed down to wives. We should repent of meanness over money and recognise the validity of housework and so forth as *real* work. Some wives have been liberated by the opportunity to have their own bank account, with the right to manage a fair share of the couple's joint income – and I don't just mean the housekeeping!

3. Repent of patronising attitudes toward female contributions and be truly open to our 'male' presuppositions being challenged, thus making room for completely new perspectives to be introduced.

4. Encourage the development of women's gifts, whatever they may be, working from the assumption that if God gave women such abilities, he meant them to be used for the benefit of all.

5. Make room for women in all levels of leadership and enable them to find the equipping and confidence to be able to operate successfully. (Men have often had far better opportunities to develop their gifts and build up their self confidence.)

In our own church we regularly enjoy women speaking and teaching and we have a leadership team which is approximately one-third women. We have not yet appointed elders (men or women) but I now have no qualms about including women, if they have the necessary qualifications. In Teamwork, the ministry team which I lead, there are already two women and I hope there will be more. I see no reason why we should not see women taking a full part in leadership teams within the churches we are building around the country, and there are many where this is already well under way.

I remember arrogantly asking God some years ago why my wife was so unspiritual. Whilst I was away at a leaders' retreat, he gave me my answer: 'She's what she is because of you!' That went right to the heart and I wept all the way home as I realised what a mess I'd made of my wife's life.

I'd starved her of my friendship, I'd left her to bring up three young children virtually single-handed, I expected her to care for a house and do all the chores, I stood by as her self-confidence and self-esteem dwindled away, I was patronising about her contributions and accused her of being possessive when she was crying out for my attention – and all this whilst I travelled around the country 'doing God's work'!

Because my repentance was real, I have since found in Pat the best friend I could possibly have, and I have been released from the feeling that women, however gifted, are a threat.

The heart of the issue, as I see it, is not in sorting out all the doctrinal issues (important though this is) but in dealing with the effects of the Fall in our attitudes and responses. If we men can purge ourselves of our fears and self-centredness and if our women friends can forgive us and break free from their resentment and hurt, together we can once more reflect the image of God in our homes, fellowships and the world in which we live.

Reference

1. Paul Tournier, *The Gift of Feeling*.

Part II:

Men and Women in Society

Jill Mowbray

Jill Mowbray has taught English for nine years in two London secondary schools and was part of a school women's group which tried to develop anti-sexist initiatives and promote staff discussion of the issues. She completed an MA in Rights in Education in 1986 and is currently working on a PhD on 'Parents and school policies on gender' at the Institute of Education, London University.

She has been heavily exposed to conservative evangelical theology, a chauvinistic church and varieties of feminism, and has managed to stay sane while exploring the tensions and differences!

7. Equal Opportunities in Education

Jill Mowbray

Introduction

Differences in the education of girls and boys have been recognised for a long time. Concern about the differences is not a new phenomenon.[1] While official reports as far back as 1923[2] have assumed sex differentiation in schooling to be right and inevitable, many within and outside education have refused to accept such differences, arguing that they simply perpetuate false assumptions about the nature of women. During the last ten years a lot of research has accumulated documenting how girls achieve less highly than boys at upper levels in the education system.[3] Many researchers have offered evidence that aspects of school organisation, teaching methods and relationships in the classroom, staffing practice, language use and the material of school texts all act to disadvantage girls and women in education.[4]

Some local authorities have written policies and instituted programmes of action and research to improve girls' educational opportunities and reduce sex-role stereotyping of girls and boys. These programmes and policies have often built upon the grassroots work of small groups of teachers who began in individual schools, drawing attention to the discrimination that existed and initiating positive action to improve girls' chances.

The popular response to work of this kind has often been to trivialise and misunderstand it. Newspapers have distorted and misrepresented the proposals as the work of a handful of activists or campaigners on the fringe at odds with the majority of parents. Resources and schemes of work have been described in such a way as to arouse red alerts in the minds of many Christians, tuned in to any hint of social change that blurs roles or disregards parental views. Yet parents, a heterogeneous group, who can't easily be characterised in one particular way, do commonly share one ideal – that their own individual children will succeed as far as possible at school, will fulfil their potential and be equipped with the skills and qualifications giving them access to employment later. (With the first two hopes Christians ought to agree, though they might have reservations about the value that our society attaches to paid work.) These aims, I suggest, unite government reports, the views of parents and proper Christian concern. There should be one difference, however. I would argue that Christians should be concerned not simply with the educational futures of their own children but for the education of all children in society (whether they are parents or not).

Anti-sexist and equal opportunity approaches to education are concerned with the kind of education that *all* children receive and the factors that lead one particular group (girls) to derive less benefit overall from the resources provided. This is important because it relates to more fundamental questions about what education is for, and who it is for. If Christians were to evaluate properly the work that is going on in this field they would find a lot to commend. God stands firmly on the side of the vulnerable and those oppressed by unequal social relationships. Christians should therefore be repentant that in this area (as in so many) it is others who have led the way in documenting systematic social injustice. Since Jesus challenged many accepted practices of his day, particularly in the dignity and status accorded to women as persons, Christians should not shrink from areas where there is a backlash from defenders of the status quo. Equal opportunities policies are bound to be resisted because they fundamentally challenge current hierarchies of status, income and the way power is distributed. Neither do they accord well with the economic and social policies of the present government, which has a vested interest in ensuring that women continue to do the bulk of unpaid caring.[5]

Christians need to investigate the huge disparities that exist between men and women in marketable qualifications and income levels. They need to absorb the accumulating evidence as to how schools prepare girls and boys for segregated employment and enhance distorted images of femininity and masculinity.[6]

Do we want to maintain the sex-segregated characteristics that make it so difficult for men to admit weakness, to be compassionate or gentle? Does it delight God that an individual's life chances are so contingent on the fact of their being born a girl or a boy? Or that our educational, legal, occupational and social systems are divided so sharply along gender lines, to the systematic advantage of men?

Unfulfilled potential

Girls and boys entering school are 'much more similar than they are different'.[7] There are no differences between males and females in general intelligence and cognitive abilities. The differences begin to occur towards the end of primary education. Girls are the higher achievers in almost every area of the school curriculum, so that before the 11+ was abolished, girls' marks had to be adjusted downwards since they were proportionally higher in the English, Mathematics and IQ tests which made up the examination. In secondary schools boys begin to show superiority over girls in mathematical skills but tend to do less well in English and reading. So having started school with similar abilities, girls are achieving highly all round in primary school, then falling behind in secondary school, particularly in scientific, mathematical and technical areas.[8] By the end of compulsory education, although the percentage of overall passes is still high, a strong demarcation line occurring between the sexes continues into higher education, youth training and work. Two questions occur: Why does it happen? and Does it matter?

1. Does it matter?

I am going to answer the second question first since we need to be convinced that the issue is a problem in order to tackle it at all. First, it could be argued that to develop a person's cognitive abilities in one sphere while limiting their development in another is a serious educational failing. More crucial, though, is the differential valuing of mathematical, technical and instrumental skills compared to verbal and affective skills in regard to employment, status and income.

History tells me
That it is not so very long since languages
Were considered very important.
Anyone who wanted to get on in the world
Needed languages as an entry qualification,
For this was how you sorted those who were capable
From those who were not.

Girls, it seems,
Were not.
They were 'naturally'
Not very good at languages
When languages were required
For leaders.

Today
It is maths and the sciences
Which are considered very important
For those who want to get on in a technological world.
Maths and sciences are the entry qualifications
Which sort those who are capable
From those who are not.

Girls, it seems
Are not.
They are 'naturally'
Not very good at maths and science
While these are required
Of leaders.[9]

'O' Level Mathematics is required as an entrance qualification to most jobs which involve further training in virtually all the professions. Careers previously viewed as predominantly female, such as hairdressing, catering and nursing, are now looking for evidence of scientific study, particularly for anyone who wants to progress beyond the most basic level.

2. Why does it happen?

Looking back at the reports which shape the education system, gender divisions are all too clear. Despite their focus being the unfulfilled potential of half the nation's children, official reports enshrine the division between preparation for work and preparation for home-making:

> With the less able girls we think that the schools can and should make more adjustments to the fact that marriage now looms larger and nearer in the pupils' eyes than it has ever done before. Their needs are more sharply differentiated than those of boys of the same age . . .[11]

> For all girls there is a group of interests relating to what many, perhaps most of them, would regard as their most important vocational concern, marriage.[12]

It followed therefore that education should capitalise on this interest and make available subjects related to home-making and child-rearing.

Same schools, different education

Schools first established as single-sex institutions tended to reflect these assumptions in their curriculum, provision of workshop space and science facilities. Moves towards comprehensivation and co-educational schooling didn't substantially alter arrangements whereby girls and boys received separate instruction for needlework, technical subjects and PE. The Plowden Report,[13] which found little curricular differentiation between the sexes in primary schools, missed many of the subtler forms of discrimination, such as classroom organisation, which have been objects of study in the last ten years. School buildings no longer stand side by side with separate entrances marked 'Girls' and

'Boys', but the fact that both sexes attend the same institution and sit in the same classroom may mask the fact that their experiences of school may be very different; that here, as in society in general, they are being prepared for different futures. Mixed schools ought to offer girls a wider choice of subjects and opportunities to learn new skills. In fact there is evidence that choices tended to become more sex-stereotyped in mixed schools; for example the 1975 DES Report found that girls were more likely to be offered a science subject than in a single-sex school, but less likely to choose it.[14] Celia Philips' research, quoted by Jenny Shaw[15] shows that girls who opted for a science subject generally chose biology and lacked the supporting sciences necessary for most careers in science.

Research by King and Clarricoates[16] suggests that gender is the fundamental organisational category in primary schools:

> Teacher: 'What must you do before you do any cooking?'
> Children: 'Roll up your sleeves and wash your hands.'
> Teacher: 'Right, girls go first.'
> The boys put on green-striped aprons, the girls flowery ones.

Clarricoates found girls and boys sitting at separate tables, in separate files for assembly and punished in different ways. Teachers attributed certain characteristics to boys and girls:
Girls: Obedient, tidy, neat, conscientious, orderly, fussy, catty, bitchy, gossiping.
Boys: Livelier, adventurous, aggressive, boisterous, self-confident, independent, energetic, couldn't care less, loyal.[17]
This drew attention to any pupils who deviated from their expectations. Pupils quickly absorbed the stereotypes and took measures to reduce the likelihood of ridicule:

> Two boys were playing happily in the Wendy House: Edward is setting the table whilst Tom is ironing. The teacher comes forward; 'Aren't you busy? What are you playing?' Edward looks at Tom, they both look sheepish. 'Batman and Robin,' states Edward vehemently. The teacher smiles and moves away.[18]

> A boy has found a snail in a wet sand box. When a girl went to touch it, the teacher said, 'Ugh, don't touch it, it's all slimy. One of the boys, pick it up and put it outside.'[19]

> A teacher in a secondary school asks a chemistry class what is special about pyrex. 'The girls will know more about this'.[20]

These examples, quoted by Sara Delamont, all illustrate how reinforcement of sex-stereotyping occurs in an incidental way as teachers try to reinforce other kinds of learning.

The timetabling of the school curriculum often includes assumptions about gender-related subject choices:

> Our timetable was so that if you did art, you couldn't do technical drawing, or woodwork or anything. No girls done woodwork. I wanted to do art so I couldn't do technical drawing – I couldn't do both.[21]

An HMI Report in 1975 found that some schools offered a subject such as technical drawing on an optional basis to all pupils, while making the condition that metalwork must have been studied earlier. Girls had not previously had any opportunity to study metalwork as part of their lower-school curriculum. Jenny Shaw believes that 'strong social pressures lie behind the apparently voluntary subject specialisation that occurs between boys and girls'[22] and that these pressures are operated by boy pupils as much as teachers, by the curriculum, or by the organisational features of school.

Teachers and pupils

Another problem in mixed schools is that girls tend to become a negative reference point for boys. 'Boys do not like being called a cissy or being compared to girls in any way'.[23] Yet many researchers found it was commonplace for teachers to ridicule a boy by suggesting his attitude or behaviour was female as a technique of classroom control or a vehicle for humour. Girls and boys endorse the message that girls are inferior in a variety of ways. Observation of lessons has shown the extent to which boys dominate in mixed classrooms, both in supplying answers and in distracting behaviour which teachers are forced to deal with if they want the lesson to continue. Girls' disinterest was more often expressed in passive ways such as reading magazines, talking quietly and arranging their hair, which teachers are more able to ignore. When teachers have been made aware of this and have tried to compensate, they have been surprised or shocked to discover that what has felt like giving 60% of their attention to girls was still only about 40%. Yet boys on these occasions often protest loudly that the girls are getting all the teacher's time, which suggests that they regard the existing situation as normal. When girls attempt to participate in discussion the response of boys is often to ridicule them and shut them up.

'Sometimes I feel like saying that I disagree, that there are other ways of looking at it, but where would it get me? My teacher thinks I'm showing off, and the boys jeer. But if I pretend I don't understand, it's very different. The teacher is sympathetic and the boys are helpful. They really respond if they can show *you* how it is done, but there's nothing but aggro if you give any signs of showing *them* how it is done' (Kathy, aged 16, Inner London Comprehensive).[24]

Surveys of teacher attitudes have found that boys may be seen as brighter, more critical, more interesting, often despite evidence to the contrary; girls on the other hand may be described as a 'faceless bunch',[25] lacking individuality, yet conscientious over written work. The question that has to be asked is, how accurate is this categorisation? And if it is true, are girls simply reflecting the stereotyped behaviour that teachers expect from them?

Of course schools don't simply exist in a vacuum. Michael Marland has written, 'Schools act as amplifiers for society's stereotypes.'[26]Right from birth messages from advertisers, greetings card manufacturers and children's books present stereotyped views of the world. Different socialisation studies have attempted to investigate how far parental expectations affect children's behaviour.[27] Taken all together these studies are inconclusive. It has not been possible to document many differences in work on parents playing with their own children. Yet adults who didn't know a child *did* appear to describe it as either female or male, solely on the basis of the visible clue of either a pink frilly dress or a blue romper suit. However it occurs, when they come to school at five children *do* appear to have internalised very strong definitions of appropriate feminine and masculine behaviour. Schools should therefore be judged on how far they mitigate or exaggerate these stereotypes. Sara Delamont contends that schools treat males and females as much more different than the outside world does.[28] She uses the title 'the Conservative School' to suggest that schools reinforce a degree of sex-stereotyping that exceeds that of the rest of society. It does this through offering out-dated role models, failing to challenge pupils' own sex-role stereotypes and enforcing exaggeratedly different behaviour and activities.

Stories to grow on

Educators have for a long time recognised the emotional potency of stories for teaching children and adults. We 'image' ourselves in the characters we see in infants' reading books and literature alike. Stories provide us with ways of articulating our own past experiences and present models for our future lives. What images of themselves do girls see in the books they encounter at school? Glenys Lobban undertook a survey of sex roles used in reading schemes. Not only did boys dominate in active, exciting roles, but they were also mentioned far more frequently.[29] A selection of prescribed 'A' level texts in English in 1978 gave fifty-three male authors and two female authors.[30] Elaine Showalter asks:

> What are the affects of this long apprenticeship in negative capability on the self-image and the self-confidence of women students? The masculine culture, reinforced by the presence of a male author . . . is so all-encompassing that few women students can maintain the sense of a positive feminine identity in the face of it. Women are estranged from their own experience and unable to perceive its shape and authenticity, in part because they do not see it mirrored and given resonance by literature. Instead they

are expected to identify as readers with a masculine experience and perspective which is presented as the human one.[31]

What are teachers, schools and local education authorities doing?

Issues of gender in education have now been the subject of research, experimentation and sometimes staffroom discussion for almost ten years. In the beginning it often seemed as though small groups of teachers in individual schools were working on areas such as the content of courses or the representation of women in textbooks with little time, resources or support. The 1975 Sex Discrimination Act provided a basis for official action by enacting that separate provision was actually illegal. The Schools Council's Sex Differentiation Project working with the Equal Opportunities Commission addressed itself to the issues of gender and schooling as a national body. In the last three years local education authorities (mostly in metropolitan areas) have produced policy documents on ending sex discrimination in conjunction with policies on anti-racism. The ILEA's policy statement includes a supporting argument which summarises much of the research I have discussed here, and commits itself to a programme of positive action aimed at overcoming sexist practices. In a small piece of research I have attempted to discover how extensive and well established work on equal opportunities was in nine secondary schools in the ILEA. Work had begun in 1975 and included the following kinds of intervention:

* a whole school policy
* staff meetings on equal opportunities
* explaining policy on equal opportunities to parents
* encouraging girls to take sciences
* encouraging girls and boys into non-traditional courses
* extending technological provision and computer literacy courses
* curriculum development in the pastoral curriculum and in Craft, Design and Technology and Child Development
* single-sex groups in Maths and Physics

* single-sex groups in Personal and Social Education
* work with advisory teachers on classroom monitoring
* examining textbooks and course material and rewriting parts of the curriculum for a more positive portrayal of girls and women
* girls' self-defence classes after school.[32]

The work is piecemeal and often small in scale, and entrenched attitudes make change difficult and slow. The fact that so much sexism pervades the 'hidden curriculum' means that even in schools where most grassroots work has been done, many teachers – male and female – remain sceptical or apathetic about adopting anti-sexist policies.

Where do we go from here?

A recent letter to the ILEA's newspaper *Contact* castigated voluntary aided schools because they were among the last to seek to implement recent policy documents on providing more equal opportunities. Among primary head teachers in Church of England schools there has often been a reluctant and cynical reaction to visits from the advisor for Equal Opportunities. A day conference on the issues of race and gender arranged by the London Institute for Contemporary Christianity (LICC) and the Association of Christian Teachers (ACT) had to be cancelled due to lack of interest. In an extreme reaction some have seen mixed Craft as a subversive plot to turn boys into homosexuals. Successful professional Christian women who have achieved highly at university and then chosen marriage and motherhood have argued that no-one or nothing prevented them from developing their abilities to the full. All these responses characterise the reaction of Christians to those concerned about gender and education.

In ten years of discussion, writing, research and innovation Christians have been virtually absent from the debate and frequently dismissive of those involved. There are various reasons. It may be partly a result of ignorance of the evidence and partly a misunderstanding of the intentions of those involved. There may also be a belief that the issues are trivial or that the enterprise is a political one. The media certainly encourage the latter two assumptions. Like other issues raised by feminists, it is very easy to portray anti-sexist educational initiatives in a way that makes them appear silly or ridiculous. But also the headway in equal opportunities policy-making has come largely from Labour authorities. The Conservative government in contrast has asserted a 'pro-family' line with a 'traditional' role for women as home-makers and carers. In the resulting polarisation of attitudes Christians are likely to feel that their most comfortable place is with the package of campaigning which argues for the banning of embryo research, changes in the abortion laws, tax and social security incentives for women to stay at home and the continuance of gender segregated education.

In this chapter I am arguing for the importance of Christians taking the issues seriously. Anti-sexist education is not about making children neuter. It is about ensuring that their opportunities in life are not determined and disadvantaged at the outset by gender.

The fact that others have done the groundwork is not a reason for Christians to stand aside. There are many aspects of the argument where Christians will differ fundamentally from some secular feminists. But the existing discussion already ranges broadly and many who are not evangelical Christians would agree that there is a place for a religious outlook in the discussion of controversial ethical issues. Christians need to be present in the discussion alongside people of other faiths and those of no faith. 'Secularism is the name for an ideology, a new closed worldview which functions very much like a new religion.'[33] A secularism which functions as a closed worldview – a methodological atheism – will lead ultimately to a closed society in which the plurality of religious experience is not possible.

As Christians we need to examine where we derive our concepts of masculinity and femininity from. If we are binding our children to conform to sexual stereotypes demanded by the world, we are denying them something of their full personhood. There are few specific passages in the Bible which tell us in any detail how we should educate children. Our concept of education must derive from our concept of *personhood*, and must involve *growing up*, developing in *maturity*, growing in *wisdom*, and exploring *truth* – all of these are biblical concepts which occur often in descriptions of the believer growing in faith (frequently paralleled with the child becoming an adult). Helpful passages are those which describe how we are created as persons in the image of God. And God's relationship with us is characterised as 'mother'-love as well as 'father'-love (for a further analysis of this subject see the chapter on spiritual gifts in the Church by Faith and Roger Forster). Are these qualities of relationship intended to be segregated as they so often are in our society, or cannot one person possess at the same time the attributes of strength and gentleness? The Bible implies, when it uses the parent/child relationship as an illustration of God's love for us, that parents want to care for their children and give them those things which will help them to achieve their full potential as human beings. The qualities required of Christians in the New Testament seem to reflect equally characteristics regarded as traditionally masculine or traditionally feminine (see Gal 5:22; Col 3:12–14; 2 Tim 2:22–25; 1 Pet 5:5–6).

To argue that girls and boys should be prepared for different destinations as homemakers and carers or aggressive competitors in the 'real' world of paid work is to accept a false and damaging division of life. Both men and women lose out as a result of this compartmentalisation. Looking in the Bible at who should be the carer of children, no impression is given that it is 'women's work'. From Proverbs[34] it seems that both parents are to be equally involved. The apostle Timothy is described as learning from his *mother*. *Fathers* are exhorted to train, teach and discipline their children. Jesus addressed both Mary and Joseph when they wanted an explanation of his three day disappearance.[35]

Jerran Barrs comments:

> Very little is said in Scripture about roles. The woman in Proverbs certainly has a life centred on the home but she is very involved out in society. Men are to reflect the fatherhood of God who loves and cares for his children, by being actively involved in the life of the home, and in raising their children.[36]

As Rosemary Dawson points out:

> Psychological arguments that women are more suited to domestic and caring work than men must be resisted. Women's overwork as home-makers and carers is not born of natural effortless predisposition, but of necessity. Women are being asked to bear the brunt of the crisis we are in. Their work overload is not inevitable; it is a product of the way society organises itself.[37]

Gender stereotypes are not only psychologically crippling; they have material consequences. It is not adequate for Christians to stand aside and leave wholeness up to people's eternal salvation. The kingdom of God implies the rule or reign of God, not just in the future but here and now. Since this world is God's Creation we must not devalue people's welfare and earthly life. At present women are massively disadvantaged in the employment market, partly because they often don't have the qualifications for more highly paid, high-status occupations, and partly because our society puts a low value on work traditionally done by women such as nursing or teaching young children.

To argue for marriage and motherhood as a solution for women is no solution. Whatever views Christians hold on women's and men's roles we should not impose particular 'choices' on others by a punitive social system that ensures there are no meaningful alternatives. A lot of women work – some by choice, some by economic necessity, many because they are heads of families. In a society which measures status by occupation many other 'goods' are linked to employment – housing, health and mental health, to name a few. It is plainly unjust that men should relatively be so much better off. Education should at least contribute to reform by a sexually inclusive curriculum and a self-conscious approach to gender issues that equips pupils to dismantle unjust sexual divisions.

Questions for discussion

1. What images of femininity/masculinity are presented in children's comics and popular teenage magazines? Collect some magazines and study them together.

2. Do birthday cards and children's toys suggest that certain kinds of behaviour and activities are appropriate for little boys and girls respectively? Collect some cards and study them together.
3. What problems would confront parents who wished to bring up children in non-stereotyped ways?
4. What kinds of difficulties are faced by men and women in adult life as a result of (a) internalising rigid stereotypes of femininity and masculinity and (b) an education system which cuts out options and restricts choices?
5. What can Christians do practically to (a) find out about equal opportunities issues and (b) get involved in positive change?

References

1. See for example articles written in the periodical *Time and Tide* between 1920 and 1923, quoted in D Spender, *Time and Tide Wait for No Man* (London, Pandora, 1984).
2. *Curriculum and Examinations in Secondary Schools* (The Norwood Report) (London, HMSO, 1943); *Fifteen to Eighteen* (The Crowther Report) (HMSO 1959); *Half Our Future* (The Newsom Report) (HMSO 1963).
3. See R Deem, *Women and Schooling* (London, RKP, 1978).
4. See the articles by Michael Marland, Lisa Serbin and Dale Spender in M Marland, *Sex Differentiation and Schooling* (London, Heinemann, 1983).
5. See J Finch and D Groves, (eds.), *A Labour of Love: women, work and caring* (London, RKP, 1983), for an account of the way women's unpaid caring contributes to society, and how unrewarded it is.
6. A very good source for charts and tables based on government surveys is *Social Trends*, published annually by HMSO, particularly the sections on Households and Families, Education, Employment, Income and Wealth. Some examples are: 'In 1983/84, 34 per cent of boys and 45 per cent of girls leaving school in England and Wales held a GCE 'O' level grade A – C or CSE grade 1 in English. Only 9 per cent of girls leaving school were

qualified at this level in Physics compared with 22 per cent of boys' (p.52); 'Women accounted for 40 per cent of the 75 thousand university first degrees awarded in 1983. There was a notable difference between men and women in the subjects studied. Only 3 per cent of university first degrees awarded to women were in engineering and technology, while 21 per cent were in language, literature and area studies; among male first degree graduates the corresponding proportions were 22 and 7 per cent respectively' (p.56); 'The gross weekly earnings of male employees span a wider range than those of female employees, which are concentrated at the lower end of the earnings scale, nearly half of non-manual men earned more than £190 per week in April 1984, compared with only a tenth of women; amongst the non-manual female employees over half earned less than £120 per week' (p.78). All examples taken from *Social Trends* No. 16, 1986 edition (London, HMSO, 1986).

7. C N Jacklin, 'Boys and girls entering school', p.17 in M Marland, op.cit.
8. See for example chaps. 6 and 7 in R Deem, *Schooling for Women's Work* (London, RKP 1980), and R Walden and V Walkerdine, *Girls and Mathematics: The Early Years* (London, Institute of Education, University of London, 1982).
9. Spender, D. and Sarah, S. (eds.), *Learning to Lose: Sexism and Education* p.128. The Women's Press, London, 1980.
10. J Bould and B Hopson, 'Sex differentiation and careers', p.130 in M Marland, op.cit.
11. Crowther Report, op. cit.
12. Newsom Report, op. cit.
13. *Children and their Primary Schools* (The Plowden Report) (London, HMSO, 1967).
14. Department of Education and Science, *Curricular Differences for Boys and Girls*, (London, HMSO, 1975).
15. J Shaw, 'Education and the individual: Schooling for girls, or mixed schooling – a mixed blessing?' in R Deem, op.cit.
16. R King, *All Things Bright and Beautiful? A Sociological*

Study of Infants' Classrooms (Chichester, Wiley, 1978); K Clarricoates, 'The importance of being Ernest . . . Emma . . . Tom . . . Jane', in R Deem, op.cit.
17. R Deem, op.cit., p.39.
18. Ibid., p.34.
19. Delamont, S. *Sex Roles and the School*, p.31, Methuen, London, 1980.
20. Ibid., p.54.
21. Sharpe 1976, p.149.
22. Shaw, p.73 in R Deem, op.cit.
23. Shaw, p.72 ibid.
24. D Spender and S Sarah, op. cit.
25. M Stanworth, *Gender and Schooling: A Study of Sexual Divisions in the Classroom* (London, WRRC Publications Collective, 1980).
26. M Marland, op.cit., p.2.
27. C N Jacklin, op.cit.
28. S Delamont in S Walker and L Barton, *Gender, Class and Education* (London, Falmer, 1983), p.93.
29. See chart quoted in C Adams and R Laurikietis, *The Gender Trap. 1: Education and Work* (London, Virago, 1976), p.41.
30. Walters, 1978, quoted in D Spender, 'Telling it how it is' in M Marland, op.cit.
31. Showalter, 1974, quoted in D Spender, ibid, p.110.
32. J Mowbray, unpublished MA dissertation, Institute of Education, University of London.
33. J Briggs, 'From Christendom to Pluralism' in D F Wright (ed.), *Essays in Evangelical Social Ethics* (Exeter, Paternoster, 1978).
34. Proverbs 10:1; 22:6; 23:13; 31:1,27.
35. Luke 2:48–51.
36. Jerram Barrs, *Equal but Different*, Cubit, 1984.
37. R Dawson, *All That Is Unseen* (London, Church House Publishing, 1986), p.29.

Bibliography

Adams, C and Laurikietis, R, *The Gender Trap: A Closer Look At Sex Roles. 1: Education and Work* (Virago, London, 1980).

Dawson, R, *All That Is Unseen: A New Look At Women And Work* (Church House Publishing, London, 1986).

Deem, R (ed.), *Schooling For Women's Work* (RKP, London, 1980).

Delamont, S, *Sex Roles and the School* (Methuen, London, 1980).

Marland, M (ed.), *Sex Differentiation and Schooling* (Heinemann, London, 1983).

Sharpe, S, *Just Like A Girl: How Girls Learn To Be Women* (Penguin, London, 1976).

Spender, D and Sarah, S (eds.), *Learning to Lose: Sexism and Education* (The Women's Press, London, 1980).

Stanworth, M, *Gender and Schooling: A Study of Sexual Divisions in the Classroom* (Women's Research and Resources Centre Publications Collective, London, 1981).

Walden, R and Walkerdine, V, *Girls and Mathematics: The Early Years*, Bedford Way Papers, 8 (Institute of Education, University of London, 1982).

Rosemary Dawson

Rosemary Dawson was Project Worker for the Women and Employment Project of the Manchester Diocesan Board for Social Responsibility/Girls Friendly Society. She is author of *And All That Is Unseen – A New Look at Women's Work*, a Report from the Industrial and Economic Affairs Committee of the General Synod Board for Social Responsibility, published 1986.

8. Men's Work, Women's Work

Rosemary Dawson

Genesis chapters 1–3 never go out of fashion. Whatever the concern, be it sin, conservation or sex, these chapters are looked to for explanations as to why the world exists at all, why it is in the mess it's in and what it should be like.

One of today's major concerns is unemployment and work. Here too recourse is frequently made by Christians to Genesis chapters 1–3. Several books and study packs I have looked at on the subject of work start here, as if in the hope that a correct exegesis will yield a definitive statement about the meaning of work and clues to the solutions to our present employment crisis. It is a vain hope. Genesis may offer us one or two helpful insights into the human experience of work, but we have to move on from there.

Three views about the experience and meaning of work can be discerned in Genesis chapters 1–3. According to one view, work is an activity inherent to human nature and is necessary for human survival: 'The Lord God took the man and put him in the garden of Eden to till it and keep it' (2:15). Another view of work is of its blessedness and creativeness. God pronounces a blessing on humanity: 'Be fruitful and multiply, and fill the earth and subdue it; and have dominion over the fish of the sea and over the birds of the air and over every living thing that moves upon the earth' (1:28). Humanity is the steward of the earth, sharing with God in the shaping and developing of Creation. This command is given jointly to the male and female, made in God's image. Neither is given dominion over the other. The third view reflects the experience of the pain and difficulty of work. Human sin affects the conditions of labour

(3:17–19). The ground is cursed because of it, and the woman's pain in childbearing is multiplied. These verses reflect the sexual division of labour, which, significantly, is described as part of the fallen order.

The writers' understandings of God's purpose in and for Creation and God's intended relationship with humanity outlined in the Genesis narrative can still illuminate our practice, particularly in our relationship with our environment. Most readers will be able to identify with the different experiences of work reflected in Genesis. What we cannot do is force out from these chapters – or any others in the Bible – an unambiguous 'biblical doctrine of work' which can be applied in detail to our present situation. There is no contemporary equivalent to biblical societies. Genesis has nothing to say about paid employment, and it is the lack of this rather than of work which is throwing our society into chaos.

Christians believe that the Bible continues to be the Word of God and feel impelled to respond to our situation in the light of it. However, to give in to the temptation fails to take our situation seriously, and reduces the stature of the biblical material, which for its own times will often have had a specific and unmistakable relevance. Likewise, the injunction which states 'if a man does not work let him not eat' cannot be used to justify the low level of unemployment benefits. The parable of the labourers in the vineyard is not about what time we turn up for work, and behaving like the lilies of the field is guaranteed to get you into trouble with your bank manager! The punchline of the parable of the talents (to them that have more will be given – to them that have not even what they have will be taken away; Mt 25:29) does not literally refer to wages, even if it does appear an accurate description of the government's wage policies.

In Genesis, the purposes of work – indeed of life, since the rigid distinctions between work and the rest of life are modern ones – are to provide for people's needs, to care for the environment and to be partners of God in creativity. But immediately a host of further questions are raised: how are people's needs to be met, how should work be shared out and how should wealth be distributed? Serious discussion of those questions requires that we know something about people's experiences (their met and unmet needs), and the present distribution of work and wealth. This means statistics – often a bitter pill – and stories, which sweeten them a bit and tell us things that statistics cannot. These questions concern the relationships between nations, groups and individuals and it is upon our understanding of current relationships that we construct our social and employment patterns. When our employment system crumbles we can blame world recession and market forces, but if we evade these questions of relationships we are evading responsibility for our fellow humans, and some of the root causes of decline.

For those seeking to make sense of relationships, the Bible may well provide more relevant comment than it does about employment. After all, are relationships not rather more basic to life than our ephemeral working patterns? Maybe so, but caution is necessary. For the potential havoc wrought by misusing Scripture here is far greater than getting the wrong end of the stick with the parable of the talents! People – especially powerless people – have to do their own theologising. That is, they have to make their own God-sense of their experience, since if they do not the powerful will do it for them. There is a Haitian proverb which says, 'If work was such a good thing, the rich would have found a way of keeping it to themselves.' It is a forceful and judgemental reminder that it is the powerful who call the tune the world over. It also hints at the justifications that the powerful have had to develop in order to maintain their position: the poor are told that work is good for them (which is not their experience). Scripture has often been misused to legitimise the social superiority of one group over another – of Jews over Greeks, of free people over slaves, of males over females (see Gal 3:27). Liberation theology has taught us that we need to be suspicious when Scripture is used in this way. Judging Scripture by Scripture means measuring its parts against the general tenor of the whole. Liberation theologians would argue that this 'general tenor' comprises the teachings of the prophets and Jesus, which consistently avow God's concern for the poor and disadvantaged and speak of God's intention to bring about a new, just order. The Bible cannot therefore be used to uphold structures which are obstacles to the Kingdom, and the behaviour and concerns of God's people must be in keeping with its values.

So far I have been talking generally about powerful and powerless groups. I now intend to look more particularly at one powerless group, namely women, in one particular sphere, namely employment, and at the questions this raises about the relationship between the sexes. From a brief survey of the facts of women's employment, I move on to look at two concepts which are thought to characterise the work of men and women. I want to argue that new understandings of these concepts are necessary if women and men are to work together and relate to one another more humanely.

Women's employment is a high profile topic. There are still the 'firsts' – the first women to make a certain grade. There are still efforts to achieve equal pay for women and to ensure genuinely equal opportunities. There is still much discussion about whether women 'ought to' go out to work. These all reflect the difficulty that society experiences in coming to terms with women's employment and the fact that employment poses problems for women that it does not for men. They may also create the misleading impression that women's employment is a new phenomenon. However, women have made up at least 30% of the labour force ever since employment statistics for women and men have been kept. Now they account for 42%. Apart from those who have left school in the last few years, very few women have never had a paid job and the periods women spend out of employment before retirement is decreasing. The falling birth rate, the tendency to return to work in between the births of children and the needs of families for women's earnings are just three of the many factors accounting for this change.

Discussion about women's employment is frequently couched in moral terms. It is seen as a problem and is dealt with in hypotheses. In spite of its high profile, people talk about women's employment without knowing the facts and with the most appalling prejudices and myths. For example, anyone who swears by the 'women take men's jobs' theory has taken no more than a cursory glance at the work women and men actually do. The distinctions between 'men's work' and 'women's work' are still very strong. When have the majority of teachers, nurses, secretaries, cleaners and caterers been men? When have men made up more than a tiny proportion of those doing part-time work, which is the form employment takes for half of all employed women? Male unemployment has risen because of the decline of the industries in which they worked, not through their being replaced by women. The industries in which women work are those service industries which have expanded since the War (particularly with the creation of the NHS) such as clerical, catering and cleaning work. These provided 1.2 million part-time jobs for women between 1961 and 1971. In manufacturing industries women are concentrated in textiles and footwear, food, drink and tobacco and light engineering. The concentration of women in a small number of industries points to the ghettoising of women in the labour market and makes the situation difficult to change.

Because women and men work in different occupations it has been easier to justify paying women lower wages than men. Overall, women's occupations are still less well rewarded than men's. It is ten years since the Equal Pay Act, and women's earnings are still only three-quarters of men's. In spite of the differential most women's earnings are not 'pin money' but provide essentials for themselves and their dependants. Four times as many families in Britain would be in poverty were it not for women's earnings.

Of civil engineers, judges and university professors 1% are women and 2% of accountants and 6% of solicitors are women. Apart from the 'female' professions of nursing, teaching and librarianship, women are greatly outnumbered in the professions. Even in these three, men will hold a disproportionate number of the senior and supervisory posts.

One explanation of the secondary position held by women in the labour market is that they and other disadvantaged groups form a 'reserve army of labour' which is called upon to fill gaps in the labour market when required. However, when the needs for employment of the priority group (white men) are not being adequately met, these groups are squeezed out. An obvious example is the World Wars, when women took over the work of the men who went to the Front and did jobs which, during peace-time, were thought to be too dangerous and dirty for women. When men returned from the Front women were told that their duty to the country was finished and they could re-establish themselves within the home once more. A more recent example which supports this theory is provided by the 50s and 60s, when the British Government actively encouraged immigrant labour in order to meet the demands of an expanding economy. Twenty years on, and the same people are made to feel that they have no right to live and work here. So the rate of unemployment for black people is twice as high as it is for whites, and it is they and women who feel the effect of the squeeze soonest and hardest. Firms which make people redundant on a 'last in, first out' or 'part-timers go first' policy are in effect getting rid of their reserve army. The Government's employment policies frequently leave women and other vulnerable groups worse off.

The facts about women's employment betray society's belief that it takes second place to men's. This rests upon another belief, namely that women's primary sphere of responsibility is the home. By implication, this is not men's responsibility. The model of a nine-to-five day, five days a week for forty years is not a realistic possibility for people (women) who care for children and other relatives, do the household shopping and maintenance work and feed and clothe those who *do* work according to this model. Ann Oakley's study of this work in 1971 revealed that it can occupy 77 hours a week,[1] and the Legal and General Insurance Company estimated its commercial value as £230 per week.[2] Housework is not recognised for the work that it is. It is usually done when those who create the mess are out of the way and so is invisible. Housewives are classed as 'economically inactive' by the General Registrar's office and even describe themselves as 'just a housewife'. Yet it is the major occupation of women in this country.

The relationships between groupings in society are reflected in its economic and social arrangements. Our employment structures are clearly weighted in favour of men and this indicates the relative values given to men and women's work. Such arrangements are not fixed; they are human creations which we can control, and to suggest otherwise is idolatrous. To ensure that they serve us rather than rule us, we have to assess their human effects, what they do to and for people and how people participate in them. If women are unfairly rewarded for their work, or if a childrearing break means the end of their career advancement, then something is wrong with the structures and they must be changed.

A theology of work therefore cannot simply look at the experiences of men. If it fails to look at women's work, housework and childcare it is because it shares society's assumptions about what is important. Even with four million unemployed and *x* million housewives, we still equate work with paid employment, and so ignore the fact that men's paid employment is founded upon an enormous amount of unpaid work – most of it done by women. A theology of work has to look at the disparities in the experience of women and men and the reasons for them, and at their different motivations and aspirations.

First, let us begin to do this by looking briefly at the concepts of ambition and service which, generally speaking, characterise the work of men and women respectively. Feminism has some important insights to offer on these issues to which Christians may also have something to contribute. The revolution in employment and the women's movement both necessitate a rethinking of the male lifestyle which has been so geared to employment that it has excluded other important facets of life. What shall it profit a man if he gains success, power and fame but does not know his own children? The changes in women's employment and lifestyle demand an overhaul of the concept of service which can be so oppressive to women, because it carries with it damaging connotations of self-negation. Service is an important Christian concept which we cannot afford to lose, but prevailing interpretations of it must be challenged. It is easy to say that Christians should lose their lives in service, but the promise that they should find them in doing so must be realised. Whatever the job, employment dominates the lives of those men who have it (and in a negative sense, of those who don't). Anna Ford, who spent three years interviewing men from all walks of life found that 'If men found it difficult to talk about their emotions, when asked about their work there was no such reticence. They visibly relaxed and began to discuss a subject they knew something about with a sense of relief and an air of confidence. In fact, it was often hard to stem the flow of technical detail ranging from cleaning the inside of boilers to trading in cocoa and coffee at sums beyond the imagination.'[3]

Because of the centrality of employment in men's lives it is upon this area that they will focus their ambition. This will not always be appropriate, as many jobs do not require ambitious people to do them. Ambition is a characteristic which does not necessarily have an outlet. For one man whom Anna Ford interviewed, success was what counted, and how it was gained or in what area scarcely seemed to matter. 'I haven't set my sights on anything in particular,' he said, 'but I know the type of position I eventually want to be in. I know that I want to be in a position of authority. I want to be recognised as an expert in whatever I'm doing.'[4]

Qualities associated with ambition are competition, single-mindedness, separateness and a preparedness to make considerable sacrifices. Men's ambition causes them to sacrifice their leisure, their mental and physical health, their relationships with other people and their environment and even their own sense of self-esteem. Some men are now acknowledging the damaging effects that their work can have on their families and refusing to subordinate their interests to the demands of a career. This can require a lot of courage, as the pressure on men to 'succeed' is immense, especially in professions where there are clearly defined career ladders. A man who resists the pressure is quite likely to have his masculinity questioned as well as receiving a less attractive salary. For many men the fire in the belly is too strong: 'There has been a conflict between my family and my work, and my family has lost because I'm ambitious, and given the chance I'd do the same again.'[5]

A case study from *Managers and their Wives*[6] illustrates the lengths to which some men are prepared to go to satisfy 'the fire in the belly'. Mr Frith has organised his private life so that it does not obstruct his career in any way. Even the time at which he got married had to be right: 'I was not too old nor too young.'[7] He does not talk very much about his work to his wife and feels that he must isolate himself from his work colleagues: 'I don't talk over my future prospects at work. I don't have people I'm friendly enough with, as they're in the race as well, you don't want to show your hand . . . one's possible best friend is one's challenger.'[8] Mr Frith recognises that he has become more tense and less flexible and his self-esteem has been affected: 'I have changed personally over the last 15 years . . . it's less easy to cope with other people[9] . . . I think I have deteriorated as a person.' One manifestation of this deterioration[10] is the adoption of behaviour of which he does not approve: 'I do bash people down. This is a good technique, rather than a way of behaviour for me. It's a good way to win, and I often hate myself for it, but it's expedient.'[11]

Is it any wonder, then, that many women are said to lack ambition and fear success? Because their work brings them into closer contact with people, they are better able to assess the cost to their relationships of being ambitious. Perhaps, with Marilyn French, we should be asking 'why women do not on the whole want to be President of General Motors and why men do'.

In the eyes of society the qualities required of ambitious people are incompatible with those which constitute womanliness. Ambitious women are labelled 'hard' or 'selfish' and classed as honorary men. The essence of womanliness is judged to be looking to the needs of others, and the success of those a woman looks after should be sufficient for her. A man who works long and hard in his job is applauded for meeting the needs of his family, but a woman who does the same will be seen either as neglecting her family or as compensating herself for the lack of one. Far from challenging such stereotyping, much literature pouring off the popular Christian presses sanctions it. There are numerous examples. The following quotations from Don Double are not untypical. Unemployed and poorly paid men will take comfort from learning that 'the scriptures clearly teach that a man who does not provide for his own family is worse than an infidel.'[12] As for women, their *raison d'etre* is to 'give pleasure, first of all to her man, and then to others including her children'.[13]

How can we reformulate the idea of ambition so that we can divest it of its harmful content and yet still affirm the forward-reaching, the motivation and the dedication which are features of it? It is good to see women achieving in the career world; the experiences and qualities they bring are invaluable. But it calls for two worried cheers rather than three whole-hearted ones. Human liberation from inhuman employment structures is not going to come about by incorporating women into the male realm. The result would be that, in addition to increased scope, responsibility and fulfilment, women would acquire the ulcers, coronaries, stress and isolation which beset ambitious men. I believe that a renewed understanding of ambition must emphasise several points.

First, ambition must not be allied with a desire to control or dominate other people. Ability and achievement are often rewarded by giving someone responsibility for others, and this responsibility inescapably involves power. But power can be shared. It need not be something to exercise over others, which reduces people to powerless objects for the sake of the enhancing of an individual's status. Ideally, sharing power entails working co-operatively rather than in isolation. If ambition and co-operation appear to be contradictions in terms, it is because ambition is so often directed towards individual gain and status rather than towards collaborative undertakings.

Rethinking what constitutes achievement also raises important questions. Success is often measured in relation to how many obstacles or people had to be overcome, the extent to which work is done in isolation, the speed with which it is carried out, and the degree of ruthlessness exercised in excluding factors other than those with which one is directly concerned. Process is subordinated to results, issuing in limited awareness of the effects of one's actions on people, groups or environments outside of one's purview. We need to discover the criteria by which we can assess the true worth of an activity. One surely has to be to ask how people have been enabled to develop or to live fuller lives as a result.

Paid employment is not the only focus worthy of ambition. Women have always known this, as they have been less identified with it and have poured their energies into unpaid activities. It is even more appropriate to stress this now because four million people are unemployed and also because so much paid work leaves little scope for personal growth and development. 'Success' usually comes to those who can 'play the system' and accept its values rather than those who oppose it.

Ambitious people generally succeed by making the present system work to their advantage. But because so much of the present system is so unjust, what is required is that our efforts should be directed not to 'making it' within today's structures but to challenging them, exposing their sinfulness and creating fairer ones. Christian ambition needs to keep in view the vision of a transformed order and to concentrate on furthering it. Its aim is to change the world. But paradoxically this is done by turning our ambition to the day-to-day things that are nearest to us, rather than to less tangible, less reachable goals. This is what I, at least, take the message of the parables to be. The changes on a personal, micro-level are the leaven in the 'macro-lump' and because everyone can look to the day-to-day, this ambition is accessible to everyone.

'Then I saw that all toil and all skill in work come from a man's envy of his neighbour' (Eccles 4:4). This is not the whole story, we hope. However, the Scriptures, from Ecclesiastes to the parable of the rich fool, question human motivations for work and challenge ambition which is directed solely towards material gain. Two other ingredients with biblical roots are helpful in this debate. One is an awareness that 'having dominion' is about having choice and responsibility, not the right to dominate others or use them for one's own ends. The second is the interdependency of the various parts of the Body of Christ. Christian ambition cannot go it alone.

I now move on to look at service, which is a feature of women's paid and unpaid work. Their paid work, as we have seen, is more often than not in the 'service industries' and is an extension of their unpaid domestic role – cleaning, catering, caring. So long as this is the case there are few complaints about women taking men's jobs.

Although the word 'service' is still used of high-status or vocational work – for example, of the Royals or brain surgeons – it generally suggests the servicing of people's needs or monotonous labour. In all modern societies, women do the major bulk of servicing work. The myth is that women are fulfilled by undertaking such work because it comes naturally to them. Only unnatural women complain about the one-sided nature of this work; 'real' women instinctively want to deny themselves and put others first.

If we were to look for a more honest explanation of why women serve we could begin by paraphrasing the Haitian proverb quoted earlier: if housework and childcare were so rewarding men would have found a way of monopolising it – or at least of sharing in it rather more than they do. In other words, we are brought back to the question of power relationships between groups – in this case between women and men.

Not surprisingly, many women resist building their self-identity and lifestyles around the principle of service, when it means servitude. Letty Russell comments, 'Women and others in modern society do not like the idea of servanthood because they see it as an impression of their own powerlessness.'[14] Because it is believed that servicing is a natural characteristic of women, its costliness and gift quality has been obscured and untold guilt has resulted among those who experience servicing differently. What comes naturally to a person, the argument goes, can be expected and is of no credit to her.

It is frightening to see how some Christian writers seek to force women into a dehumanising servicing role. 'God intends his wife to submit. He created her that way,' is their view.[15] Submission to a husband is a way of demonstrating your love for God. It is disobedient to God to resist the husband's authority. In fact, a Christian woman's service is not discussed except insofar as it relates to her husband, home and family. However, with reference to these three, it is interpreted in meticulous detail. It means having your husband's meals ready when he comes home, having a tidy home, children and hairdo whenever he's around. It is about having all the buttons on his shirts and clean socks in his drawer. 'Little things can mean such a lot.'[16] What's little about keeping a home and children tidy? These things mean nothing if they are not freely given.

However, if we are going to reject such ideas about women's servanthood, what do we replace them with? Service is too essential a Christian concept to dismiss altogether. Here I will suggest a couple of considerations which serve as correctives to the traditional teaching.

First, Christians must not equate women's service primarily with submission. By submission I mean in this instance the willy-nilly bowing to the will of another and an avoidance of adult responsibility and decision making. It has been an accepted Christian commonplace that Pride is Sin Number One. Women, however, are more likely to err in the other direction by underestimating and therefore under-utilising their strengths. The occasional practice of submission may be virtuous and helpful for those who are habitually proud. But this kind of submission 'is in fact an element of sinfulness in which women refuse to accept their full created status as partners with men in the work of God's mission in the world,'[17] says Letty Russell. The woman who always submits and only does what she is told will never find out the extent of the gifts she can use in God's service. And the people she serves will not develop if they do not learn how to do things for themselves. Nor will they learn how to relate to people as equals and form reciprocal relationships.

Secondly, women's sphere of service is wider than the home and the PTA. It is worth pointing out that Jesus rejected the belief that women's role was necessarily a servicing one, and that he put motherhood firmly in its place as one calling among others. Mary was encouraged to sit at his feet and learn as the male disciples did. The blessing from the woman in the crowd upon 'the womb that bore you and the breasts that you sucked' met with the response from Jesus, 'Blessed rather are those who hear the word of God and keep it' (Lk 11:27–28). His question, 'Who is my mother?' (Mt 12:48) was not a denial of his relationship to his mother, but an acknowledgement of the network of relationships, wider than his immediate kin, of which he was a part.

A popular misconception about feminism is that it undervalues the role of motherhood. I find little in feminist writing to evidence this belief. Feminism does – and should – challenge the idealisation of motherhood which ignores the realities and hardships of that role. It also claims that for most mothers additional outlets for self-expression and sources of satisfaction are necessary.

Being a good and faithful servant will mean washing people's feet. It will mean feeding the hungry, giving drinks to the thirsty, visiting the sick and those in prison, healing and comforting and all the things that women do daily for children, partners and ageing relatives. Yet it will mean other things too. No one's responsibility for other people stops at the garden gate. Feeding the hungry beyond the gate requires Christians to campaign, and in some cases to undertake collective and political action. The nurturers and comforters are God's servants, but so too are the prophets, the agitators and the disrupters, those who dream dreams not only of domestic harmony but of a world turned upside down.

Thirdly, there are lessons about service to be learnt from the example of Jesus, who became a servant not in order that people could dominate him, but in order that he could liberate them. Jesus' service did not entail self-negation or the hiding of his skills under a bushel. His self-emptying for others did not prevent him from making some momentous claims about himself or from finding time to be alone, away from the demands of others. Only by doing this could his service become the powerful vehicle of a liberating work. A central strand in Jesus' preaching was the challenging of power relationships operating in his society. His reinterpretation of messiahship as the way of the suffering servant overturned contemporary views about the nature of God's kingdom.

This discussion about ambition and service is essentially about discipleship and the human need for fulfilment through work. I have sought to challenge understandings of Christian discipleship which simply reflect today's accepted gender roles and characteristics. Many people experience these as oppressive because they fail to take into account our needs for different forms of self-expression. Ambition and service do not need to be seen as an either/or option, but rather as complementary. Maybe then women will cease to apologise for sometimes putting their own interests first or for going all-out for a certain goal, and men will learn that the fact that service-work is done by women does not mean that the women who do it are weak or inferior. Ambition and service are two necessary facets of the response of women and men to the call of radical discipleship. It is our duty as Christ's followers to live lives which incorporate both.

Questions for discussion

1. Share your experiences of upbringing and education and consider how these have affected your attitudes to work and employment.
2. What ambitions have you had/do you have? Do you experience guilt about being ambitious in certain areas? Where have your ambitions stemmed from?
3. What do you understand by (a) vocation and (b) service? Are they the same thing?
4. List the kinds of work you have done, including significant unpaid activities. List the purposes, frustrations and rewards of the work undertaken.
5. Consider any differences in the responses to these questions made by women and men in the group.

References

1. Ann Oakley, *Housewife* (Penguin Books 1976) p. 6.
2. Chris Beals, 'Work? You must be joking' in *RESPOND!* (Tees-side Industrial Mission 1984) p. 3.
3. Anna Ford, *Men* (Corgi Books 1985) p. 206.
4. Ibid., p. 218.
5. Ibid., p. 220.
6. J M and R G Paul, *Managers and their Wives* (Pelican 1972) pp. 81–90.
7. Ibid., p. 87.
8. Ibid., p. 85.

9. Ibid., p. 87.
10. Ibid., p. 88.
11. Ibid., p. 89.
12. Don Double, *For best results follow the Maker's Instructions* (Marshalls) p. 21.
13. Ibid., p. 39.
14. Letty Russell, *Human Liberation in a Feminist Perspective – A Theology* (Philadelphia, Westminster Press, 1974) p. 142.
15. Don Double, ibid., p. 29.
16. Ibid., p. 35.
17. Letty Russell, ibid., p. 144.

Bibliography

Baker Miller, Jean, *Towards a new psychology of women*, (Pelican, 1978).

Dawson, Rosemary, *And all that is Unseen: A new look at Women and Work* (Church Information Office 1986).

Morris, Jo, *No More Peanuts: An Evaluation of Women's Work* (National Council for Civil Liberties 1983).

Oakley, Ann, *Subject Women* (Fontana 1981).

Acknowledgement

I am indebted to Anne Borrowdale for discussing this chapter with me and, in particular, for sharing her ideas on service which form part of her PhD thesis.

Helena Terry

Helena Terry graduated in Politics at Lancaster University in 1984 and is currently working as Research Assistant for a Liberal MP at Westminster. Her commitment to reconciling Christianity and feminism started at university where she worked as a voluntary member of a refuge for battered women, whilst still a member of the Christain Union. She has been a student at the London Institute for Contemporary Christianity and has researched into women in the military, and prostitution.

9. Women in Politics – Is the Personal Political?

Helena Terry

'Politics are not women's business and would distract them from their proper duties; women do not desire the suffrage, but would rather be without it; women are sufficiently represented by the representation of their male relatives and connections; women have power enough already.' These were some of the arguments against female suffrage, quoted by its proponent John Stuart Mill, in a debate on the Representation of the People Bill in 1867. Women ratepayers gained the right to vote in municipal elections only two years later, in 1869. But only after the defeat of twenty-eight Bills for women's suffrage between 1870 and 1914 did women over twenty-one eventually win the parliamentary vote in 1928.

In 1986, nearly 60 years on, there were only twenty-six female MPs out of a total of 650, including a female Prime Minister, and 64 women in the House of Lords out of a total of 1,171. Despite their legal access to formal politics, the structural process which determines who gets what, where, when and how, women are sorely unrepresented at every level in our political system. Only 19% of local councillors were women in 1985; an increase of only 7% in twenty years.

'A woman's place is in the House' is the slogan of the 300 Group, an all-party campaign to promote women's representation in politics. Three hundred is approximately half the number of MPs in the House of Commons, and so theoretically there should be 300 women MPs. But in fact there are twenty-six female MPs against 624 male ones. One therefore needs to ask, why is it, when women have had the vote for over fifty years, that there are so few female MPs? Do we still believe that 'politics are not women's business'?

Some do, arguing that politics is best left to men, who are better equipped to do the job, whilst others believe that there are so few female MPs because women are more interested in children and family life than political power.

It is easy to assume that the small number of women in the House of Commons (fewer than 3%) must reflect a lack of political interest among women as a whole. A number of facts, however, argue against the theory that women are simply apolitical. To begin with, women are the most politically active section of the population. They make up between 50% and 60% of the membership of the major political parties and are thus more keen than men to acknowledge a political affiliation.

There is a growing number of people who believe that politics is just as much women's business as men's, but suggest that what women and men understand as 'politics' may be different. The 'politics of Westminster' that speaks of reducing the level of inflation, controlling defence spending and pushing through Bills has been and still is essentially organised by men. The media tell us that this is 'important politics', as it attempts to secure the future of our country and our freedom as individuals.

Women, having been excluded from the 'formal' political system until the last half-century or so, have largely held domestic responsibilities, especially those of child rearing. From this very different position in society many women have developed an alternative agenda and conception of political priorities.

The feminist movement in the 1960s coined the phrase 'the personal is political and the political is personal'. This was an attempt to broaden the commonly accepted narrow definition of politics, arguing that any negotiation for power, whether it be over housework, conversation or sex is political. Personal interactions and activities may seem far removed from Westminster, but are considerably influenced by its decisions.

Discrimination

In some parts of the world, women fare a great deal better in the political stakes. For example, women make up between 23% and 28% of the national leglislature of Norway, Sweden, and Denmark. Women are better represented in Italy and Ireland than in Britain, and neither of these countries is particularly renowned for its support of women's liberation.

Britain has remained unresponsive to the changed status of women, recognised in leglislation by successive governments, but, neither cultural attitudes nor the length of time women have had access to the political system seem to explain this phenomenon. It is the political system itself that needs to be examined, particularly the ways in which candidates are selected and elected. All the countries previously mentioned, with a high proportion of women elected, use proportional representation of one form or another. This is helpful to women candidates.

With the British, single-member, first-past-the-post system the electorate is presented with one candidate for each party, and party selectors must choose the candidate most likely to win. Because the public perception of a 'politician' has been and largely continues to be one of a white, middle-class man, the parties, each competing for precious seats, tend to play safe. A woman candidate, as in many other spheres, has to be as good as and usually better than her male competitors even to be considered for selection. Women are therefore all too seldom selected for winnable seats and rarely for safe ones.

There was an incident recently in which a local party selection committee for a prospective parliamentary candidate asked the only married woman on the shortlist what she would do with her children if she were selected. She replied that they were all over twenty-one and capable of looking after themselves, but what did the married male competitors propose to do with theirs? Such examples are common, and together create a significant impediment to women reaching political power.

However, the discrimination does not stop there. Once

elected as an MP a woman enters the male world of Westminster, which closely resembles a boy's public school, and is often faced with juggling the two demanding jobs of representing a constituency, and maintaining a family. Shirley Williams, an ex-MP, when criticised for being late or looking scruffy, succinctly highlighted the tensions of being a woman MP when she commented that what she needed was 'a wife'!

Stacey and Price, in their study of *Women, Power and Politics*[1], initally ask why there are so few female MPs, but realising the considerable hurdles and discrimination that women in politics face, go on to ask, 'How has women's involvement in politics possibly come about in so short a period of time?'

There is no doubt that in recent years women in Britain have increasingly become involved in politics, but mainly in protest at Greenham Common, with the miners' strike in 1985 and through the Women's Movement rather than at Westminster. Women, in all kinds of different ways and often on single issues such as education or housing, have been waking up to the fact that politics are 'women's business', that women are *not* 'sufficiently represented by the representation of their male relatives' and that they do *not* have 'power enough already'.

Politics is not the whole answer to women's aspirations, and much needs to be worked out between women and men on a personal and family basis, but as long as there remain strong pressures on women to conform to a male politician's view of the world, there will be no real possibility of women working out their personal problems in isolation from political activity.

'The personal is political and the political is personal'

That is a neat catchphrase, but what does it mean? It recognises that women cannot retreat into purely personal activities in work, education, childcare, health, personal relationships, retirement or any other facet of their lives as long as they are at the sharp end of policies which cut child-care, women's pension rights, social security payments, job opportunities and wages. Women cannot escape 'politics' as they pay more than their fair share of taxes, do more 'community care' and miss out on programmes of public investment and when public services are geared to the interests of men, their needs, their career patterns, their daily lives and their attitudes towards women.

So the personal is political and feminists want to incorporate that truth into the political agenda of the day, and in doing so make politics more relevant to the everyday lives of women and men. Yet, as with most other issues, there is division between different feminist schools of thought over the issues of women in politics. Radical feminists, who stress the evils of patriarchy and the consistent oppression of women by men, argue that women, being the subordinate group, should not attempt to join in the structures or systems of their 'oppressors' but should create new, separate organisations themselves. Mary Daly, an American radical feminist, thus paralleled women trying to enter male political systems with blacks trying to join the Ku-Klux-Klan, the most violently racist group seen in America in the 1960s. Using this analysis, Margaret Thatcher is understood as the key collaborator with 'the enemy' to maintain the oppression of women. Given her appalling track record so far on women's rights, considering her sex, there is perhaps some truth in what may initially appear to be a bizarre suggestion.

Liberal feminists, on the other hand, tend to opt for a more integrationist approach, believing that women must enter the system to change it. It is only by having more women involved in politics and fighting for justice and fairness between the sexes that women's general position in society will improve.

It is difficult to assess whether women in politics can change the position of women in society as there are so few women MPs, but the evidence is hopeful. When in 1979 women entered Parliament in significant numbers for the first time, with the percentage rising from five to sixteen, there was an immediate and significant concern with equality issues. It appears therefore that men do not 'sufficiently represent' the rights of the other half of the population, despite a fairly popular belief to the contrary, and at the end of the day women are left to keep up the interests of their own sex.

Although women's politics need to be affirmed and encouraged outside Parliament as they organise themselves on a smaller scale, the evidence shows that women MPs can significantly help women. They need not necessarily conform to the male hierarchy of power, nor imbibe its attitudes and values, as radical feminists fear they will, becoming, like Margaret Thatcher, 'the best man among them'.

The Biblical view

What does the Bible have to say about women in politics? Does the biblical perspective reflect the view that 'politics are not women's business' and would 'distract them from their proper duties'? John Stott promotes the equal involvement in politics by the two sexes, claiming that 'Their resemblance to God and their stewardship of his earth were from the beginning shared equally since both sexes where equally created by God.'[2] Stott adds, 'We are equally called to rule the earth and to co-operate with the Creator in the development of its wealth for the common good.'[3] So the responsibilities of stewardship, ruling, co-operation and development of wealth for the common good were intended to be just as much a woman's concern as a man's. Yet this creational ordinance, like others, has become distorted by the disobedience of human beings to the will of God. Consequently men have come to dominate the political sphere (as they do other spheres) which should ideally be administered jointly by women and men.

Those who believe that God intends a 'woman's place' to be in the home but not the House of Commons often call on the predominance of male political leadership in the Bible to justify their case, but conveniently avoid the powerful leadership of Deborah and the diplomatic skills of Esther, prefering to focus on the 'ideal wife' of Proverbs chapter 31, who incidentally fulfils the 1980s-style 'superwoman' role of combining managing a home with a successful business career: 'She considers a field and buys it; with the fruit of her hands she plants a vineyard . . . She perceives that her merchandise is profitable.'[4]

Jesus sought to redefine the 'politics' of his day, as feminists do today, by challenging the values and standards of the established political system. Although he never held political office, Jesus's ministry had definite political implications in that he distinguished between the oppressed and their oppressors and constantly sought justice for the underdog in society.

Jesus was involved in human issues with their political implications, yet held no formal political office in the Jewish establishment of his day. His whole ministry was political in the sense that it called for a new way of living together as women and men in community – a form of politics with a model of service based on love and not on authoritarian, hierarchical control, a model with which most feminists could easily identify.

Jesus upset the male establishment by his challenging behaviour and by rejecting the patriarchal structures that treated women as property and denied them citizenship. On many occasions Jesus intervened in situations where women were being degraded by the sexist values and structures of Jewish society and sought to bring them dignity and autonomy, which as human beings they deserved. He affirmed the prostitute who poured expensive perfume on his feet, he encouraged Mary to be educated by him, and he trusted Mary Magdalene enough to deliver the news of his resurrection through her.

The way in which Jesus dealt with the woman caught in adultery not only exposed the double standard of sexuality practised in Jewish society (which is still prevalent in our society today) but also demonstrated his integrated approach to structural and personal issues, deeming both equally important. For the woman the personal certainly was political – a private activity, the circumstances of which we know nothing, was dragged out into the open by the Pharisees, whose main concern was to catch Jesus out. Jesus, in characteristic style, twisted the issue away from the personal sexual immorality of the woman to the structural hypocrisy of the system which the Pharisees represented with the words, 'Let him who is guilty cast the first stone.'

Throughout his ministry Jesus often challenged the priorities and 'important political issues' of the day, just as feminists do today, arguing that the system is biased in favour of one section of society and does not recognise those which it oppresses. In the same way that feminists want to bring a more human, caring, compassionate approach to the cold, clinical world of male politics, so Jesus often used the vulnerable, sensitive and intimate experiences of women to expose the harsh, legalistic, and unjust Jewish system. Although there were no Greenham Commons, no miners' wives initiatives or political parties for Jesus to encourage women to join in his day, there seems nothing in his attitude and behaviour towards women to suggest that he would not have done, had they been there.

Summary

Politics, therefore, are 'women's business' according to the biblical agenda and political careers could well be included in their 'proper duties'. John Stott comments, 'The resolute desire of women to know, be and develop themselves, and to use their gifts in the service of the world, is so obviously God's will for them, that to deny or frustrate this is an extremely serious oppression. It is a woman's right and responsibility to discover herself, her identity and her vocation',[5] which could be in politics.

However, just as gaining the vote for women fully in 1928 did not mean equal access to political responsibility for women and men, likewise the achievement of 300 seats in the House of Commons by women would not indicate their equality of influence with men, because of the patriarchal nature of the system they are entering. Therefore true justice for women in politics is not merely a question of getting more women MPs into power (although evidence shows this is helpful), but also of allowing women, in different ways, to change the political agenda that for so long has been dictated by men essentially for men.

A recently elected female MP asked during Parliamentary

Question Time whether hairdressing facilities for female MPs could be provided as there was only a male barbers in the House. Her perfectly reasonable request – which one would have expected not to be necessary, given that she is one of twenty-six women MPs – was met with considerable laughter from male colleagues who seemed to find the proposal trivial and thus highly amusing. This relatively minor incident clearly exposed the chauvinistic and patronising atmosphere of the formal political system towards women and made one wonder what a different world it would be if women had contributed to the system from the outset. One feels sure that not only would there be hairdressing facilities for women, but also a creche, reduced and more flexible working hours, less superflous ritualistic procedure and a shift in political priorities, using a more personal rather than structural approach. For example, the viability of a particular employment strategy would not be judged solely in terms of economic efficiency but also as to whether it offered flexibility and choice over childcare.

'The personal is political' is a short statement that describes a potentially long process of change in our understanding of politics, which would bring value and credibility to women's contribution to it and enable them to participate in this important sphere on their own terms.

Questions for discussion

Theoretical

1. Why is politics perceived as a male domain?
2. Considering the notion, 'the personal is political', to what extent can we adopt this integrated approach to power as Christians?
3. How can a Christian stewardship of resources based on an equal partnership between women and men be promoted in our formal political system?

Practical

1. What is the ratio of female to male councillors on your local council?
2. Is your MP a woman? If not, have any women stood for the seat in recent years? If so, why did they not get elected?

3. How can you encourage women to get involved in politics both at local and national level? (For example, you could babysit for a woman activist.)
4. How can you encourage men to examine the sexism of the political structures which they control and which deter female participation?

References

1. M Stacey and M Price, *Women, Power and Politics* (London, Tavistock publications, 1981).
2. John Stott, *Issues Facing Christians Today* (Basingstoke, Marshalls, 1984), p.237.
3. Ibid., p. 239.
4. Proverbs 31:16,18, RSV.
5. John Stott, op. cit., p. 248.

Bibliography

Rogers, Barbara, *52% Getting Women's Power into Politics* (London, The Women's Press, 1983).

Phyllis Thompson

Phyllis Thompson is a trained teacher. She has worked for ZEBRA, a race relations project in East London, for four years, which has involved her in race issues at home and abroad. She is currently co-ordinator of a literacy scheme in Hammersmith and works as a District Youth and Education Director for the New Testament Church of God at both a local and a national level.

10. Women and Racism – A Double Agenda

Phyllis Thompson

This chapter can be seen as a response rather than a pace setter, and is particularly concerned with the double agenda of issues facing black women. By virtue of our colour, sex and prescribed position in society, black women are at the sharp end of relationships and institutions contaminated by racism and sexism. Our experience, vision and understanding of Scripture rarely informs traditional Christian thinking, even within the denominations in which we form the majority. Expositors claim that Scripture transcends cultural and traditional values and is not subject to human prescribed power. However, it has become increasingly clear that unless certain checks are applied the Christian message carries with it a bias towards those with invested power, who then interpret, authorise and structure Scripture into 'theology'.

Our Western tradition

Western theology comes from a decidedly male, white tradition. Consequently, it all too easily underrates the female prototype as well as the female imagery of God clearly evident within Scripture (Gen 1:27; Jer 66:13; Mt 23:37). If our humanity is a reflection of God's image, as biblical teaching claims it is, then in being Christian each of us is a participant in the celebration of sex, colour and race as a unique expression of God's likeness, in harmony with our black brothers and sisters. Together we represent the Truth about the image of God and the Truth about the family of God. The Bible teaches that the nations of the world will bring splendour, glory and honour into the new Jerusalem (Rev 21:24–26). John Stott comments that 'if they will enrich human life and community in the end, then they can begin to do so now.'[1]

Challenging traditional views

Race and gender, then, are basic attributes of all people, and cannot be overlooked when considering the relationship between men, women and God. Unless we agree that these issues warrant Christian attention, we may well find ourselves upholding beliefs and values which in effect trap and convict black people (women in particular) as impure and headless images of our Creator.

The Church's response

The level of awareness and understanding of women's experience in society varies amongst churchpeople. Inevitably this affects the Church's willingness to join with others in strengthening the female voice where it has been weak or non-existent. Finding a common voice is not easy, and all too often it reveals major differences between even black and white Christian women. It is sadly evident that racist and sexist attitudes remain embedded even within our Christian fellowships.

Confronting this problem in our midst challenges us to go back to biblical roots, in order to establish and recognise our common status as women and men of God. As we have seen, this means recognising our common humanity as people (male, female, black and white) created in the image of God.

Biblical roots

The Bible declares that God has made of one blood all nations on the earth (Acts 17:26). Scripture speaks of one race – the human race. The races were not created to live independently but to live in interdependence and to learn to share the earth's resources. Creation points to the fact that this is God's world, not ours, even though we have responsibility to steward its resources. Biblical teaching cuts right across racial, national and cultural pride, pointing rather to our need of each other and our duty towards each other as neighbours.

In the doctrine of sin, the Bible declares that all have sinned (Rom 5:12). Sin has permeated every part of human life and society, with the result that injustice and conflict arise. It is important to remember that all are sinners, irrespectively of colour, class or nationality. This means that minority groups are no more sinful than majority groups; they are both composed of sinners and exhibit the traits of sin. Anything that separates people is sin, whether it be pride of race or culture, prejudice or discrimination in the treatment of others.

The doctrine of salvation shows that Christ's death on the Cross has broken down the great divide between Jew and Gentile (Eph 2:11–22). It brought into being a new community composed of women and men of every race and culture, joined together in mutual love and worship of their Lord (Rev 5:9–10, 7:9; Gal 3:28), expressed in mutual concern and practical service for each other.

The doctrine of God in Scripture states that because God is sovereign and in control of nations and their destinies, he has ultimate power over the existing authorities and governments which are part of his provision for the world (Rom 13:1–7). They therefore have a duty to practise justice and to exercise compassion, even though very often they do not do so. The Old Testament gives specific instructions about how to treat the foreigner and alien (Ex 23:9; Lev 19:34; Deut 10:19). They were to be loved, accepted as equals, welcomed and provided for, making sure that they were not ill-treated but rather that they obtained justice. To go against these injunctions was to bring upon oneself the wrath of God.

From this, the following points need to be noted:

(i) Discrimination against any ethnic minority group cannot be justified on any grounds.

(ii) Political and social expediency can never take the place of moral imperatives. As someone has said, when national loyalty becomes an -ism and takes priority over moral imperatives, all kinds of evil appear.

(iii) Because of our calling to be 'salt', we Christians must not only be sure of not siding with the oppressor but must act positively and stand up for righteousness and justice in the treatment of minority groups (Patrick Sookhdeo).[2] It is interesting that in Matthew chapter 25, which deals with the final judgement, Jesus pictures himself as a stranger, an immigrant and an alien, and then bases his judgement on the reception and treatment of this type of person.

Both men and women suffer from institutionalised racism as well as prejudice from individuals within the society in which they live. The effects of social and economic deprivation, accentuated by government policy and media hysteria, are all taking their toll on immigrant communities. Whilst some, especially the young and many women, are resigned to their 'inferior' position, new political forces within these groups are emerging. Their direction and the extent of their influence has yet to be seen. The expression of violence is symptomatic of a sickness which desperately needs curing.

What stance are Christians to take? Will the Church assert moral rights and principles over unjust political and cultural expediencies, or will we continue to compromise? Are we willing to assert with biblical authority the unity of all races? Are we willing to get our hands dirty by getting involved in the needs of the immigrant community, even if this means alienation from some of our own people? These questions must be answered by each individual Christian and each Christian community.

At the same time, being in touch with our own needs (whether male or female) should enable us to understand better the needs of others, and so will increase our ability to empathise. Women supporting women's issues therefore should not be seen as inward-looking or self-obsessed, but as helping to establish a clearer vision of the part that women can play for the benefit of the entire body of Christ and its ministry.

Care needs to be taken to ensure that contempt is not stirred amongst those who resist change. Our aim should be to foster growth and maturity amongst all believers, motivated by the love of Christ. Otherwise efforts all too often become divisive and counter-productive. If dialogue is entered into from a position of insecurity and a lack of confidence and clarity, it is easy to become defensive and aggressive. Unfortunately in the Christian Church we have not always been above this.

In search of a theology which speaks of our experience

For some black women, life is full of racist and sexist overtures and attacks have become commonplace. So much so that in some cases they hardly recognise that anything is wrong. For example, a woman who experiences verbal and physical sexist assaults in her home will often say 'men are like that'. Likewise, some black people (men and women) who constantly put up with racist remarks all too easily conclude, 'Well what else can I expect? That's the way these people behave.' Many women have difficulty looking at their own lives apart from their families. Their lives can only be described – and therefore only become meaningful – when seen through the lives of their children and husbands. Church attendance is appreciated as an escape from home routine and the demands that follow. Such women feel that sexism and racism are problems 'out there' which do not apply to them. Indeed, to raise these issues in church can easily be seen as a threat to peoples' comfort. Racism and sexism are often seen as 'problems' in themselves. Consequently, we hear white Christians claim that too much emphasis is placed on the plight of blacks whilst black Christian women equally disqualify sexism from their own experience, assuming that it is 'something to do with white women'.

However, if the Christian Church is to have any credibility for black women, including those who are conscious of their political positions, it must have a theology for women, with more than light reference to race. The Church needs to present a God who has Good News for our real-life experience and to be able to value and accommodate the contribution of black women into its life and ministry. Alice Walker, although not a professed Christian, through the voice of one of her characters in *Colour Purple*[3] puts this plea more succinctly: 'If he (God) ever listened to poor coloured women the world would be a different place, I can tell you.'

Black women in black churches

I remember sitting in a Bible study led by a black female pastor who with reference to Isaiah 3:12 declared that because the English nation had erred from Christian standards it was being cursed with a female monarch and Prime Minister. She was quite oblivious to the fact that the implications could equally apply to the fellowship over which she was responsible. In my denomination women are barred from committees and responsibilities which would involve making doctrinal decisions. Women pastors exist in name only, since they cannot administer the sacrament or a number of other ceremonies. They are active in the youth and Christian educational department. However, when there are too many women in these areas it gives cause for concern, since those ministries are regarded as in-service training for potential pastors. Ira Brooks, one of the few who is bold enough to voice his concern for the plight of women, writes:

> Like race, the true value and position of women in black-led pentecostalism has never been faced squarely. If the 9ruling hierarchy of these churches are guilty of racism in the way they relate to their coloured counterpart then, similarly, black leadership is guilty of sexism by its attitudes to female members collectively.[4]

The issue of women in partnership with men in the ministry needs to be a priority on our church agendas. Otherwise we simply endorse the existing systems in society and perpetuate the failure of white Christian churches in this area. As mentioned earlier, many black Christian women don't understand what sexism is, basically because they have not given much thought to it. Survival against the odds created by racism has been the main concern. However, some of our younger women are beginning to question their position in our churches and their involvement in leadership. One such member reflects, 'In my denomination, where the membership has at least a 75% female majority, no one ever asks for my opinion on the various issues which concern me. No one bothers to ask me how I feel, yet they, a body of men, dictate to me even about basic matters such as what to wear. If I have children I certainly will not bring them up in this church if things carry on the way they are now.' We really need to establish amongst ourselves where we stand on such issues. We need to establish our own definition of liberation from sexism within our homes, churches and society at large.

The voice of black women is resonant of multiple underprivileged experiences. Black women in western societies experience the sharp end of racist and sexist socialisation and the mentality that comes with it. James Cone's question might be asked in this context: 'What is the gospel, and how is it different from my own social condition?'[5] Not only do we need a gospel which speaks to us and brings sense to our lives, but we need a gospel which will enable us to rise above the conditions in which we find ourselves. *New Society*,[6] using information available from the Policy Studies Institute (1984), portrays the disparity between the life-experience, aspirations and achievements of black people and white people in England today. In crucial areas such as education, housing, employment and civil rights, racial discrimination is very much in evidence in spite of the various Equal Opportunities Policies and Race Relations Acts. Theressa Hoover has suggested in her Essay, 'Black Women and the Churches: Triple Jeopardy'[7] that the black Christian woman on one level experiences a triple jeopardy: 'To confront the inequalities of women and the inequalities of blacks, and to have the responsibilities of a dedication to the church.'

We need to hear from a God who brings meaning to our lives and a meaning which can be applied to other experiences. For to put God on the side of women instead of men conceptualises a female God or a black God which would be as idolatrous as that of a white male God. Neither concept presents the biblical God. If anti-sexism and anti-racism are about equal opportunities and human rights based on a biblical understanding of what it means to be made in God's image, then our task as black and white women is to lead Christian thinking to a clearer interpretation of God's dealing with us in our humanity.

To look at the realities of sexism and of racism is to confront the experiences of the poor and the least valued members of society. But how are we to deal with this beyond rhetoric? Do we have the Christian framework from which to work? Should we join hands with non-Christians? If we are to make our case relevant to the world, what are some of the issues for which we have to find biblical perspectives and then apply both inside and outside our churches?

Suggestions for action

Education and training are two examples of these issues. Education in the home, in Christian and non-Christian educational institutions and through life-experience and the media is a process through which we are taught how to think about ourselves and our potential. From pre-school days there is the tendency to channel girls towards activities which are home-related rather than academic and business-related. Therefore even at the infant state interests are cultivated in subjects which lead to training and work. Thankfully this is changing and much of the positive changes in women's lives can be accredited to the current practices in education. However, although the ratio between males and females entering primary education systems reflects that of the sex ratio worldwide, being educated does not necessarily lead women to specialist training in non-traditional spheres:

SCHOOL ENROLMENT OVER THE DECADE

	1975		1985	
	GIRLS	BOYS	GIRLS	BOYS
PRIMARY SCHOOL				
Rich World	92.9	92.6	93.1	92.9
Poor World	54.1	70.6	65.1	78.4
World Average	64.0	76.3	71.2	81.6

SECONDARY SCHOOL				
Rich World	83.6	80.5	89.9	87.3
Poor World	28.5	41.5	37.1	48.1
World Average	45.0	53.3	49.8	57.5
FURTHER EDUCATION				
Rich World	28.0	32.8	31.9	34.7
Poor World	6.2	12.4	9.8	16.1
World Average	13.6	19.3	16.0	21.3

Percentage of age group enrolled in appropriate level of education.

Source: 'Tendances et projections des effectifs scolares par degré d'enseignement et par âge. 1960–2000 (évaluées en 1982)' UNESCO, 1984.

From the above table[8] one can deduce that women constitute the poorest of the poor in terms of opportunities in education as Jill Mowbray outlines more fully in her chapter in this book. The implications are great both worldwide and from a more local perspective. *New Society* states that 40% of the 1.7 million black people in Britain were born in the United Kingdom. It also states the undying high hopes black people have of redeeming their social status through education, particularly of the young. But education figures of achievement and under-achievement show a disportionate rate for the black population as well as women in relation to the white male population. Perhaps Christian women involved in all aspects of education and training need to consider and create collective strategies to promote more opportunities and support for black women to fulfil their educational potential. But what of education and training which takes place in our churches, whether formally or informally? Many ideas for action would become apparent if both men and women were to take a radical look at the situation as it is – that is, who receives what kind of education and training within the local churches.

Buchi Emecheta, speaking from her African experience, questions current challenges concerning roles and division of labour, emphasising fundamental differences between African and Western perceptions:

What is demeaning about looking after the home I live in? One of the greatest pleasures in life is to sleep between nice crisp cotton sheets. What is bad in my preparing them for myself?

Our mothers prepared their sleeping places, not for their men, but for themselves. And if they felt like bringing a man there, then it was so. But what do you learn in the West? You learn that such jobs are low. And, of course, the makers of society give such jobs to women. So what is the result? The most important chores that make us human are regarded as low.

I had my photograph taken once in my 'office' where I do my writing. The photo-journalist was a staunch feminist, and was so angry that my 'office' was my kitchen and that packets of breakfast cereals were in the background. I was letting the women's movement down by allowing such a photograph to be taken.

But that was where I worked, because it was warmer, because it was convenient for me to be able to see my family when I put my typewriter to one side. I tried in vain to tell her that. In my kitchen I felt I was doing more for the peace of the world than the nuclear scientist: in our kitchens we raise all the future Reagans, or the future Jesuses. In our kitchen we wash for them and cook for them. In our kitchen they learn to love and to hate. And we send them out from our kitchens to be grown men and women.

What greater work is there than that? I do not think it low. A mother with a family is an economist, a nurse, a painter and diplomat and more. Those who wish to control and influence the future generation by giving birth and nurturing the young should not be looked down upon. If I had my way it would be the highest paid job in the world. We think it is low because society says so. But it is time we said 'It is not so. We will train all people – men and women – in housework.'[9]

Thankfully more Christian men are seeing their role within the home as a valid part of their Christian commitment. This is commented on more fully elsewhere in the book. A step towards positive change along these lines would not only give women opportunities to do 'men's' jobs but give men the opportunity to do 'women's' jobs and enable both to contribute to human development as their abilities allow rather than as society (and at times, the Church) dictates.

Women, men and power

So often in both Church and state in matters where there is the need for important decisions or complex organisation, the men are visibly in charge and the women are seen to be providing the tea or typing the documents produced by the men. If this does not present a true picture at the local level, it is certainly more likely to be the case at a national level.

Feminists argue that the domestic role allocated to women is the most serious impediment to their progress to power in a man's world. Others like Buchi Emecheta assert that if domestic work received the credit it should, more men and women might appreciate and revalue the power which exists there. Feminists are campaigning for a reaffirmation of feminine and masculine roles on equal and just terms.

In secular society the tendency is for men to have roles which have a lot of power and women to have those which at best carry a lot of responsibilities but little power. Christian teaching puts power firmly in the hand of God. Power tempered with our human weaknesses, soon develops into selfish exploitation and defensive mechanisms based on fear.

Positive discrimination?

The responsibility of Christian men and women is to make our lives available to God so that he can bring his presence into the world through us. Positive discrimination with reference to sex and race, if successful, ensures that those most discriminated against gain a proportional share in the rights and responsibilities of our common humanity and Christian witness. However, positive discrimination presents problems if this actually takes place. Irrational objections to women doing certain things are not uncommon. For example, a Catholic woman faced with the choice of accepting the

Eucharist from a female server said, 'a woman is just ordinary, like myself. When she gives out the Eucharist my mind wanders to events which she might have been involved in during the day, such as arguments with her children and husband. Every woman has her place. It is not in the hierarchy of the Church.' This woman is a typical example of the psychological plight facing many. She needs to 'step back' and ask herself a number of questions. First, she would need convincing as to her reasons for doing so. James Cone believes that 'the Christian gospel is God's Good News to victims, in that their humanity is not determined by their victimisation'.[10] Black and white women, therefore, do not have to relegate themselves to the place allocated to them by the powers of this world. Their perceptions, lives and ministries need not be controlled by social conditioning. God, in his infinite love and wisdom, invites us to see beyond present restrictions. We might be bound to social values and positions but the Word of God is not bound. It remains the source of our hope and our basis for change. Jesus died to free men and women from social and psychological hangups. The story in John chapter 4 of the Samaritan woman shows, much to her doubt and surprise, that Jesus had time for her, a woman void of esteemed social status, in his ministry. The ministry of Jesus remains the same today:

1. Jesus seeks to meet people. He meets us regardless of our labels and social status. Nevertheless, we respond to him out of our social context and experience with the cultural belief and language they afford.
2. Women can find self-esteem and self-worth in Jesus. Like the Samaritan woman we too can find the power in him to share the Good News with those in our communities.
3. Only in the power of the Spirit can we worship him as he really is, for it is his Spirit that enables us to have the faith to accept that there is no difference between races and sexes. We are all the same, needing his forgiveness and strength (Gal 3:28).

Can two walk together unless they agree?

There are significant parallels between anti-sexism and anti-racism. Each aims to free people from exploitation based on biological factors. Black and white women approach the issues of sexism and racism from different social experiences, and this interferes with our Christian pilgrimage. White women's experience is rooted in the controlling and dominant race whilst black women's experience comes from the controlled and dominated race. In effect we bring to focus the different feelings, attitudes and language associated with those racial groups when we meet. We cannot find and use a common voice until we have listened to each other, and in that process discussed our way of seeing and doing things in the light of our unequal experiences. I know that many of us, black and white, have deep-rooted resentment towards each other's race. Of course, we say things like, 'Some of our very good friends are black [or white]'. Equally we may claim to see 'people' and not 'colour'. But we should observe our responses when we hear of some of the atrocities which go on in our communities and we should note the speed at which we search for reasons for or against getting involved, whether in support or combat. White and black people have been heard to assert that 'too many blacks in one place is bound to generate problems.' The sad truth is that black people can also be heard reflecting this racist equation: 'black equals problems.'

Where the battle lies

Christians against racism and sexism do not see whites or men as the enemies. Racism and sexism are evils which in effect push certain groups of people to the periphery of society, where they are treated as less than human. All attitudes and actions of this kind are sinful. And any study of the relationship between men and women in communion with God and Kingdom life will bring to light the command to value life and treat people as people, no less than we would like them to treat us, irrespective of race and gender. As Christians, we have to learn to hate sin and not the sinner.

This is a maxim which the 'sinned against' needs to remember, however painful (see Mt 5:43–48).

There is a big difference between the motives of 'people-led' and 'Spirit-led' anti-racist and anti-sexist movements. The former will ultimately lead to the exclusion of men and whites whilst the latter seeks reconciliation. In many local fellowships, the one or two women who challenge racist and sexist behaviour are often treated with contempt and hostility. It can be a lonely road where the majority lack the confidence and security needed to help strengthen the voice of women on these issues. This is often through fear of being labelled extremists or even worldly and unholy. Talking together not only helps to clarify understanding and establish knowledge, it gives moral support to those who need it and inspiration to the uninspired.

Talking and listening

The process of talking together might not be as easy as it sounds. Many women would be embarrassed to speak out in discussion groups about racism and sexism as it affects their lives. Often women are silent, not because they have nothing to say but because they have never had the opportunity to speak out on the subject, so they are not used to doing so. Given the space and opportunity to gain confidence, women are enabled to raise their awareness and commitment in these areas. This becomes an important part of the process of finding a voice and making sense of both the personal and collective experience.

There will always be some who 'opt out' of any discussion or confrontation. However, for those who take up the challenge, mixed discussion groups, seminars and workshops are ways through which people can openly and honestly face up to the issues personally and collectively. Although men should not be excluded from leadership roles in these sessions, it is good practice for women to have the opportunity to develop their public speaking skills. We often hear that there are not enough good women speakers. The fact remains that women (black and white alike) still don't get as much opportunity as men to gain the necessary experience.

What can be done?

Taking sexism and racism seriously in turn leads to a more general concern for those who are forced in other ways to live their lives as second-class citizens. For example, in education Parent-Teacher Associations could draw up an equal opportunities policy for schools or Supplementary Education; in housing, one could support tenants' groups in campaigns for particular facilities or improvements; in family health, young mums' groups could be set up; in unemployment, self-help groups for young unemployed men and women could be supported. The issues and methods will obviously depend on the kinds of resources which are available to the group and the working styles most appropriate for the members. A 'social concern' group might be initiated within a church or between a group of neighbouring churches. The same groups might support existing campaigns or pressure groups to combat racism, contribute to pamphlets and papers or organise inter-racial events, to mention a few other possibilities.

These activities might seem on the surface to relegate women concerned with racial issues to the perimeter of the Church and in activities quite distant from 'soul winning'. This might be the case if it takes place in isolation, as a separate element of the total life of the fellowship. As previously mentioned, all such activities should be carried out with the desire for reconciliation; reconciliation between people and God, and between the Church and the poor and destitute. At all times individual churches and groups of Christians involved in social concern should be careful not to lose the vision for evangelism. The aim of all Christian activity must be to bring every aspect of our lives into the redemptive purpose of Christ.

Eradicating sexism and racism from our lives, churches and communities disturbs both our comfort and silence. To take up the challenge might cost us the loss of friendships and involve us in political action. This is the very reason why many evangelicals and pentecostals cover up the issues with spirituality. Jesus is indeed the answer, but he becomes the answer, for example, to black people relegated to the poorest and ill-resourced corners of communities, not only when we commit our lives to him but when he is allowed to show us how to make the place a better area for black and white people to live in. It is not easy as a black individual to accept this. It is easier and more in my interest to move out to an up-market area. It is also comfortable to opt for the compromise of moving out but returning to work, whether paid or voluntarily, in the socially deprived and ghetto areas.

Theological training

To take up the challenge is not easy, but men and women, black and white, are equally called to rescue the lost from personal sin and the situations in which they are sinned against. Since theological colleges are places where church leaders receive vocational training, we need to check that 'women's studies' and issues to do with race are given appropriate places on the syllabuses and in the curriculums. This is not so much a bid for equal rights as a plea for relevant training of leaders for today's Church. Whilst the Church should not package Scripture to suit people, it does need to study Scripture diligently for the Word of God for contemporary Christians and the issues they face.

For the present, we need to focus on the realities of racism and sexism but we should not lose sight of the fact that they are only aspects of our experience. They are certainly not its sum total. We should take time also to celebrate the differences we bring to the body of Christ as women and men, black and white. Maybe we should not only be re-reading Scripture to discover the 'motherhood' of God but also to bring to our attention the references to factions within the Gentile race.

Questions for discussion

1. Who gets what training in your church and for what purpose? Is there any anti-racist and anti-sexist component in the training?
2. How might women make an impact on the decision-making process at leadership level in the churches?

3. Do you think a theology arising out of the experience of black women has any relevance for others? What is this?
4. What might some of the spin-offs be if women in black-led and white-led churches were to meet regularly and take to task issues of common concern?
5. How might our brothers be encouraged to help us to facilitate the potential of women in the church, particularly in relation to Galatians 3:28?

References

1. John Stott, *Issues Facing Christian Today*, (Marshall Pickering) p. 207.
2. Patrick Sookhdeo, 'A matter of Black and White', *Cubit* (UCCF Magazine), Autumn 1981.
3. Alice Walker, *The Colour Purple* (Women's Press 1983).
4. Ira V Brooks, *Another Gentleman to the Ministry* (Compeer Press Ltd, Birmingham) p. 109.
5. James H Cone and Gayraud S Willmore, 'New Roles in the Ministry: A Theological Appraisal' from *Black Theology: A Documentary History 1966–1977*, USA, (Orbis Books, 1979) p. 391–398,
6. *New Society*, 17 January, 1986.
7. Teressa Hoover, from *Black Theology: A Documentary History 1966–1977*, ed. J H Cone and G S Willmore, (Orbis Books, 1979).
8. *New Internationalist*, Issue 149, July 1985, p. 24.
9. *New Internationalist*, Issue 149, July 1985, p. 9.
10. Cone and Willmore, op. cit., p. 329.

Bibliography

Cosslam, Sue and Hobbs, Maurice, *The New Humanity: A Study Pack for Christians in a Multi-Racial Society* (Evangelical Christians for Racial Justice (ECRJ), Birmingham, August 84, May 85, August 86).

Wallis, Jim, *The New Radical* (Abingdon Press, Nashville, Tenn. USA, 1983).

Helpful addresses

Institute of Race Relations: 2–6 Leek Street, London WC1X 9HS.

Evangelical Christians for Racial Justice (ECRJ): 12 Bell Barn Shopping Centre, Gregoe Street, Birmingham, West Midlands B15 2D2.

Veronica Zundel

Veronica Zundel is a writer and editor. She is a regular columnist for *Christian Woman*, winning the 'Best Specialist Columnist' in the 1983 Magazine Publishing Awards, and assistant editor of *Third Way*, an evangelical magazine which aims to deal biblically with social and political issues. Based in London, she is currently chairperson of Men Women and God.

11. Women, Men and the Media

Veronica Zundel

'What she has done will also be told'
(Mk 14:9; Mt 26:13).

As I stood waiting at the bus stop, an empty bus drew up with the sign DRIVER UNDER INSTRUCTION in its window. I glanced casually into the cab and saw, to my surprise, that the driver was a young and attractive woman. The incident reminded me that things are changing. But it also brought home with renewed poignancy how rare it was to see such a positive image of a woman at work. Had I ever seen a woman bus driver in television drama? I couldn't remember doing so. If ever one should appear, I fear it would be as a comic figure, regularly denting her bus as she garaged it.

Broadcasting, newspapers, advertising, cinema and popular literature are major forces influencing our views of society. How women and men appear in these media must inevitably have a profound effect on how they are seen and see themselves in everyday life. Let us take a closer look at how this happens.

Not seen

The 1977 report of the Annan Committee on the future of broadcasting in Britain found that over 70% of television characters were men.[1] In other words, on television women were, quite literally, less visible than men – in fact only 30% visible. This phenomenon reinforces the subconscious idea (often held even among those with a concern for fair representation) that women are a minority, a kind of sub-group of humanity. But in fact women form over 50% of the population.

When women *are* shown on television, only some categories of women, and some aspects of women's lives, are seen. American research in the 1970s showed that most male television characters were single (about 60%).[2] By contrast, 70% of female characters were married. Women, then, are brought into the scene mainly as wives, as adjuncts to men.

Advertising is even more selective. The same American research found that 75% of women in television advertisements were in either the kitchen or the bathroom. The message is clear: a woman's life consists of cooking, cleaning and beautifying herself (activities which, incidentally, are hard to reconcile!). Of course, advertisers rely on market research, and it is true that women are still the greatest consumers of domestic products. At the same time, there can hardly be a better demonstration of the 'vicious circle': men are not seen in the media using the cooker or washing machine, so the view is reinforced that this is women's work, so the men are reluctant to do it, so they are not seen in the media doing it . . .

Meanwhile, women as workers outside the home are shown largely in traditional female, low-paid, mainly low-status jobs: as cleaners, shop assistants, waitresses, factory workers, nurses, secretaries. Think of the soap operas. *Coronation Street* offers us Hilda Ogden, cleaner; Bet Lynch, barmaid; Vera Duckworth, machinist in a clothing sweatshop; and various assorted transport cafe staff. Switch to *Eastenders*, and the picture is only marginally different: Ethel, cleaner; Angie Watts, barmaid; Pauline Fowler, launderette attendant; Sue Osman, transport cafe proprietress. There are the odd exceptions: Andy, male nurse, and Tony Carpenter's upwardly mobile wife Hannah. But exceptions they remain; the Square's doctor is still white and male.

Other more 'up-market' drama may show the occasional woman lawyer or business executive (though frequently in a 'female' business such as cosmetics, or else as part of a family firm, inheriting rather than earning her position), and police series centred around woman officers are increasingly popular. However, in the average office drama the overwhelming picture is still of woman as the managing director's wife, secretary, mistress or tea lady – not the managing director.

Reality?

It might be objected that television drama simply reflects social reality. But 'seeing is believing', and what we watch also profoundly *influences* reality. The models girls and women are given will affect their aspirations and choices, as will become clearer if we examine some of the newer dramas centred on 'career women'.

An increasing number of series are responding to a changing society and showing women in responsible and challenging jobs. But all too often the lead character is just a beautiful female counterpart of the stereotyped handsome, glamorous, ruthless male, with added 'feminine wiles'. Or else she is a 'rich bitch', hard as her own nail polish and 'deadlier than the male', as in many boardroom dramas (which spend as much time in the bedroom as in the boardroom). Alternatively she may be shown to bring a more 'womanly', human dimension to her work and be less involved in direct physical confrontation (*The Gentle Touch* is a significant title here).

The more realistic examples of this new drama do show an awareness of the conflicts between work and home often faced by married women. Mary Beth Lacey of *Cagney and Lacey* struggles to be both a good cop and a good mother (her husband Harvey has no corresponding conflicts between being a worker and being a father). There are no television drama heroines, however, who *succeed* in both work and family relationships. Overall, the message is that if you want to be a 'real' woman, you had better stay at home; if you are set on a career, you will have to sacrifice marriage (like Christine Cagney).

Advertising, too, is somewhat ambivalent about social changes. A recent advert for detergent makes great comic capital of a little girl watching Daddy wash dishes. His hands are not so soft as Mummy's, since they are not immersed in the advertised liquid so often. Clearly a man washing dishes is still seen as basically 'helping with his wife's job' and fair game for laughter.

Such categorisation is not just a matter of confining women to certain limited areas of life. It confines men just as much. The man who has chosen to be a full-time carer for children, or the man working in a job traditionally regarded as female, or the man who wants to express 'feminine' emotions, is as little likely to see a positive reflection of his life on the small screen as the woman living in what is regarded as 'a man's world'.

Type casting

Overlaid on the basic stereotype of 'man as worker, woman as homemaker' are a host of other stock ways of pigeonholing the sexes.

Little girl equals 'Daddy's little darling', while little boy equals adventurer, explorer. Teenage girl equals sexually vulnerable (Michelle Fowler of *Eastenders*), while teenage boy equals 'a bit of a lad' (Nigel in *No place like home*). Young woman equals sexually enticing, with several sub-categories (the innocent virgin just waiting to be seduced, the 'dumb blonde' or 'sex kitten' manipulating men by apparent stupidity, the sexually aggressive Amazon whom only a truly strong man will subdue, and so on). Middle-aged woman equals nagging wife, nagging mother, discontented housewife ripe for an 'affair'; middle-aged man, on the other hand, is in the prime of life and at the height of his career (if, in mid-life crisis, he has an affair with a young woman, this is nothing like as ridiculous as his wife fancying the milkman). Old woman equals kindly grandmother, comic 'silly old moo', or worst of all, mother-in-law; old man is a fumbling 'dirty old man', lusting after young girls.

Both sexes are stereotyped, but in the case of women the stereotyping has a special element. Women tend to be defined entirely in terms of their sexuality and the presence or absence of sexual attractiveness. The process can be carried to absurd lengths, even in news reporting. On a random check of *The Star*, I found the following story: '*Bedtime secret of TV's genius*. Brainy Jennifer Keaveney romped away with the Mastermind title – thanks to late-night swotting sessions in bed. She revealed that her husband spent hours questioning her on her subjects until she was word perfect.' I wonder whether a *male* Mastermind winner would be reported the same way!

In television news and documentary programmes, while there are now a large number of women presenters and reporters, it is easy to see that for certain jobs (newsreaders, for instance, or presenters of 'soft' news programmes such as breakfast television) one of the main qualifications is to be both young and attractive. Women in these positions may have excellent journalistic qualifications and experience but they seem to disappear mysteriously from the screen as soon as they reach forty! In the words of one BBC senior producer: 'Women on the screen are nothing to do with equality; where is a woman with the same position as Robin Day?'

Whatever is true . . .

Why should any of this matter to Christian women and men? Perhaps the best answer is provided by Paul's well known exhortation to the Christians at Philippi: 'Whatever is true, whatever is noble, whatever is right, whatever is pure, whatever is lovely, whatever is admirable – if anything is excellent or praiseworthy – think about such things' (Phil 4:8). I believe it is very significant that 'whatever is *true*' comes first in this list. Attention to truthfulness provides the foundation for identifying whether something qualifies under all the other headings: noble, right, pure, lovely, and so on.

It is clear that today's news and entertainment media are often far from qualifying under the criterion of truth. They do not simply reflect an already distorted world; they distort it further by 'editing out' much of that world's experience and reducing it to a few well-worn formulae. And nowhere is this more evident than in the portrayal of women's lives and relations between men and women.

In reponding to this untruthfulness, it is not enough just to campaign for the suppression of certain topics and images as 'offensive'. To object to 'Page Three' girls because they are bare-breasted is to miss the point; plenty of women in traditional African cultures go bare-breasted with no loss of dignity or modesty. The real offence against truth is that the 'Page Three' image reduces a woman to *nothing but* a pair of bare breasts and an inviting smile. Moralists who would cover the breasts but leave the smile just as inviting actually change nothing.

The missing half

Of course, the press and broadcast media are not self-created, but are produced by people. The media are one of the professional fields most open to women, and large numbers of women work in them. So why has this, so far, influenced the output so little? To answer this we need to look at where women are in the media.

Recent research[3] by Monica Sims, Director of Programmes for BBC Radio, shows that 38% of the total monthly-paid BBC staff (i.e., excluding weekly-paid categories such as cleaners) are women. But if we remove the secretarial and clerical grades, the percentage of women drops to 26%. Among those actually involved in creating programmes, then, only a quarter of staff are women.

Nowadays women are entering BBC training schemes in greater numbers than ever before. But even so, when trained they tend to stay at the lower (and therefore less influential) levels. In Band 2, which includes Studio Managers, Researchers, Station Assistants (i.e., largely 'back-up' jobs), women predominate at 51%. As the grade rises, the percentage of women drops, until at Band 5 level (including Heads of Department, Correspondents and Senior Television Producers) they are just 8%.

Independent broadcasting companies do little better. Thames Television in 1985 had one woman in thirty-six employees at higher grades; and even the innovative Channel 4, whose very existence arises out of a concern to broadcast for neglected constituencies, had nineteen women in seventy-two management staff, and eight in twenty-five senior managers.

As in other fields, the major obstacle for married women

trying to develop their broadcasting career is lack of child care, and lack of help in re-entering work after a break (especially when technology is changing so rapidly). Age discrimination also means that women over forty re-entering the profession are often seen as 'over the hill' (rather than as having gained valuable experience). And yet, as one employee observes, 'these are the very women who can contribute ideas and programmes which would have something in common with approximately 50% of the viewing public.' Another, commenting on the 'old boy network' operating in the bars after hours and on the 'workaholism' of many male broadcasters, asks: 'Are men whose entire social life is the BBC more likely to have a clever grasp of public opinion and viewers' concerns than those women who spend time at parent teacher meetings and community groups?' Perhaps the most pertinent comment is that of Monica Sims herself: 'An organisation which serves the whole population needs the contribution of both men and women at all levels. This is not just a matter of legal equality, but a belief that women can bring different qualities of style, thought and feeling to the benefit of the Corporation as a whole and to the image it presents to the public.'

For women only

What of the area where women form an overwhelming majority, both in staff and readership: the women's magazines?

Traditionally, women's magazines have concentrated on a narrow range of interests seen to be 'women's sphere' (titles like *Woman's Realm* reflect this): domestic cares, fashion and beauty, romance, glamour. Newer magazines like *Cosmopolitan* have broadened the range, aiming at the sophisticated young 'woman-about-town', but still concentrate on women in relation to men, whether as 'lovers' or career competitors. The ill-fated *Working Woman* made a brave attempt to break out and address women in their own right, but quickly sank. At the younger end of the market, titles like *My Guy* tell their own story: procuring and hanging on to a boyfriend now has to start as young as eleven or twelve.

Another range of magazines like the long-running *Spare Rib*, the newer *Everywoman* and *Women's Review*, as well as younger, more leisure-oriented newcomers such as *Mizz* and *Etcetera*, reflect the continuing feminist debate. But there are pluses and minuses to the whole idea of women's publications.

On the plus side, magazines or programmes specially for women do at least mean that women's daily experience is not ignored completely, even if it is filtered through a limited view of what that experience is or should be. On the minus side, they mean that women can still be seen as a 'special interest group' instead of more than half of humanity. While there are women's magazines and women's pages in newspapers, the rest of the press can ignore women or treat them as 'special' (interviewing women politicians or film directors, for instance, on the basis of their novelty value as women). *Woman's Hour* is an excellent and praiseworthy programme, but many producers and reporters (and hopefully listeners) would rejoice if it became redundant because adequate opportunities for women broadcasters and coverage for the issues it deals with were provided elsewhere.

Whose Church?

Finally, the Church itself has to be examined as a purveyor of media, both in print and other forms. What image does Christian communication present of men's and women's lives and relation to each other?

Even the briefest look at Christian publications, publicity material for parachurch organisations and even worship itself reveals a depressing picture. Articles, books and teaching materials in both text and illustrations reinforce the assumption that every woman is a wife and mother and that this is her main occupation. Church leaders are assumed to be male, even though many Protestant denominations now ordain women; phrases like 'the preacher and his congregation' and 'ministers and their wives' abound. Female speakers are introduced by the names of their famous husbands: a recent book advert boasted a contribution by 'Mrs Billy Graham'.

Although it has been estimated that roughly 10% of the Bible is made up of stories about women, it is rare if not impossible to find a church where even five sermons a year are devoted to this material. Even when preaching or writing does deal with Sarah, Deborah, Hannah, Ruth, Esther or Mary, they are usually approached in terms of their excellence as wives, mothers or 'the good woman behind every good man'.

Little attention is given to inclusive language in liturgy. Anglicans (using a prayer book published in 1980!) are forced every week to pray 'for men of every race' and proclaim faith in a Christ who came 'for us men and our salvation'. Anyone who doubts the influence of such language should consider the hesitation of a mixed congregation in a recent experimental liturgy I attended in Cambridge, where men as well as women had to identify themselves as 'daughters'. Men who might earlier have blithely asserted that of course 'sons' included everyone thought again when they themselves felt excluded!

New images

I began this chapter with a real-life image which had 'opened up the world' for me a little. Such images *are*, slowly, beginning to appear in the media. Applause is due to drama series such as *Juliet Bravo* for portraying a woman at work without glamorising or sensationalising. Also encouraging is the emergence of excellent female comedians such as Victoria Wood: women who can make people laugh by their shrewd observation instead of by losing their clothes. Developments like these demonstrate that a concern for fair representation need not lead to 'worthiness' but can produce good entertainment in which one sex in not always the joker and the other the joke.

In the less 'popular' area of non-commercial cinema, I still remember vividly the shock of recognition as I watched Claudia Weill's delightful film *Girl Friends*, the story of a friendship between two young New York women and what happens when one of them marries. For the first time, here was a portrayal of women's lives and relationships *seen from the inside*, a story in which I could recognise myself. Since then I have had a similar sensation on reading some women novelists, such as Antonia White or Rosamund Lehmann.

That experience is a pointer for the Christian communicator. When people can see their own lives reflected, explored and transformed in a story, it can become what I heard one writer call 'a healing story'. If I see someone like myself responding to God's grace, I can believe that there is grace for me too.

As society starts to reassess the lives of women and men and combat the distortion which false understandings have produced, the media *are* beginning to reflect the changes, however tentatively. Surely Christians who look for 'a new earth' as well as 'a new heaven' can play a significant part in this process.

Discussion and action

1. Spend a Saturday morning watching children's commercial TV. What view of girls' and boys' interests is presented by the programmes? By the adverts?
2. Monitor a week's TV viewing, making a note of anything you find offensive or untruthful. At the end of the week compare your findings with others in a group.
3. Make a collage of pictures, headlines and adverts dealing with men and women from weekly magazines. What overall picture emerges?
4. Collect as many Christian publications as you can (study books, novels, Bible reading notes, Sunday school materials) which deal with Bible women. (In a group, ask different people to collect different types of literature.) Share them out and compare them with the original Bible texts. What has been added? What does it assume?
5. With a concordance, find all the parables of Jesus in which a woman is the central figure. What qualities does the woman show in each case? How often does she represent God? What can you learn about Jesus' use of women in communication?

References

1. *Report of the Committee on the Future of Broadcasting* (London, HMSO, August 1977) Cmnd 6753.
2. See Gaye Tuchman, 'The symbolic annihilation of women by the mass media' in Stanley Cohen and Jock Young, *The manufacture of news* (Constable 1981).
3. *Women in BBC management* (internal BBC report, 1985).

Further reading

Carol Adams and Rae Laurikietis, *The Gender Trap 3: Messages and Images* (Virago, London). A basic introduction to media stereotyping, written for schools and colleges, with useful list of books, films and organisations.
Germaine Greer, *The Obstacle Race* (Picador, London) and Joanna Russ, *How to suppress women's writing* (Women's Press, London). Two books charting how women's contributions have been discouraged or ignored in painting and literature.

Organisations

Women's Media Action Group (A Woman's Place, Hungerford House, Victoria Embankment, London WC2) monitors the media and provides a newsletter, speakers and information. The group is working on a code of practice for the Advertising Standards Authority.
Women in Media (The Fawcett Society, 46 Harleyford Road, London SE11) is a campaigning group of women working in the media.

Part III:

Is Biology Destiny?

12. The Future of the Family

Elaine Storkey

In this chapter I shall be looking at the social aspect of the family from a Christian perspective. This means I will need to look at different theories of the family and at the differences between the normative structure of the family and the actuality of the relationships between people living together in Britain today. We'll be glancing at some statistics about the way people live and the way families have changed. We'll also look at the way the family relates to other institutions such as work and the Church.

General thesis

To make it easier to follow I want to put all this material into a general thesis.

1. Christians have almost always supported the family as being part of God's plan for us. This has varied with different underlying theological evaluations of the place and meaning of the family, but on the whole it has been recognised as a good rather than a bad thing by Christians.

2. Today this is becoming a minority view to some extent. People, especially politicians, pay lip-service to the family but social practices and even government policies reveal something very different. The consensus about the family which appeared to be based on a Christian world-view has broken down, as one of the casualties of the decline in the whole world-view itself. So, in our contemporary society the family is under attack from many different quarters.

3. How we understand the attack and what we do about it is one of the most crucial issues facing Christianity today.

The danger is that because we don't have a Christian view of the family but have instead already accepted one kind of secular humanist view or another, we may well find ourselves reacting in a purely moralistic or even self-righteous way, and thus failing to be the salt and light in society which Jesus Christ expects his Body to be.

What is the family?

There are a number of different Christian views of the family. I don't want to get bogged down in sociological distinctions between extended and nuclear, because both kinds of family are affirmed by Scripture. The Bible recognises the specific relationships of wife-husband-children (Ephesians chapters 5 and 6) but also puts the nuclear family within the context of a broader extended family and its pattern of responsibilities (Mark 7:9–13; 1 Tim 5:4–6). The family in broad Christian terms, then, is a kinship network, based initially on blood ties and love.

But the way in which we understand the family in a more detailed sense, and especially how it relates to other parts of society, is more complex. There are a number of pro-family views which have been adopted by different Christian traditions, not all of which, however, are faithful to a Scriptural perspective.

The pro-family camp

1. The Catholic or sacramental view

Here celibacy is regarded highly and is seen as a vocation, but marriage and the family are seen as made sacred by God's special grace through the Church. This is an example of the classic sacred-secular split, where God's domain is the 'sacred' but where parts of the secular, natural world can be sacramentalised by the Church. Thus by a special service marriage loses its 'worldliness' of being just a bodily union.

2. The Calvinist view

This, the view which I would personally espouse, has a much more earthy view of the family. The Reformers were anxious to stress the companionable aspects of marriage rather than procreation, and both marriage and the family are seen as rooted in Creation. They do not need to be 'sanctified' by the Church because they are already part of God's world. Theologically the family reflects the covenant of God's love and is defined by the normative principles laid down in Scripture. Troth, commitment, openness, patience, faithfulness, hospitality, discipline and forgiveness all operate within the family community. Within these norms the institution of the family can unfold and intimacy can develop. But this view recognises that as well as being a creation ordinance the family is also affected by sin, which has repercussions we will look at later.

3. The functionalist view

It is interesting to note how this basically secular view has embedded itself in much Christian thinking. This 'consensus' view of the family found frequently among the 'moral majority' accepts and reinforces the family as a Good Thing. The family undergirds all of society and performs very important functions. Often these are seen as being socialisation functions, as the family passes on social values and taboos to the next generation; an economic function, as the family provides the basic unit for consumption; and a sexual function, as the family regulates sexual activity and ensures a safe, stable environment for offspring to be born into. The family therefore is important not because it is a covenanting community or a normative institution but because it is *functional* for society.

4. The romantic view

A very different view is the romantic view of the family, which says the family is all about close relationships: it is all about love and care, about intimacy, about togetherness.

Structures are unimportant. Norms or principles of family living can be cold and static. Instead the family should be an emotionally bonding community. Of course, it has to be agreed that all this is a very important part of what the family is. Some of the most 'successful' Christian families operate along these lines. Yet that is often because undergirding their view of the family is a very strong scriptural understanding about relationships. The trouble with this perspective on its own, however, is that it can become self-indulgent, introspective and fragile. There is sometimes little framework for understanding or handling conflict. Worst of all, it can deteriorate into sentimentality, where a myth about the family lies uneasily with the reality of day-to-day existence.

5. The Christian modelling view

A final position I want to consider here is one for which again I have much sympathy, although I do not hold it. It says the family is about both structure *and* relationships. The structures are already outlined in some detail in Scripture, for the Bible gives us not just norms and principles but actual patterns of family organisation. The Old Testament offers a land-based, extended family model which we should translate and re-establish in our contemporary culture, and which we have moved from at our own loss.

These views have informed and directed the way Christians and many others have seen the family in society. The last position has recently had some interesting and surprising echoes in the impressive research done by Germaine Greer in *Sex and Destiny*. For the most part, however, evidence is that the influence of the pro-family positions has enormously waned in Britain and indeed in the West as a whole. Instead, both in theory and practice the family has come under attack. I want now to examine where the attacks are coming from and what forms they take.

The anti-family camp

First, the attack is coming from the theorists. And whatever we feel about those who theorise rather than practise, it is undoubtedly true that they enormously influence the way we all live and behave. It is the theorists and not just the practitioners who work, for example, in the media: the theorists write scripts for television, present us with the news, produce radio documentaries, write columns in the newspapers. They devise educational programmes for our schools, write textbooks for our children, direct the training of social workers, work out our political economy, advise our politicians. It is also theorists who train our ordinands and future Christian ministers. It was through the work of a sociological theorist that a certain theological training institution told me a couple of years back, 'We don't study the Bible much any more. We've come to realise that context is much more important than text.'

So the fact that an attack on the family is coming from the theorists should not be taken lightly. We should take it with the utmost gravity. It should make our flesh creep. For what they theorise about in one generation very often becomes practice in the next. And our generations are getting shorter.

What is more, the attack is not uniformly from one theoretical perspective. It is coming with equal strength from both the left-wing, Marxist and right-wing, individualist perspectives.

1. The Marxist view

Many of the Marxists are sociologists and have much influence. They are saying that the family is simply a pawn, a social device in the hands of an elitist minority who use it to reinforce a certain social and economic structure in society. The division of labour along class and gender lines has depended upon having a certain family structure to undergird it. If man had not become the breadwinner through the effects of the Industrial Revolution, we would not have had a pliable labour force willing to accept gross inequalities in order that their dependants might survive. What is more, the Marxists argue, although the right-wing constantly presents itself as pro-family, wherever profits or capital are under threat, the glossy veneer drops off to reveal very ugly beetle-ridden, rotting wood underneath. They can and do illustrate this by pointing to our present government, who whilst paying lip-service to the family, put a three-line whip on the Sunday Trading Bill which would have produced a massive deterioration in the quality of the 'family day' of the week. Where profits matter, families don't.

2. The radical feminist view

Radical feminist sociologists also attack the family, for like the Marxists, they see the family as being used, this time to reinforce patriarchy. The creation of a special sphere for women in the home and a different sphere for men at work or in the decision-making bodies of our society has meant that we have a society where everything is generated along gender lines. Women are left powerless and dependent on the good will of men. Many of my own radical feminist colleagues feel there can be no freedom for women whilst the traditional family exists. Because men will always use their privileges and advantages in their own self-interest, women will be always there to prop up the male status quo. As long as women are the ones to have children, male power will not wane. Fifteen years ago we all laughed and shuddered at Shulamith Firestone's suggestion of transplanting human embryos into the uteri of cows or pigs or even adapting male bodies to bear children. During the last year a much publicised article in the *Daily Telegraph* claimed that the time will be shortly upon us when with a small routine operation, male anatomy can be adapted so that a man can carry a child to full term. Recently in the USA a feminist medical researcher told a conference that we were not far off the position where we would be able to reproduce without sperm altogether, by splitting the human egg. Only female children could be born that way, but if the idea caught on, men would be redundant anyway, and women's oppression would be over. Just theories? They have an alarming tendency to become practice.

3. The right wing libertarian view

This position also attacks the family, for the family is by nature anti-individualist. It puts restraints on the individual.

It produces anxiety, neuroses and often deep unhappiness. What is more, they say, family responsibilities get in the way of my living the kind of life which is best for me. Marital constraints mean that I cannot enjoy sexual relations with those I would like to have them with. Families produce repression in society – they squeeze the individual, they eat away at his time or her initiative. They socialise children into conformism. The family is how the bureaucrats drain the life out of the individual. Freedom, then, means negating the family and once more extolling individualist virtues such as self-help from the youngest possible age, entrepreneurship and looking after number one.

4. The 'communal' theorist view

This attack on the family takes the other position from the one outlined above. Today's family is anti-community, they argue. It is isolated and privatised. Everything takes place within the home, where people live individual lives enclosed within four walls. Leisure is brought into the home and away from the community. Modern domestic conveniences mean that people do not need to join one another in their chores or their transport. We travel in individual family cars. We exclude outsiders like the single person, the childless couple, the widowed, the elderly. Families have become self-centred and self-congratulatory. They protect themselves with fences and walls and burglar alarms. The community does not matter in any significant sense.

These are just some of the sociological theories which abound. However, the attack on the family also comes from a second front. There is concrete evidence that the family is under attack in real people's lives. In a deeply practical sense, family life is changing very quickly in our society. An article in *New Society* by a homosexual writer argues that Christmas is the family's last revenge on society for trying to kill it off. But what happens at Christmas? Is it a time for the family to renew its strength, to wait on the Incarnate Lord and then mount with wings like eagles? Hardly. It's a time when mothers wear themselves out in the kitchen, many fathers spend a lot more time at the pub and children are overindulged with the mountains of materialist rubbish that the shops have been pushing out at us for weeks. It is a time when guilt over elderly relatives and in-laws is assuaged by an invitation to Christmas dinner and a chair in front of the TV. Even at the height of its celebration, of its revenge on society, is our contemporary family any more than a collection of individuals around a television set?

There are two aspects to the evidence of the attack on the family in daily living. The first is the deterioration of relationships. There is now a large volume of case studies in family therapy which indicate that many things of a deeply worrying nature are going on behind the closed doors of the Englishman's castle. I am writing a book on the search for intimacy and looking at how people are increasingly abandoning their search within the family. Intimate relationships are complex and elusive, but families so often relate in terms of roles and prescribed patterns than as whole, needy and open people. Studies of relations between wives and husbands and between parents and children suggest that needs are not being met within a family context. Men and women are now further apart, in spite of all this new consciousness.

The other aspect to the evidence is that of family structure. We still have an image of the British average family, with a husband who goes out to work and a wife who stays at home with her 2.5 children. This is fast becoming an unreality. If you glance at a few of the figures on the information sheet, completed from government statistics and social trends research publications, you'll see that some of our cherished ideas of the family are now history. Most people do not live in a 'family'. More than half of the population live in households containing only one or two people.

A large proportion of people living together will not be married. A quarter of all first marriage partners will have cohabited; two-thirds of all later marriages.

At least a third of all marriages in 1987 are remarriages. The majority of these include divorcees. First marriages have been declining in number since the end of the 1960s.

Nearly a fifth of all pregnancies are terminated by abortion. This, of course, was always assumed to mean there would be a drop in the illegitimacy rate. In fact this has gone up 100% since the Abortion Act was passed. It is now about 16% of all births. When we include babies born to women who have married but are now divorced or cohabiting, the figure reaches almost 30%.

There are over one million one-parent families with dependent children in Britain, and this doesn't include single women living with their parents.

The divorce rate has more than doubled since the early 1920s. Marital breakdown is growing in every area of society. It has greatly increased with the Church, and the marriages of Christian ministers too are more prone to breakdown than ever before.

A mere observation of the impact these figures have when translated into people's lives around us can cause a sick feeling in the pit of one's stomach. This is the Britain we live in. And, of course, people say that the fact that people marry for the second and third time ought to give us encouragement. However, it doesn't, because they also divorce for the second and third time and in larger numbers and with shorter periods in between. It leads others to say, 'Well, what do you expect? This is what we have been saying. The family has failed. It has failed because it is not a good way of arranging living patterns. Christian morality is wrong again. How irrelevant can you get?'

Facing the challenge

How do we Christians face the challenge which these attacks on the family pose? I think we do it rather badly. As I list some of my own observations, see if you've spotted them too or have noted any more.

1. The moralistic reaction

This tries to recall people to some universal moral standard which they are neglecting. It assumes an undergirding Christian vindication of the family in all its forms and goes all out to remind people of their moral responsibilities. For example, we must blame working mothers and latch-key children for the decline of the moral fibre of society.

2. The functionalist reaction

This is similarly conservative. It sees as important the need to re-establish the function the family once played in society. It urges for the re-acceptance of traditional family roles – domestic women and manly men. It argues that we need the family still for the *functions* it performs in society.

3. The sacramentalist reaction

This is essentially a Catholic reaction. The Pope is sent round the world to reassert the values of the family. The right to birth control is denied. If we try to increase the strength of the Church, the family will come back into line.

4. The escapist reaction

This stems from a head-in-the-sand mentality. It contends that 'We must hold on to the ideology even though the actuality says something different.' This is nowhere more evident than in some parts of the USA. The Christian Right extol the importance of the family in American life. The family is surrounded by a halo. Adverts sell the family, and the family is used to sell everything – films, holidays, products. There is an obsession with important families: Dallas, Dynasty, even our own Royal Family.

So there exists a romantic and sentimental fascination with the family which has been exploited by Christianity. But it is unreal, because when you look at the breakdown of the family in the USA, it is substantial. A massive dissonance exists between the ideal and the actuality. The guts have gone. Sentimentality is left, plus Bing Crosby and *A White Christmas*.

5. The Anglican and Free Church reaction

This attitude says, 'Let's have a family service!' This reaction is in fact very grim indeed, for the family doesn't really exist for most Anglican churches except for one Sunday in a month. As with many denominations, church meetings are structured in such a way that they bring additional pressure upon families rather than supporting or relieving them. The negative vibes given to someone who doesn't support church meetings can be very strong. Frankly, in the families of full-time Christian workers the strains can be enormous, and yet they are the ones who are having to set a family example to the rest of the community.

Last year I spoke at a conference for full-time Christian workers. Both husbands and wives were there, and most of the people knew the others well. They were wonderful people who had given their all to serving Christ. There were, however, problems which some of the families were known to be facing. After I had given the main address the conference convenor – a wise, concerned man – suggested I might like to get together with the husbands and wives in separate sessions. The result was striking. The forty or so women sat in a big circle, and after a few gentle introductions began to talk openly to me and to each other. They wanted to talk about their relationships, about the frustrations of their husbands' work, about anxieties over their children. They wanted to share their concerns about the lack of intimacy, time, sharing and involvement they had with their husbands. They told of the financial pressures, pressures on family life, and from other people's demands and expectations. It was open, loving, warm communication. They shared from their hearts. I left the group feeling we had encountered each other as real people and that Christ had been there ministering to our needs. Then I went to the men's group. They were sitting formally in rows and I was given the speaker's chair at the front. They wanted to talk about the theology of headship, the theology of divorce. Something cerebral; something abstract; nothing too personal. It was only when I had pointed out to them the difference between the two groups that there was silence. And then quietly, from the back, one of the men asked humbly, 'Will you tell us what our wives said, please?'

Family relationships *are* personal. They do matter. They

are where most of us take our identity from. They affect all of us in ways too profound to go into in this brief chapter.

How, then, are we going to see the family, and how are we going to address the attack on it. I want to conclude with just a few observations.

We need to recognise that although the family is God's idea it is still a human institution. The family *per se* is not necessarily a good thing. A certain form of the family might be a very bad thing. For the family, due to being a creation ordinance, has been thoroughly affected by sin. I want to claim that what we are seeing breaking down in society is not in fact the Christian family. The Christian family has not so much been tried and found wanting, as not tried at all. I believe that what we are witnessing is the breakdown of a humanism which has gripped every part of our culture and which has embedded itself very strongly in family life. Because humanist ideologies are so pervasive we have not detected this. The same humanism which shapes our knowledge and our theories of knowledge also directs the families of our nation. But it is a world-view which cannot produce the goods. It is an idol with clay feet. Those institutions in our society which are already vulnerable because they are built on intimate relationships will crumble once they have sold themselves into humanist slavery, rather than living in the freedom of the living God.

What we need to do, therefore, is not to defend the traditional family, or to get mixed up with trying to re-establish patriarchy or even certain forms of family organisation, but to look initially at the Christian biblical *norms* for the family and at ways of living within these ourselves.

People are living sad and tragic lives, caught up in a humanism they don't fully understand but have inherited from our culture. We need to recognise this. We then need to be able to move from sin to redemption.

It is naive to think, as some do, that we can use the family to fight the devil. In one sense the devil captured our British and American families years ago. Yet in another sense the family has God's thumbprint on it. It is marred and misdirected but can be redeemed, reformed and renewed. However, a lot depends on us. Are we going to take it seriously? Are *we* going to recognise the integrity and the meaning of the family or are we too going to continue to pay lip service only, and then point the finger when people's lives disintegrate.

All too often we don't see results because we don't ask. God can give us insight and wisdom. His spirit can equip us for the task ahead. Let us be convinced, therefore, that the job is a real one.

Questions for discussion

1. What view of the family do you think you have been holding, even unconsciously?
2. How many people do you know who discuss gender roles and family roles before they are married? How much would you say is taken for granted?
3. How would you describe your own experiences of family, taking the one you know best as your focus?
4. Can you list all the barriers to communication in the family which you have come across during the last month? How many of these are permanent ones?
5. What do you think ought to be the Christian's attitude to divorce?
6. Do you know any families which you would call 'successful' families? What does this mean for you, and what makes them successful?

Bibliography

Atkins, Anne, *Split Image* (Hodder & Stoughton 1987).
Evans, Mary, *Woman in the Bible* (Paternoster 1983).
Gittins, Diana, *The Question of the Family* (Macmillan 1985).
Green, Wendy, *The Future of the Family* (Mowbrays 1985).
Lees, Shirley, *The Role of Women* (IVP 1984).
Mount, Fedinand, *The Subversive Family*
Oakley, Ann, *From Here to Maternity* (Pelican 1985).
Storkey, Elaine, *What's Right With Feminism* (SPCK/Third Way 1985).

Tony Walter

Tony Walter is a freelance author based in Bath. He has written prolifically on a wide range of subjects. His most well known books include *Hope on the Dole*, *Fair Shares*, *A Long Way From Home* and *All you Love is Need*. He lectures in sociology part-time at Trinity College Bristol, and is speaking increasingly at home and overseas. His most recent book is *Basic Income: Escaping the Poverty Trap*, to be published in 1988 by Marion Boyars.

13. Breadwinning – Provision of God or Man?

Tony Walter

A convent commissioned a Christian artist to do a sculpture on the theme of 'work', based on Joseph the carpenter, husband of Mary. To get ideas the artist went to his Bible. To his surprise he found the theme of Joseph as worker totally absent from the Gospels, which mention only once – later in Jesus' ministry (Mt 13:55) – that his father was a carpenter. Joseph's specific job, according to the Gospels, is not so much to work in order to support the holy family as to protect and look after the child and his mother during the flight to and from Egypt (Matthew chapter 2). Without this nurture and protection, Jesus would have died an infant. This, then, is the role of Joseph in the scheme of salvation, which the resulting sculpture depicts beautifully.

The nuns, like most of us, had assumed that Joseph's role as husband and father was to work to provide the material wherewithal for dependent wife and family. Think of all those Sunday school pictures of Joseph with his son in the carpenter's shop. The nuns wanted a depiction of this kind of scene to glorify the Christian husband at his work. In this chapter I want to show how this is a recent idea, a product of the Industrial Revolution rather than a biblical concept. I will describe how our ideas about breadwinning have been formed in the past 150 years, then we can go back and see what the Bible actually says.

History

1. Peasant life

In peasant societies the basic economic unit is the household. This may be a small nuclear family of mum, dad and dependent kids or a larger extended family including other kin, depending on the particular society. In medieval Europe it was generally just the small nuclear family. This unit grows most of its food and makes most of its utensils. What it cannot grow or make for itself it is as likely to obtain by exchange as to buy with money. (However, money is becoming increasingly necessary in peasant societies today, as the modern world impinges onto the remoter parts of the world.)

In this household economy all adults and children work. There is no division between breadwinners and dependants. The only dependants are the very sick and infants. Indeed, in most peasant societies women and not men produce most of the food. Even today, throughout the world more women work on the land than do men. Men, women and children work alongside one another.

This does not mean, however, that they do the same tasks. In virtually every known human society there is a strict division between men's work and women's work. In hunter-gatherer societies the women usually gather berries, nuts and grubs while the men hunt. In agricultural-pastoral societies, such as Israel in the time of David, typically the women and girls look after the fields while the men and boys look after the herds and flocks.

Peasants, then, live in households where (a) all members are involved in the same household economy and (b) there is a strict division between women's work and men's work. Developments in Western Europe were to change this.

2. Craftspersons

For centuries in Britain and the USA and for millennia in Latin countries and the middle East there have been a good number of families such as Joseph's or St Paul's, carrying on a trade as shoemakers, carpenters, tentmakers, weavers and so on, selling their wares. I do not know how such households were organised in New Testament times, but if we go back as far as records allow in England, to the middle ages, we find husband and wife working together in their trade and there were even independent female craftspersons. If there was a battle between the sexes, it was roughly between economic equals.

By 1600, however, Protestant reformers were having none of this, believing that the Scriptures call the woman to be a dutiful wife subservient to her husband, while he is free to run the business. He could come and go at will while she had to stay at home as his dependant and as his property. William Perkins in his *Christian Oeconomie, or, A Short Survey of the Right Manner of Erecting and Ordering a Family, according to the Scriptures*, published in London in 1609, was one of countless tracts which reproved women who took the 'libertie of wandring, and straying abroad from her owne house, without the man's knowledge and consent'. The medieval equality between housewife and husband (one 'bonded' to the house) changed, for bourgeois tradespeople at least, into a situation in which a wife was bonded to the house and a husband free to wander.[1] (So much so that today we are astonished to discover the origin of the word 'husband'!)

3. Wage labour

Throughout the middle ages in England the market, where things are bought and sold for money, was steadily expanding into the major element in material life. Less and less could be produced for oneself or bartered for; more and more had to be bought. So the poor household had to send one or more of its members out to be wage labourers, bringing home a wage with which the household could buy the necessities of life. This was often made necessary because of the expropriation of the peasants' land, as with the Enclosure Acts and in Scotland the Highland Clearances. At first (and this is still often the case in the Third World today) wages were so low that all able-bodied members of the household – women, men, children – went out to earn money.

By the mid-nineteenth century evangelical philanthropists like Lord Shaftesbury were horrified that women and children were working often half-naked alongside unrelated men, brutalised by the conditions in the factories of industrial Britain. Various laws were passed restricting the hours and ages at which children could work; and married women were once again exhorted to stay at home, creating loving homes that could redeem their menfolk on their return from the brutalities of life in the factories.

Many households were now split into earners and dependants, those who work for money outside the home and those who use that money to provide a nest in which human beings can be safely produced and re-produced for toil in the world. The household was divided into breadwinners and dependants, and life into work and home, the public and the private.

Sermons instructing the wife to busy herself creating a godly home were common. Perhaps this was a valid Christian response to the brutalities of the Industrial Revolution, but a certain timelessness came to be associated with this arrangement, as though this was how households were actually organised in the Bible and how they should be organised forever. However, households in the Old Testament at least were usually peasant or craft households, and could not have been divided into breadwinners and dependants. Certainly the 'good wife' of Proverbs chapter 31 is not a financial dependant. Yet this misunderstanding still persists.

From Victorian times onwards fathers were largely absent from the home. For children the father became a rather remote figure, returning, it seemed to many children, only to judge and to punish. One survey shows that today only one child in ten has spent any substantial period of time alone with his or her father. Since we see God as our heavenly Father, is it surprising that many today see him as a rather remote figure, oscillating between punitiveness and irrelevance?

4. Individualism

At the same time as furthering this rigid structure of breadwinners and homemakers, the Victorian era also saw the flourishing of a very different idea: liberalism. This stressed the individual and his or her (usually his) talents over against traditional social roles. Liberals believed that those with personal talent should climb, via education, to the top. Many evangelicals assented to this.

Liberalism, individualism and meritocratic ideas clearly meshed poorly, however, with that other Victorian idea of 'me woman, me homemaker; you man, you breadwinner'. Some women were not good homemakers by nature, and had talent instead for politics or music; some men were superb cooks, and lousy at financial management. Just at the moment when a rigid structure was being affirmed so the seeds of discontent were being sown. The Victorian era is strewn with talented women who aspired to 'male' preserves and had to fight against the odds to have their talents recognised.

Today many evangelical Christians are the cultural children of this contradictory Victorian period. On the one hand, many of us are still taught very strictly about the place of women in the home (and presumably the duties of men to go out and support their families). Indeed, such teaching seems to be having something of a revival. Yet at the same time we are taught about stewardship – God has given each of us unique talents which we are to use in his service. We are not to bury our talents.

The only way of reconciling these two teachings is to believe that God gives only certain talents to women (talents to do with childraising and homemaking) and only certain talents to men (talents to do with working for money in a post-industrial society). For those who happen to have the 'appropriate' talents, the two teachings can happily co-exist. For those who do not, much heartsearching ensues. I will suggest at the end of this chapter that we have inherited here a false dilemma and that the Bible provides keys that our evangelical tradition seems to have temporarily mislaid.

At the very least, there does seem to be a certain asymmetry about the Victorian evangelical formulation. Clearly, God has given women a unique biological ability to bear and suckle children. But nature has not given men any such unique and essential ability that has any necessary implications outside of the bedroom. Men's breadwinning role today derives not from biology, but from history – in particular from capitalism and from our puritan and evangelical forebears. Biology may be destiny for women, but there is no evidence of male roles today being determined by biology. In the computer age, the majority of jobs in manufacturing may even be more suited to the dexterity of female fingers than to male brawn.

Today

The Victorian evangelical ideal of wives at home was never fully implemented. Many poorer women had to go out to work. The number of married women with paid jobs has fluctuated considerably over the decades since then. The most recent fluctuation has been a steady increase since a rather low figure in the 1950s. In Britain in 1983 there were in employment 11.7 million men, and 9 million women (of whom 4 million worked part-time). In other words, almost as many women as men have paid jobs, and most women who have paid work have a full-time job. Almost as many married women of working age (68%) have a paid job or are looking for one as do non-married women (74%). The big difference when it comes to going out to work is not between unmarried and married women but between those with pre-school children and those without. Of those women with pre-school children, only 6% have a full-time paid job, and 19% a part-time paid job. The fear that mothers are abandoning their young children in droves in order to go out to work is simply not borne out by the facts. Women with pre-school children stand out as the one group of fit adults who are not significantly involved in the labour force.

By contrast, more *men* with pre-school children are in paid work and work longer hours than any other group of men, presumably in order to make up the income lost because the mother is not earning. There really is little cause for alarm about working mums, but there should be far more concern about working *parents*. It's their dads, not their mums, that young children hardly see.

The shift from manufacturing to service industries has been associated with employers tending to lay off full-time men and take on part-time women. Wives and daughters now contribute more to the household income than at any time since the last war. However, *responsibility* for bringing in the money is still overwhelmingly the man's, just as responsibility for housework is still overwhelmingly the woman's. The fact that women earn more money now and some men do more housework does not mean that the ultimate responsibility for these areas is any less strictly divided. Many wives understand this when it comes to housework; he may help, but it's her responsibility. I'm not sure, though, how many wives realise that earning money – a free choice for the better off among them – is still a duty and a burden for their husband.

Finally, a comment about a recent development of particular importance for Christian views on the subject. The declining fortunes of the Church of England mean that today a vicar and a dependent wife and two children have an income below the supplementary benefit level and are entitled to Family Income Supplement. More and more clergy wives are going out to work, often to keep their families out of poverty, sometimes because the wife has a professional qualification she wishes to use. Clerical husbands frequently look after children after school while mum is out earning the major share of the bread. Ministers in other mainline denominations are usually in the same position. At the same time, current conservative Christian teaching on the family, whether evangelical or Catholic, is insisting that wives stay at home. Quite soon, and possibly quite suddenly, the Church is going to wake up to the absurdity and hypocrisy of a situation in which families are being exhorted to do what the majority of the families of Christian leaders cannot or will not do. A recent lecture at the London Bible College elicited considerable questioning among the students of the simple female homemaker/male breadwinner formulation. Many of them understood that it simply will not be viable for them. These are the Christian leaders of tomorrow.

Psychology

Historically, we have arrived at a position in which the husband is still generally expected to be the main breadwinner, but there are contradictions within this (for example, liberal views about talent, or ministerial salaries). Psychologically, we find much the same situation: there are processes operating in most families today that support the man as breadwinner, co-existing with contradictory processes. Let's look briefly at some of them.

Many husbands quite clearly want to be the breadwinner. Many feel a failure if they are unemployed and cannot support their family; many don't like the idea of their wife going out to work, because they feel it reflects badly on their ability to support her. But this is to oversimplify. Let's look at this in more detail.

1. Ambivalence

Many husbands have mixed feelings about going out to work. Work is often hard, brutish or boring. We all know for ourselves that, as the Bible describes it, work is a curse as well as a mandate. In every European language the word for 'labour' also signifies pain, effort and birth pangs. Is it any wonder we feel that Monday morning feeling of reluctance to go back t' mill? Barbara Ehrenreich in her book *The Hearts of Men*[2] documents how in the past thirty-five years in North America men have become less committed to breadwinning. This *preceded* the women's movement; it is a change in men's feelings, not a response to female liberation. Yet it co-exists in the States with a still powerful and largely male work ethic. To me, this suggests deep ambivalence among men about work and breadwinning.

2. Wives

Secondly many wives want their husbands to be the main breadwinner. Susie Orbach and Louise Eichenbaum[3] have written about the desire of most women to depend on a man. They suggest that, typically, little girls are encouraged to give rather than receive love, and so grow up insecure, craving the love they feel their mothers never gave them. They desire this love from their husbands above all else, yet know deep down that he is unlikely to be able to give emotionally all she craves. I wonder whether in this kind of marriage wives trade the unobtainable emotional security for a financial security?

Another possibility is raised by Ehrenreich. Aside from the question of security, a high-earning husband excuses the wife from having to go out to work. Once the children are in school, and certainly once they have left home, the wife is free to spend her day as she pleases in a way not enjoyed by her husband. Ehrenreich suggests that this is why so many conservative middle class women in the USA fought against the Equal Rights Amendment which would have put women on an equal footing with men. Equal wages would have meant that the real value of husbands' wages would have declined and more wives would have had to go out to work. It is not only men who, in an affluent society, want an easy life!

3. Lifecycle

Thirdly, many households in Britain and the USA do not allocate jobs, paid and unpaid, simply according to gender. The recent work of British sociologist Ray Pahl[4] suggests that the experience of working jointly for a household economy may be much more alive than we are led to believe by the Victorian ideology of 'home' being different from 'work'. Most of the households Pahl and his colleagues talked to on the Isle of Sheppey understood that they needed a certain income, and made decisions according to each member's stage in life as much as by their gender. So wives and daughters went out to work when extra money was needed and when there were no dependants at home to look after. The young woman who gave up work on starting motherhood and then went back again ten years later had not undergone two conversions about proper gender roles; she and her husband had simply made rational decisions about how to maximise household income and how to get the work done at various stages in their family's life.

There is no space to go in detail into these kinds of processes. Suffice it to say that there is considerable evidence not only that many husbands remain the chief breadwinner because they want it that way, but also that many wives want it that way too; that many husbands are rather more ambivalent than at first sight appears, and that one's stage in the lifecycle as much as gender influences who does what and when.

What the Bible says

For most families today, and for most families who have ever lived, producing the goods and/or getting the money to feed and clothe the family is and has been the joint responsibility of all adult members of the household. This was so in Bible times and remains so today. Given this, what has the Bible to say? I must confess it does not say to me what apparently it said to puritan and evangelical divines of previous centuries.

1. Who provides?

The first passage in the Bible about work is remarkable for not being gender-specific. The mandate in Genesis 1:28 to be fruitful, multiply and subdue the earth is given to both male and female. There is nothing in the Creation account to suggest that man is a worker, with woman his dependant. In the account of the Fall in Genesis chapter 3, part of the curse on woman is that man will rule over her, but this is very far from validating or justifying the economic dependence which so many women today experience. It is a curse, not a mandate. Certainly, the curse of agricultural work (verses 17–19) is directed to Adam, but as we are all now very well aware through the information provided by Third World aid agencies, it is women who do most of the agricultural labour in the world, and they are in practice afflicted by the curse on Adam's toil even more than men are. Jesus was content for himself and his disciples to be materially provided for in their ministry by women such as Mary Magdalene, Joanna and Susanna (Lk 8:1–3). There is nothing in the accounts of Creation, Fall or the Gospels that allocates breadwinning specifically to men.

The consistent biblical view about money and resources is that they are provided not by men but by God. To get bogged down in seeking texts to help us decide what a man or woman should provide is to miss the entire point, even if such texts could be found. Rather, the hope in God as provider goes right through both Old and New Testaments. It is particularly clear in the Sermon on the Mount (Matthew chapters 6 and 7), where Jesus reassures us that if our heavenly Father looks after the birds of the air, who neither sow nor reap nor gather into barns, he will most certainly look after us. And in the wandering in the desert, the provision to the children of Israel of manna and quails and then the promise of a land flowing with milk and honey are an assurance that when we trust God we will be provided for. As Walter Brueggeman[5] has so clearly shown, it was when Israel tried to fend for herself, and moreover took a pride in fending for herself, that things always went wrong.

I find this really liberating. It cuts through the secular uncertainty as to whether we are created for dependence (as many women and feminist authors such as Orbach believe) or independence (as many men and feminist authors such as Dowling believe). To know that ultimately we can rely on God lifts us out of this oscillation between craving for dependence and yearning for independence, enabling us to get on with our work in freedom from this kind of psychological bondage.

In many a marriage the husband prides himself on being the provider, not acknowledging his dependence on God, while the wife understands her dependence but looks to her husband to provide for her both emotionally and materially, something he may be unable to do. Surely the Christian hope is that both partners jointly can look to God as the ultimate provider, taking the pressure to be like God off the man and making the woman more realistic about where ultimate security lies. Both can then become co-workers under God.

Note that last sentence. Belief in the Great Provider does not mean we just sit back and wait for manna to drop out of heaven. The desert was a special situation. Admittedly the lilies and the grass that Jesus refers to in Matthew chapter 6 do not toil, but the birds of the air he also mentions have to do their bit. They have to build their nests, catch their prey and feed their young. Jesus' point is that we need not be anxious. They work, but they do not have delusions of grandeur about being the ultimate provider for their families.

So the practicalities work out like this. With reason, care and prayer, work out how to divide up the labour in your household, and review this regularly. Direct your attention to God the provider, not hubbie the provider. And fear not, because your heavenly Father will feed you. I do not say this lightly; overcoming anxiety about supporting a family is something I struggle with. I am still a pilgrim on this road with you, and am undoubtedly one of the 'men of little faith' that Jesus addresses (Mt 6:30).

2. Stewardship and sacrifice

It is easy in a secular and individualistic age to see stewardship in terms of 'I have certain talents and owe it to myself to use them'. I glory in my talents, and I come into conflict with you if yours do not complement mine. That is not a Christian view of stewardship, but a secular view of self-fulfilment. What is stressed in the Bible is not talents as possessions of the individual, but talents as given by God. Moreover, they are given to the individual as a member of family, household or Church. Using them is a response we jointly make to God's goodness as the Great Provider. Though there is certainly a conflict between a secular individualist view of talent and the rigid Victorian evangelical view of men's work and women's work, there is no conflict between stewarding the God-given gifts within a household, and viewing God as the ultimate provider and upholder of that household.

There may well be periods in the lifecycle of a family when husband or wife will choose to relinquish certain God-given gifts for the sake of the family. In the words of Ecclesiastes (3:1), 'For everything there is a season, and a time for every matter under heaven.' A wife may well give up paid work which she is very good at for a few years in order to have children. A husband may well give up hobbies or service in the local church in order to spend time with his family. He may sacrifice career opportunities that would involve disruption to his family, or to support a growing family he may take work that does not use the talents he most enjoys.

Occasionally we find a family where he looks after the

children while she goes out to earn full-time. Usually this is because the couple see this as the most sensible and practical way of using their various talents and callings, given the constraints of their situation and for the time being. I find it difficult to see how one can object to this, as some seem to, on biblical grounds – especially when some clergy and missionary families feel called to live this way!

Many wives are used to sacrificing themselves for their families. The Bible, however, calls *husbands* to sacrificial living.[6] Paul's famous passage in Ephesians (5:23–33) about the husband being the head of the wife has nothing to do with authority as we understand it in a natural, earthly sense. Paul goes out of his way to explain that this headship involves the self-sacrificing love that Christ shows to the Church. The authority of Christ is the authority of one who loves sacrificially, and one can only suppose that most husbands have, through their selfishness, forfeited this Christ-like authority. They descend into the domination described in Genesis 3:16.

The implication of this for work seems to be that, in a good marriage, stewardship is tempered with sacrifice. Work in the biblical view is about glorifying God and serving one another; since work is often hard, that may mean sacrifice. It is important that such sacrifices be made not in response to unbiblical and sexist ideas about the division of labour, but jointly with a view to stewarding the various talents God has given the entire household. Then service and sacrifice can be made willingly, with joy and a sense of partnership. Lots of sensible families, by no means all Christian, do precisely that.

The key issue about stewardship on which we should be clear is 'To *whom* are we, as stewards, responsible?' Most husbands and wives today have a concept of stewardship, but they see themselves as responsible not to God but to their family, to their spouse, or to their children. Their ultimate reference point is the family, and in this sense their family is their god. A few ecologically-minded families see themselves as responsible to the Earth. For the Christian family, though, both individual and family are ultimately responsible as stewards to God. The family is responsible to God for how it uses its gifts, skills and resources. There is a covenant between God and the family in which God gives the assurance of provision and the family responds in trust. That is the covenant which sustains any temporary agreement between a couple as to who does what for the time being.

Questions for discussion

1. If you have lived in or visited a Third World country, how did men and women there share out the work? Who worked harder?
2. If you know a couple which has reversed roles, why have they done this and how is the arrangement working? What pressures do they find?
3. What kind of work (paid or unpaid) a) do you enjoy? b) are you good at? c) do you do? If married, compare your spouse's answers.
4. In what ways do you think your culture has shaped your attitudes to earning and childcare?
5. Why do you think many Christians confuse God's curse (Gen 3:16–19) with his mandate (Gen 1:26–31)?
6. What practical difference does it make for a woman and a man to see their talents not as personal possessions but as gifts from God?

References

1. George, M, 'From "Goodwife" to "Mistress": the transformation of the female in bourgeois culture', *Science and Society*, 37 (2), 1973.
2. London, Pluto, 1983.
3. *What Do Women Want?* (London, Fontana, 1984). See also Colette Dowling, *The Cinderella Complex* (Fontana 1982).
4. *Divisions of Labour* (Oxford, Blackwell, 1984).
5. *The Lord* (London, SPCK, 1978).
6. By this standard, it seems wrong that women should be discriminated against by employers (in terms of wages and prospects) because they have spent a few years rearing children.

"WHAT FEARFUL
WONDER IS
THIS" CRIES
JOSEPH "THAT
THE CRADLE
I FASHIONED
IS TODAY MADE
GREATER THAN
THE ARKS OF
NOAH AND OF
MOSES, FOR
IN IT IS HELD
EMMANUEL,
WHO SAVES US
SAINT
JOSEPH
FROM THE FLOOD
OF DEATH, WHO
IS GLORIOUSLY
ENTHRONED ON
THE CHERUBIM."
PRAY FOR US
THEREFORE, SAINT
JOSEPH, THAT
THROUGH THE
WORD MADE
FLESH, OUR
WORKS MAY BE
MADE BEARERS
OF HIS GRACE.

Kathy Keay

Kathy Keay has worked for ten years with different evangelical organisations in the UK, during which time she has developed an increasing commitment to issues relating to gender and faith.

She has travelled widely throughout Africa, India and Europe, mainly on the OM ship LOGOS and as a staff worker for UCCF. Whilst preparing for an M.Litt on 'Discrimination as Heresy', she studied feminist related issues as a student at the London Institute for Contemporary Christianity. As Communications Secretary for Evangelical Alliance, she ran the original MWG conference and later founded the MWG Trust. She continues to speak and write on Women and Christianity and is now an editor with Lion publishing, and an associate member of the Iona Community.

14. The Single Person and the Kingdom of God

Kathy Keay

In most western societies single people are on the increase: the unmarried, divorcees, the widowed, single parents – of both sexes and all ages. Huge numbers of the population live on their own. Already there are over four and a half million in Britain, and the figure is increasing by 120,000 a year. Official estimates indicate that by 1990 the number of people living alone in the UK will have risen to six million. In the light of these facts it is important to ask, What place has the single person in the Kingdom of God? In this chapter I intend to outline some of the prevailing attitudes held towards single people. I will then look at some major issues facing single people today, look at what the Bible says, and conclude by asking, How can the local church accept, involve and learn from single people in her midst?

Prevailing attitudes

Everyone reading this will be influenced by their own experience of singleness. It is foolish therefore, to presuppose that the experience of all single people is the same, any more than that of all married people. Some love it, others hate it. And whilst there has been an increasing trend towards supporting the independence of the single lifestyle in society, prevailing attitudes and structures in most churches all too often reinforce the view that to be single as an adult is unnatural, and has somehow to be 'accounted for'.

Unnatural

In traditional Africa, India and the Far East, and within Asian and West Indian communities in Britain, most single people, especially women are not catered for as individuals. Usually they live in family households, until they marry. Arranged marriages are still practised, and marriage is seen as both the norm and the passport to adulthood. In the West however, where many leave home for college in their late teens, where romantic love and free choice (in theory) prevail, where people seek intimacy in relationships often at the expense of permanence and where there is no clear point at which we become 'adult', the situation is much more complex.

A threat, an escape

In spite of clear biblical teaching which affirms singleness, some see it as a threat to stable family life. When Christian women or men pursue a different lifestyle, people accept it for a few years, then strongly infer that it is time 'to settle down'. Those who choose not to marry are seen by others as independent, even selfish people who refuse to take on 'normal' adult responsibilities. Referring to a single man in his late twenties struggling with the tedium of a nine-to-five job, and wanting to do more for God with his life, a married friend of mine said, 'what he needs is a wife and a mortgage, that would soon sort him out.'

At the same time, it is when a couple are going through a particularly tough time in their own marriage that at least one person is tempted to remember with nostalgia the freedom of being single (usually the man), or envy unmarried friends who have more time to themselves (usually the woman). Although they believe marriage to be the norm, and are probably quite happily married themselves, the single life is seen paradoxically as an escape, a desirable empty space 'out there' somewhere, where the individual is free to be without distractions or demands.

It is easy to think that the grass is greener elsewhere. Married people, especially within the Church, need to learn to accept the unmarried as they are without envying or pitying them because they haven't 'made it to the altar'.

A curse, calling, or course

Most contemporary evangelical literature puts the single life in one of two categories. In her book, *Single*, Margaret Clarkson concludes that singleness is the result of the Fall, as 'there was no singleness in Eden'.[1] This is a common view held by many Christians today. The message is clear: being single is unfortunate, even a curse, but with God's help we can make the best of it.

In sharp contrast, others believe that singleness is a gift from God. Though many remain unconvinced that it is better to remain single, particularly when those who give them counsel are usually married.

Two examples of popular evangelical books which seek to present a positive attitude to being single are *Getting The Most Out Of Being Single* by Gien Karssen[2] and *Your Half Of The Apple* by Gini Andrews[3]. Gien Karssen concludes that God does not make mistakes. If you are single, you have been granted the special gift of singleness.

Whilst these books contain much wisdom and practical advice, their basic premise is not entirely convincing. The lack of eligible single men in our churches and a desire to stay faithful to God's Word are in fact the main reason why most single women are not married. Others have decided to give a few years to their career, in the hope of getting married at some point, and a few believe that being single is the only way they can serve God fully, whether at home or abroad.

The important thing is surely not whether we are married or single, but whether or not we are living in expectation of God's coming Kingdom.

What are the issues?

Ultimately, the crisis and challenge of being single is the crisis and challenge of being ourselves. Everyone, whether married or not, is faced with basic human questions of identity (who am I?), vocation (what am I here for?), relationships (to whom do I belong?) and security (where does my ultimate fulfilment lie?). At times these questions become painful and acute, particularly for the single person who has not chosen to be single. And learning to be real with one another, to build trust and to communicate what really matters takes time. Being single at twenty is not the same as being single at thirty or forty, and being a single parent or a widow is also different from being someone who has never married. Although there are similarities between the lives of all single people, there are particular issues for those who have never married, which the Church needs to take more seriously.

Childlessness

Married couples without children recognise the growing oppression of childlessness. It is rarely understood that for some single women, this can be as real for them even without being married. The least maternal, once they hear the biological clock ticking, have to face the fact that their own child-bearing years are quickly passing. For Christian women in their twenties and thirties this can be extremely painful, especially when a good number find themselves approached by non-Christian men at work (married and unmarried), and saying no does not guarantee that a suitable Christian partner will appear out of the blue either. To remain single and childless in these circumstances takes courage, tenacity and a good deal of faith. Women who have found this predicament too painful have married non-Christians, or have decided to have a child out of marriage.

In most cases this issue also becomes a crisis of faith, where the individual is tempted to ask, 'Why has God let me down?' or even, 'What have I done to deserve this?' Counselling someone who feels the oppression of singleness must be handled carefully although whilst the church remains an institution that is largely run by married people, sensitive counselling in this area is hard to find. As long as they continue to present marriage and family life as the norm, church people should not be surprised when Christian single people marry divorcees, get into difficult relationships or simply withdraw because the family pressure in church communicates more powerfully than the good news of God's Kingdom.

'I couldn't believe it', said Julie. 'I went to talk to Mrs X about how awful it's been lately being on my own, especially with that married guy at work always after me, and I was quoted Isaiah 54:1: "Sing, O barren women; you who never bore a child: burst into song, shout for joy, you who were never in labour; for more are the children of the desolate woman than of her who has a husband', says the Lord."

'She told me that it would be a good idea to get stuck into some evangelistic work, maybe amongst kids, and said that if I did it well, my life would be even more fruitful in the end than hers (she has four children and another on the way).'

Women like Julie have every reason to be angry with this kind of response. Verses such as Isaiah 54:1 are often quoted out of context in an attempt to offer quick compensation to single women for their singleness and childlessness. Scripture teaches that sharing the good news of the gospel is the responsibility of all believers, and nowhere indicates that it should or can be a substitute for marriage or family life. The point here is that within God's sovereignty, there are all kinds of ways in which our lives can be fruitful. A woman's value no longer depends on her ability to produce children. As members of God's Kingdom, we need to learn how to bear one another's pain, and when we have earnt the right to speak, encourage one another towards lives of greater fruitfulness, however that is best expressed.

Breadwinning – not a soft option

Most single people, whether male or female, have to earn their own living. The way in which this is done varies according to the individual's education, gifts, experience and employment opportunities, and, whether or not they have known and responded to God's call on their life. Usually breadwinning means paid employment outside of the home involving the traditional nine-to-five routine, unless the person is part of a Christian community with a shared income, voluntarily unemployed, or is supported by a local church or mission society. Some find their work fulfilling, whilst an increasing number have no jobs at all. Single professionals soon find that responsibility increases, and whilst men are trained to expect this, most women are not. Christian professional women often lack support and understanding from people within the Church. At worst, they are seen to be 'competing in a man's world', 'uninterested in family life', 'a threat to their married Christian sisters', which by definition is often interpreted to mean being feminist, whether this is true or not. After several years in professional life many women (and men for that matter) want a break or change of routine as much as the wife at home longs for a break from her routines. This is usually not possible for the single person, as he or she has no alternative breadwinner to fall back on. It is easy to admire, even envy the well-dressed, single professional whose busy life introduces him/her to many interesting people. Indeed, many enjoy their jobs, but primarily they are simply earning their living.

Decision-making

Just as road signs on the motorway are not addressed to pedestrians or yachtsmen, single women find that most of society's wisdom is simply not addressed to them.'[4] This is also the case within the Christian tradition. Our scriptures were written within a strong patriarchal culture. The Book of Proverbs, for example, contains many wise sayings, written from a father to his sons. Men are warned not to keep company with loose or contentious women, vivid descriptions of whom are given in several chapters (Prov 5:3; 7:5–23). The author writes, 'Listen, my sons, to a father's instruction. Pay attention and gain understanding. When I was a boy in my father's house. . . .' Nowhere is similar advice given by a mother to her daughters. Indeed until recently, no one looked for women's experience in Scripture, and the single woman was always protected by her nearest male next of kin. Hence, single women are not warned in the Bible about walking alone at night or how to react in the event of mugging or rape. They knew neither the opportunites nor the vulnerabilities which many single women face today, and were seen and respected at best always within the context of home and family.

New order

Within the Gospels, however, we see emerging a new order for women as well as men, unmarried as well as married, based on personal relationships with Jesus, and a lifestyle together in obedience to his commands. The challenges Jesus presents are not always easy, especially for women who are used to other people taking care of their lives for them. In some Christian circles today the challenges of Jesus still need to be heard. Within the House Churches and wherever the shepherding* principle is practised, single women are all too easily prevented from growing up and having to take responsibility before God for their own lives. In her book *The Cinderella Complex*,[5] Colette Dowling emphasises how many women actually fear this.

In contrast, the Bible is full of general principles which help the believer to make responsible decisions. No one should have to make major decisions without the advice and counsel of trusted friends or family. However, our freedom to choose is an important God-given part of our humanity which should not be delegated to someone else, unless unusual circumstances prevail.

The challenge Jesus presents when he says 'follow me', calls all believers, women and men, single and married, to leave what is safe and familiar and journey with Him into the unknown. Whilst this may not always mean geographically, it certainly means that in every other way we must be prepared to lay aside our prejudices and preconceived ideas, in order to become more like Him.

As single Christians journey with Christ, they are perhaps

* The principle that single women are ultimately responsible to a man or a couple in their local fellowship. The intention at best is for this to become a support to her. In practise it often means riding roughshod over the freewill of the individual in the name of 'shepherding', and has developed into a fairly rigid pattern of female to male submission, cf Fear and Forgiveness: a Masculine Confession.

freer to choose more unconventional paths, though this takes courage and it is not always easy to understand the relationship between the choices we make and the sovereignty of God in our lives. Single women anxious to do what is right, can be particularly susceptable to unhelpful guidance, even 'words from the Lord', as church tradition teaches them to submit and receive. It is the men's task to study and teach God's Word; it is the woman's to learn in humble obedience. Many lives have been almost ruined because women have jetisoned natural instinct and common sense, for advice from 'spiritual shepherds' who hardly know them. With no close partner to confide in, the single person needs all the more to become part of a recognised, believing community where s/he is known and loved, and where the spiritual and social climate helps him/her to mature as a person, growing in obedience to Christ's commands.

1. The sexual celibate

It has taken the present threat of AIDS to awaken people to the possibility of celibacy as a positive alternative lifestyle. For single Christians however, celibacy has always been an issue. Most will admit that staying celibate is the hardest aspect of staying single, particularly in a climate where personal identity is so closely identified with sexuality and sexual behaviour.

Most popular evangelical literature focuses on sex within marriage (e.g. Tim LaHaye's *The Act of Marriage*[6]) or guidelines for teenagers (Joyce Huggett's *Two into One*[7] and *Just Good Friends*[8]). Little is written on adult sexuality for single people, perhaps because it is assumed that singleness and celibacy come automatically. In most people's lives nothing could be further from the truth.

With an increasing tolerance developing over recent years towards different sexual practices (including homosexual partnerships), it is important to return to the Bible in order to work out a theology of sexuality which is both convincing and practical for single people today.

A thorough study of I Corinthians chapter 7 will help here. Paul was all too aware that to remain celibate was far from easy in Corinth, as in our own society today, where people are surrounded by sexual immorality on every side. He advised people to marry rather than to burn with lust or live in immorality, advocating that if at all possible it was however, better to remain single.

The reason why most single people find Paul's teaching hard, is because they have not chosen to be single. Even amongst the most God-fearing single christians, there are those who do not find this teaching liberating. They know that sex at its best brings with it affirmation, closeness, intimacy and a unique sense of belonging which are basic human needs. Although not all married people experience this within their marriages, they have the potential to do so. Single people, whether heterosexual or not, often live for months even years without any meaningful physical contact with another person. This can be extremely tough, particularly during times of stress when the need for support and emotional succour is real, and temptation if it presents itself, the harder to resist. How a single person finds the necessary encouragement during these times is extremely important. The support of friends and a local community is usually vital, and needs to be nurtured, not only during times of crises.

2. Masturbation

'Ethical judgements about masturbation run all the way from viewing it as a sin more serious than fornication, adultery or rape to placing it in the same category as head scratching.'[9] Masturbation is particularly an issue for single Christians who are required to say 'No' to sex outside of marriage. Whilst most evangelical writers (mainly women) have avoided speaking directly on the subject, others (usually men) have taken a more positive attitude, often within a broader context. John White,[10] Lewis Smedes[11] and Richard Foster[12] for example, have all aimed to be true to what they understand to be a biblical view of human sexuality (in so far as it speaks of the subject), whilst at the same time seeking to dispel the disproportionate sense of guilt often associated with this practice. Many important questions surface: is masturbation morally acceptable for a disciple of Christ? Could it be a gift from God to enable us to avoid promiscuous sex, as some have suggested? What about the sexual fantasies which are inevitably associated with it? Richard Foster rightly states that these questions, and many more, are the concern of every believer, women as well as men.

Our sexuality affects our entire human personality. There is no one who is totally free of the tensions and temptations of being a sexual being. How then, does the sexual celibate come to terms with his or her sexuality?

Richard Foster reminds us that masturbation is not physically harmful; secondly, the Bible nowhere deals with it directly. There are no specific prohibitions, as there are for example with adultery or homosexual practices.

Whilst accepting that masturbation is not inherently wrong or sinful, it is simply not true that we have to become a slave to our sexuality and sexual demands. Our bodies have to be disciplined in different ways, whether we are talking about sloth, gluttony or sex. At times of acute anxiety or distress, obsessive behaviour of any kind may take over but with God's grace, it *is* possible to emerge from any such behaviour more whole and at peace with oneself.

It is naive to think that all single people are inexperienced sexually. Jesus must have wrestled with his sexuality, though, unlike us, he did not sin. He understands more than anyone the struggles of the sexual celibate and can bring forgiveness, healing and freedom from all that harms us in this area.

An increasing number of children and young women experience sexual abuse (often within the home) long before they enter any meaningful sexual relationship with their own consent. Women who are raped, whether at sixteen or forty, say that the experience never entirely leaves them, affecting them and their sexual behaviour for the rest of their lives. Single women are particularly vulnerable to rape and abuse outside of the home, as they tend to be out at night, often don't have their own transport and are not always in the company of someone who will see them home. Churches should be encouraged to organise corporate transport for women and should not be shocked or surprised if a woman in their congregation is attacked or raped. It can happen to anyone.

3. Broken relationships

Broken relationship also leave scars. Whilst a divorce is publicly recognised and the parting of the couple often publicly mourned, many single people have experienced as acute pain with broken relationships, though this is rarely recognised by others because it never led to marriage. In a society where there appears to be a crisis of commitment and where Christians are encouraged to maintain a high view of marriage, there are many Christian single people who admit to being badly let down by Christian partners who 'just can't go through with it'. The readjustments necessary for those in this situation are different from the divorced, though often equally demanding. Christian marriage preparation classes could help such people work this through. Older Christian people later come to recognise that in not committing themselves to marry earlier they have in fact committed themselves, often without realising it, to a life of equally great demands by remaining on their own. Some remain single by choice, whilst others remain so by default. In different ways, both need affirmation and support. Few churches provide opportunities to talk about these matters, and single people don't always want to be huddled together in a separate 'singles' group to do so.

The need for acceptance

Single women often fall into the categories of 'sirens' or 'jolly sisters', depending on their sexual attractiveness. The attractive often admit to being more sexually harassed in the world and held at arm's length in church, whilst their plainer sisters are accepted more easily as whole people wherever they are. Everyone needs the loving, affirming presence of Jesus to liberate and transform their lives, and there must be no discrimination as to who receives it. The awkward and the attractive are all part of the Kingdom, and we must receive each other as such wherever we are. Unless our churches become places where the teaching and example of Jesus is reinforced in this way, then they will only be 'clanging cymbals' in the ears of those who need to experience the love of Jesus most (1 Corinthians 13:1).

What the Bible says

Many of the problems which single people experience stem from a lack of biblical teaching on this subject within the local church.

Created

Perhaps the main problem surrounding singleness is the tendency to see celibacy almost exclusively in negative terms – the absence of marriage and the denial of sexuality. This view has been held by many throughout Christendom, who believe that sexuality is shameful – even the source of original sin. Looking into Church history and the writings of the early Church fathers, 'one would be excused from thinking that God had an oral-genital fixation.'[13] However, the biblical starting point for both married and single people is identical: people (men and women) are made in the image of God as emotional, sexual, intellectual, spiritual and social beings.

The Creation narrative in Genesis chapter 2 clearly spells this out. Although the injunction that it is not good for us to be alone refers specifically to marriage, it also implies the need we all have for wider human relationships of kinship and community. The Bible teaches that though God is essentially one being, he has always been in relationship (Gen 1:26). Made in God's image, women and men are made likewise to be in relationship. Just as a successful marriage depends on how a couple grow in their special relationship within the wider social context of other relationships, so a full single life depends on openness and growth in relationships with others.

Fallen

Both these truths have to be seen from the perspective of our fallenness. Because of the long term effects of our human disobedience against God, all relationships are now imperfect

(Gen 3:16), and human sexuality has become twisted, exploited and degraded in a thousand different ways (Gen 3:10). Over-optimistic views of the single life or marriage are therefore unrealistic. The alienation, hurt and mistrust which exists within and between us is a direct result of the Fall. D. H. Lawrence described it in many of his novels as 'the blackness in the center'. Single and married people struggle with it in different ways, often with equal intensity. There can never in this age be a return to the perfect relationship and the completely unspoilt experience of sexuality described in Genesis chapter two. The only true basis for the single life, then, is to acknowledge that we are sexual beings who need loving relationships within the wider community. The problems encountered in singleness should not be seen primarily as the consequences of not being married but as the inevitable consequences of a fallen humanity.

Written from cultures where arranged marriages were the norm, the Bible has a surprising amount to say on the subject of singleness. There is no concept of a celibate priesthood in the Old Testament, although commitment to God challenged the norm of society then, as it still does today. For example, Jeremiah was commanded not to marry (Jer 16:1–4), Ezekiel was a widower (Ezek 24:16– 18), Paul rejoiced in the freedom singleness gave him (1 Cor 7:7) and above all, Christ himself never married. Being single according to the Bible is a God-given alternative to marriage (Mt 19:12). It is seen as a good state with advantages and disadvantages, just like marriage. It is neither superior or inferior, although at certain times in the history of the Church it has been seen as both. At its best it is a gift from God (1 Cor 7:7) – a charismatic gift which few may recognise, but which is given as a means of grace as much to some as marriage is given to others. For most people it is better to marry (1 Cor 7:26–27, 39–40). Each individual must be honest beore God and seek to make the most of whatever situation he or she is in at the time.

Perhaps the most striking fact which emerges from the Bible is how little we know about the marital status of so many Bible characters – for example, Daniel, Jonah, Habakkuk, Miriam, Elijah, John the Baptist, all the disciples other than

Peter, Timothy and Titus. All too often our evaluation of others is based on marital or professional status. This should not be. All believers are called to live distinctive lives which speak to others about the Kingdom of God regardless of our marital status.

Jesus, our model

Throughout Old Testament times and until the coming of Jesus the calling of God for everyone was seen in terms of marriage. It is because many Christians today consider this teaching to be the total Christian view that singleness is often seen negatively, having to be justified in a way that marriage does not. This view fails to recognise the truly revolutionary change brought about by the life and teaching of Jesus. Celibacy for the disciples became a state into which they were called as an integral part of their discipleship. In the fullness of the kingdom of God, says Jesus, there will be no marrying (Mt 22:30). In the present age some will live in the state originally set out in Creation (i.e. marriage) whilst others will live in anticipation of what is to come in the presence of the kingdom of God here and now.

At the heart of our faith is a God who chose to live out his human life as a single person.

It is often stressed that Jesus came as a man, but rarely that he was single. His relationships with his disciples were extremely important – in the garden of Gethsemane he counted a lot on their presence and understanding (Mk 14:32–42), even though they let him down. With Peter, James and John (Mk 9:2–14, 33) he seems to have confided at a deeper level, and with one whom we know as the beloved disciple (Jn 19:26) he had a particularly close relationship.

It is these disciples which Jesus regarded ultimately as 'family', just as many single people today regard their friends as family, more than their 'natural' family or the local church family whose immediate preoccupations prevent deeper relationships from developing.

Jesus and family

Rather than uphold the model of the nuclear family as *the* model for dependence, growth and security, Jesus knew all too well how easily families can remain self-sufficient, closed units which can even be at odds with life in the kingdom of God. After his visit to the temple as a twelve-year-old he replies to an anxious father and mother, 'Did you not know that I must be in my Father's house?' (Lk 2:48–49). In this instance Mary is clearly thinking of Jesus' security within his immediate family, whilst Jesus himself has already perceived that new experience of family in which he would find his meaning and security as an adult. Similarly, when he is told that Mary and his family are waiting for him he asks, 'Who are my mother and my brothers? . . . Whoever does the will of God is both brother and sister and mother' (Mk 3:33–35). Whilst not wishing to underestimate the importance of family responsibilities and child bearing, Jesus nevertheless put both firmly within their place. To the women who call after him, 'blessed is she who has given you suck' he replies, 'Rather blessed is the one who follows the will of God and does it'. To the man who wishes to bury his father, Jesus replies, 'let the dead bury the dead – come follow me.' For single women in particular, Jesus challenges traditional roles and values. His encounter with Mary and Martha affirms both women, but he encourages Mary to sit at his feet and learn from him, stating that this was better than being concerned primarily about domestic affairs (Lk 10:38–42).

The local church and single people

With the constant emphasis within the Church these days on marriage and the family then it is not unreasonable for the unmarried to ask, 'where do I fit in?'

Most clergy will surely not forget the relief it was to find a wife by the time they started (or during) their first curacy, because it is simply not easy to survive long term in a local church set up where marriage is seen as the norm.

The personal and practical implications can be enormous, though rarely do churches acknowledge them. Our sermon illustrations, bookstalls, church events, the Family service, and social life, heavily presume that we are all married or should be, and if we are not, well never mind.[14] How then can the church accept, integrate and learn from single people in her midst? In the Grove booklet, *A Place in the Family: the single person in the local church*,[15] the authors outline five ways in which a church can exist as family. Whilst this is helpful, this very family emphasis can, however, confuse those who see in the Gospels, a model for the kingdom which does not borrow from the nuclear family ideal. This needs to be taken more seriously and efforts made to re-examine what Jesus taught about the Kingdom, so that we are all included without distinction. The structure of nuclear family life today, makes it very difficult for some single people to identify the kingdom with any notion of family when, by and large families tend to remain by nature insular and self pre-occupied.

How can the church help?

The local church can however develop a more outward looking attitude. I have been particularly helped when moving to a new area, with moving in, decorating, helping to put up shelves, lending tools, and supported generally when domestic crises occur. When I belonged to Pip 'n' Jay in Bristol, and was travelling all over the West Country doing student work, the church was a tremendous support.

If I needed a heater or a fridge, they appeared. Someone in the congregation regularly mended my car; others did some typing and cooked meals in bulk, while others prayed for me (and still do even though I'm no longer there). A church like this, which is practical and prayerful, is a model to aim for. It encourages its members (whether married or single) to make their needs known. By meeting them, it breaks down many barriers which we in our self-sufficiency erect.

Single people have no wedding presents to help them set up home and don't always want to be the gracious receiver of cast-offs from married friends, however well meaning they may be.

I have received money and housewarming presents from

friends who have been sensitive to my situation – usually those who have married later or who have learnt to survive on low salaries in Christian work. Members of the local church have all kinds of hidden potential which is waiting to be released – some could develop recreational activities. Regular programmes could be set up to explore and develop peoples natural and spiritual gifts and interests. For example, why not hold a series of creative workshops including music, dance, drama, art, craft and writing groups, all of which could meet simultaneously, and work on the theme Images of God. Encouraging Christians in the arts has long been neglected within church life, to our own loss. Single people may wish to run photography or computer classes and banner workshops or to organise sports. Don't presume that the Sunday school and youth group are what they ought to be doing. Recreational activities should never replace spiritual responsibilities within a church, but every possible means should be taken to break down barriers between single and married members in a congregation, in order to emphasise our common membership of God's Kingdom.

Conclusion

While not wanting to denigrate the good gift of marriage, and be unsympathetic to the demands which family life creates, it is time, nevertheless that churches started to take more notice of the single people in their congregations. And even to recognise that the swing from the celibate priesthood to marriage has perhaps created a marriage ghetto mentality which is in danger of becoming self-obsessive in its desire to preserve itself.

The Grove booklet, *A Place in the Family*, recommends that every church appoints a working party to look at the dynamic of relationships between married and single church members, and to see where the gaps are and how things can change. Membership of the working parties should include married and single people of both sexes and all ages. It is my hope that many reading this chapter will do this and thereby help to build a local congregation which is a more realistic reflection of the Kingdom of God. And lastly to acknowledge that within the clamour of our late 20th century existence, there is great potential for meeting God and personal renewal, if with His help, we can come to terms with the empty spaces in our lives.

Questions for discussion

1. What are some of the main issues facing single people today? What are the pros and cons of being unmarried?
2. How are they different from the pros and cons of being married?
3. Study 1 Corinthians chapter 7. How does Paul's teaching apply to single people today?
   (a) What is meant by 'the things of the Lord?'
   (b) Is it true that the single person has more time than those who are married?
   (c) What different lifestyles are practised by single people in your church?
4. On what basis do members of your congregation relate?
5. How can barriers be broken down between married and single people within your church?
6. What can be done to help meet the needs of both?

References

1. *Single*, Margaret Clarksan (Kingsway 1980).
2. *Getting the most out of being single*, Gien Karssen (Nav Press 1982).
3. *Your Half of the Apple*, Gini Andrews.
4. *The Single Woman in the Family of God*, Margaret Britton (Epworth 1982).
5. *The Cinderella Complex*, Colette Dowling (Fontana 1982).
6. *The Act of Marriage*, Tim la Haye (Marshall Pickering 1984).
7. *Two into One*, Joyce Hugget (IVP 1981).
8. *Just Good Friends*, Joyce Huggett (IVP).
9. *Money, Sex and Power*, Richard Foster (Hodder & Stoughton 1985).
10. *Eros Defiled*, John White (IVP 1978).
11. *Sex in the Real World*, Lewis Smedes (Lion).

12. Richard Foster, op. cit.
13. *Poverty Chastity and Obedience*, John Bell and Graham Manle. (Wild Goose Publications, 1986).
14. Kathy Keay, 'Single Minded', *Church of England Newspaper*, July 10, 1987.
15. David Gillett, Anne Long, Ruth Fowke, *A Place in the Family: The Single Person in the Local Church* (Grove booklet 1981).

15. Grievous Bodily Harm – Responses to Rape

Helena Terry

'I tried to wash his memory off my body'... 'I cringe with fear when men are around.'

Women have always been vulnerable to physical and sexual abuse of thc most severe kinds. And far from abating, they appear to be on the increase. Inspite of all the progress made over the last decade through the women's movement, women continue to be violated in a whole variety of ways. This chapter will look at what is meant by violence against women. It will concentrate on rape and current responses to rape, and conclude by suggesting ways in which the church can positively respond.

Definitions

The concise Oxford dictionary defines violence as the unlawful exercise of physical force; intimidation. To violate is to transgress; to infringe; to treat profanely or with disrespect. All these definitions need to be held together when thinking about violence against women. In so doing, we recognise that anything which physically and psychologically assaults, exploits and degrades women, also degrades those who are responsible for their assault, exploitation and degradation (usually men). Violence against women is, then, a man's problem as well as a woman's, especially if there are men reading this who claim to have a relationship with God. Advertising, pornography, rape and prostitution are undoubtedly the major ways through which women are violated, although every time they are consciously ignored, manipulated or jeered at, they are also being violated.

Advertising

It is not difficult to find examples of ads which play heavily on women as sex objects in order to sell their products. The extent to which this happens is almost so familiar to us that we scarcely realise how damaging and humiliating some women feel it to be. The message is clear: if you're the right shape and size, you're okay, you're acceptable. If you're not, then you're out. Many women get caught in the most awful treadmills in order to look like the popular images of women portrayed in the media. The worst instances of this can lead to anorexia – a killing disease which all too often starts when women think they are too fat to be acceptable, and set out to lose weight.

Pornography

'Pornographic images show man with power over woman. The woman is any woman stapled to a page. The images of pornography tell us that men are always potent, and that women are always willing.'[1]

Pornography has become a highly profitable industry, which sells a perverse but widely acceptable image of women entirely on the basis of their sexuality. Whilst amongst women's magazines in the USA, during the mid 1980s, *Family Circle* tops the bill selling some 7,004,000, from 1985–6, an estimated 4,100,000 copies of *Playboy* (all editions) were circulated in over thirteen different countries. The women who feature regularly in these magazines often admit to being bored by it all, but do it for the money. Others get conned into it and hooked, not realising that flattery from the cameramen means nothing to them once they get what they want.

Prostitution

'The worst part of prostitution is that you are obliged not to sell sex only, but your humanity. That's the worst part of it, that what you're selling is your human dignity.'[2].

Prostitution has never been a woman's institution, although it has often thrived historically where poverty has been rife, and in many cases is still a quick way of earning hard cash. However, the image of the 'happy hooker' has little to do with reality. Many girls are sold into prostitution by poor families. Once in the system, it is hard to get out. In the international prostitution network, women are merely commodities. Prostitutes are traded and exchanged among pimps, marriage catalogues offer women for sale. Despite growing protests and exposure, the trade is flourishing and widespread.

Sex tours to South East Asia for men, represent an extreme of exploitation for women. Prostitution exists in all countries, regardless of its legal status, although under different laws, the treatment of prostitutes varies widely.

The International Feminist Network against Sexual Slavery is active in over 25 countries, though the Church has been slow to involve itself in this area to any significant degree.[3]

Rape

Rape is probably the most under-reported, fastest growing and least convicted crime in the world. It has long been considered only as a crime against property – women being seen as men's property. Now it is beginning to be recognised for what it is: a crime of violence and power, and a violation of women's civil rights of the worst kind.

Men of all ages and backgrounds rape women, often within their own homes. Rape even in families is not a secret any more. Understandably, rape is perhaps the greatest of a woman's fears.

A hidden crime

Two thousand women in Britain reported to the police last year that they had been raped; thousands more alleged other sexual offences. But the reported incidence hides rather than reveals the enormity of the situation, because most women who suffer these appalling experiences don't report them.

Between 1979 and 1986, rape figures were reported to have risen by 22 per cent, though this rise varied from area to area, and rape became a more publicized issue as a result. However the increase is more likely to be due to a greater reporting of the crime, in response to attempts by the police and the legal profession to deal more sympathetically with rape victims. The *London Rape Crisis Centre* estimates that there are between 5000 and 6000 rapes a year. Yet only 25 per cent of the women who ring them report to the police.

Various feminist pressure groups like *Women Against Rape*, and *Women Against Violence Against Women*, have helped to draw attention to the often sexist and insensitive way rape victims are treated by the authorities, and encouraging changes are taking place; for example, police stations are providing more comfortable facilities for rape victims and taking more care to ensure that women staff are available. However the legal procedure involved in trying to bring a rapist to court can still be a humiliating and draining experience for many women, who feel that to be raped is quite enough in itself.

Living in fear

It is difficult to identify whether the recent heightened public awareness of rape has curbed or actually accentuated women's fear of it, and which tendency is in fact more helpful in preventing rape from happening. Evidence from rapists shows that they are much more likely to attack a woman who looks fearful, who appears to be a 'victim', rather than one who appears calm and confident.

Women are taught as little girls to be afraid of 'strange men', who offer them sweets, or lifts in their cars and as adults to keep their doors locked, not to be alone, and not to look or act in any way that might 'provoke' men to rape them. This fear of rape is reinforced by various forms if intimidation from men, ranging from the supposedly 'harmless' wolf-whistle in the street, to different types of sexual harassment and forms of physical violation which only just fall outside the technical definition of rape.

Myths

The offence of rape is legally defined in the 1976 *Sexual Offences Act* as when a man 'has unlawful (*ie* extra-marital) sexual intercourse with a woman without her consent, and at the time he knows that she does not consent to the intercourse or is reckless as to whether or not she consents to it'.

Despite growing public awareness about rape, two important 'myths' still seem to persist in society, fuelled by the tabloid press: that 'women quite enjoy rape really', and 'anyway it only happens to scantily clad blondes in dark alleys and is committed by sex-fiends who can't control themselves'. In reality, rape is rarely just 'unwanted sex', but an extremely violent, and often life-threatening, experience involving the use of weapons, such as knives, bottles and guns, A Women's Safety Survey conducted by *Women Against Rape* in 1985 revealed that 75 per cent of rapists were known to their victims, and other surveys show that 80 per cent of rapes are planned, and take place during the day, often in the victim's own home. The legal acknowledgement of rape in marriage remains a key feminist demand. Because it is one of the most difficult issues on which to legislate, in the meantime such wife-abuse will sadly continue unchecked.

Rape is understandably a central concern to feminists, who have orgainzed campaigns such as WAR and WAVAW, not only to break the 'silence' over the horrors of rape, but also to argue that rape is the inevitable physical expression of a patriarchal society, in which men dominate women. The *London Rape Crisis Centre* believe that 'the greatest myth of all is the one which tells us that rape is an aberration removed from the ways in which men relate to women, emotionally, sexually and physically. Our experiences over the past eight years have shown us that rape is the extreme and logical conclusion of this relationship'.[4]

A man's problem

The *Centre* understands rape as essentially a man's problem, rather than a woman's one, which it is commonly perceived as. Although the workers at the *Centre* respect a woman's right to choose to interact with men again after she has been raped, they believe that for the immediate process of counselling and support, women don't want men to be involved and are relieved to discover that it is an all-female set-up. One worker summed it up by asking 'How can men counsel women about rape when it is them that are doing it to the women?'

Susan Brownmiller, a radical feminist, argues that a rapist is an ordinary 'normal' man, and rape for a man is a 'normal' biological act, albeit a violent and woman-hating one. In *Against Our Will*, she concludes that rape is 'nothing more or less than a conscious process of intimidation by which all men keep all women in a state of fear'[5]. Thus all men are potential rapists, and all women are potential victims. It is this radical feminist understanding of male sexuality as inherently violent and aggressive and sexual violence as merely an extension of 'normal' heterosexual behaviour that led to the complete exclusion of men from meetings, and to initiatives such as SCUM – the *Society for Cutting Up Men* – in the USA in the 1970s.

Germaine Greer also claims that rape is nothing other than the expression of woman-hatred. 'The act is one of murderous aggression spawned in self-loathing, and enacted upon the hated other. Men do not themselves know the depth of their hatred'[6].

Man-hating?

In response to assertions that 'all men are potential rapists', many Christians may well share Mary Stott's reaction: 'Some women, indeed, are saying some exceedingly nasty things about men these days'. Of these 'nasty things', she says, 'the most horrific I ever had to listen to was at a *Women in Media* discussion on "What has man hating to do with feminism". One woman actually said that looking at her eight year old son she saw a potential rapist. I ended up at that meeting almost in tears, and had to be briskly reminded by younger colleagues that bitter experiences drive some feminists to get off their chests in this sort of way their anger at the way male-dominated society had treated them.'[7]

One hopes that the last thing Christian women want is to perceive all men to be their 'enemy'. But they still experience the uncertainty of walking alone, even in a park in broad daylight, and the awkward 'necessity', that most men can ignore, to arrange a lift home from evening engagements, or alternatively leaving early before it gets too dark. Such restrictions on women's autonomy and liberty in our society are a tragic manifestation of the unequal power relations between the sexes, and something that Christians should not accept as somehow inevitable or 'natural'. Women may well 'need' to be walked home by men, for example, but not because they are essentially more vulnerable or 'require male protection', but due to the threat of violence from other men. Rape is no more a woman's problem, than a man's, and both sexes need to work together to overcome this most awful injustice.

Forgiveness and justice

So how are women to 'love their enemy'?

'I pleaded with them not to kill me' . . . 'Imagine being penetrated with a knife'. How are these women meant to 'love' the men who raped them, and men in general?

The much publicized vicarage rape in early 1987 provides a clear example of the forgiveness that is required, but which was obviously so costly to deliver. The vicar in whose home the woman was raped promptly offered forgiveness to her attackers.

'The unstinting offer of forgiveness from an innocent victim shook an angry public,' commented one writer. The fact that this offer was not dependent on the remorse of the guilty was made very clear. So was the heartfelt longing that these men should nevertheless seek the forgiveness of God.'[8]

However such forgiveness still goes hand in hand with a need for justice. The forgiving man also felt a sense of righteous anger. 'So while I keep hatred and vindictiveness at bay, and I can hold forgiveness and a need for justice in tension with the other, I have every right to feel anger at the evil done that day'.[9]

On the issue of justice, it is interesting that in the Old Testament rape was punishable by death, as it still is in many Arab countries today. Although this no doubt reflected to some extent the partiarchal understanding of rape as essentially a crime against a man's property, an attitude that still lingers today in various forms, it also revealed that rape was viewed as a serious 'crime', not merely a trivial misfortune. Whilst capital punishment may not be the most appropriate form of justice for rape today, it would be encouraging to see rape taken as seriously in our legal system as *the* most unacceptable crime against women.

In contrast, both the media and the courts in the vicarage case seem to have fallen short of this ideal. By law the anonymity of the rape victim need not be respected by the media until a definite crime of rape has been recognized, and photos of the woman raped in the Ealing vicarage appeared in some papers immediately the event took place. But once the fact of her rape had been established, media attention focused largely on the vicar's injuries.

Although it is obviously difficult for journalists to give attention to an individual whose identity must remain secret, the horrendous nature of rape and the implications for the wellbeing of the woman concerned were scarcely covered. The vicar's bruises, although serious, were surely nothing compared to the distressing and humiliating ordeal that the woman experienced, and yet little serious attention or sympathy was offered to the victim in her suffering.

The comments of the judge, Mr Justice Leonard, in passing sentence on the two men convicted of her rape, seemed to trivialize the crime of rape in a similar way. In giving McColl, a 22 year old, an eight year sentence, he said, 'Because of your age, and because I have been told the trauma suffered by the victim was not so great, and because of your penitence and your saving her the ordeal of going to the witness box, I shall take a lenient course with you . . .'[10] The judge also paid tribute to the woman's moral resources in her response to the rape. Yet surely this does not diminish the guilt of her assailants or the danger which their liberty will present to others. The courts tend to take the view that a man accused of rape should be rewarded for pleading guilty because that plea spares the victim the anguish of appearing in the witness box. The motive for that convention is obviously humane, but its consistency with justice is more questionable.

The vicar was 'appalled' by this lack of understanding shown by the judge. 'The judge seemed to assume that because we were Christians everything was allright. But we were still suffering.'[11]

Disturbing attitudes

The raped woman was equally shocked (as were many others) at the way the judge seemed to treat rape and burglary as roughly comparable crimes. The two men who raped her received sentences of eight and ten years, whilst the third participant who had no part in the rape, got fourteen years. It does appear that Justice Leonard can be defended in this instance, because the third man, Horscroft, seems to have led and planned the enterprise, and his sentence took into account several other offences to which he had admitted. Yet further scrutiny of the judge's comments reveal some disturbing attitudes about rape that are all too common. In his statement, when passing sentence, he also said, 'What happened was that a perfectly innocent young girl with no previous sexual experience was subjected by you, McColl, to a horrifying experience. You aggravated what you did by the general filthiness of your behaviour'. And in giving details of the attack he added: 'It was not *simply* (my italics) a matter of intercourse . . .'[12]

Mr Justice Leonard seems to be implying from these comments firstly, that if a woman *is* sexually experienced then rape is not quite so much of a violation to her. This view is often exemplified when prostitutes, for instance, are less likely to be believed if they say they have been raped than 'nice, respectable women'. Even if they are believed, it is felt that, given their trade, it is all part of a day's work. Of the Yorkshire Ripper's victims, there was much more public outrage when an 'innocent' Sunday school teacher was raped and killed, than when a prostitute was one of his prey. It is also perhaps worth questioning whether it is appropriate to describe a women in her early twenties as an 'innocent young girl'. Secondly, by the use of the word 'simply' he implies that rape which consists of 'straight' sexual intercourse is somehow better, more acceptable even, than more 'filthy' activities. This reinforces the notion that women quite enjoy rape really, after all it's only 'rough sex' if it doesn't involve too much violence.

Reflecting on this particular rape case, one only hopes that the woman, like the vicar, will eventually feel able to 'love her enemy' in the men who so cruelly violated her, and also develop good personal relationships with men in the future.

Rapist as victim

A Christian understanding of rape must surely recognize both raped and rapist as 'victims' in a fallen world, where the intended mutual respect between the sexes has been distorted, perhaps most grotesquely in this form of violence.

In contrast to the dogmatic radical feminist analysis of rape, which although understandable is ultimately so destructive, it is encouraging that Lynne Segal, a socialist feminist, in her recent book which challenges many current feminist orthodoxies, rejects the notion that 'all men are potential rapists', and recognizes that men too are 'victims' in rape:

'Behind rape and battery of women, which are not habitual to most men, there is a particular history to uncover. It is a history tied in with the cultural reality described by object-relation feminists, where sexual performance in men is one very important way of confirming 'masculinity', mixed up with guilt and anxiety over sex and resentment towards and fear of women. Men who rape are frequently manifesting a contemptible inadequacy and weakness if not mental disturbance . . .'[13]

Ray Wyre, an experienced counsellor in the treatment and assessment of male sex offenders, identifies four main types of rapist, which although not neat categories, are useful to explain some of the complex reasons why men rape women.[14] It is interesting that in his counselling he found that linking a rapist to one of the types seemed to give them 'permission' to talk as they felt he knew all about their motivations and behaviour patterns.

In the case of the 'sexual rapist', it is not necessarily true that rape is purely an act of power. Sexual rapists lack social and life skills, and are often obsessed with sexual inadequacy. They have very poor self-images, and feel that the only way they can satisfy unusually strong sexual urges is by attack. Wyre mentions one rapist who hopes his 'victims' will enjoy the affection and attention he imagines he is giving them. He says of his attacks on women 'All I want is to be loved and cared for'.

'Anger rapists' are usually men with a woman in their lives whom they see as dominant and whom they fear and resent. They displace their anger by attacking other women, with the main aim of dominating, degrading and controlling them. They act agrily, may use weapons and severe forms of physical and verbal abuse.

'Sociopathic rapists' are offenders who are primarily criminal or anti-social, are interested in 'conquest sex', and would resent being classified as sex offenders. Finally, 'sadistic rapists' are specifically aroused by their victim's fear, pain and potential death, and may go to any lengths to indulge it. Sadist are least accessible to being diverted by any ploy their victim might attempt.

These examples of the complexity and depth of human depravity clearly demonstrate the rapist as 'victim', and expose the castration solution as wildly simplistic. Such measures may assuage the personal anger of some victims and the public indignation but they do little to diminish the incidence of rape. Instead of long gaol sentences, constructive forms of group therapy and counselling need to be provided for sex offenders, who are unlikely to mend their ways purely via imprisonment. Like alcoholics they are not helped at all by being locked up for a period, and then released into a world of temptation.

Uncomfortable truths

Wyre claims that 'Women have been protesting about rape for years, and could continue doing so for many more still, but men are not listening to what women are saying. Now that I am saying the same things and recounting the uncomfortable truths I have learned from ten years of talking to offenders, suddenly men are listening *because* I am a man. It comes from the same side of the fence as it were. Normal men believe that rapists are a breed apart. But when I point out that insisting on sex, despite verbal refusal by the woman and some physical resistance, might constitute rape, a common response is "Well in that case I've raped lots of women".'

As part of his research Wyre asked convicted sex offenders to complete a questionnaire about their attitudes to women – the meaning of a low slung dress, does 'no' mean 'yes', is agreeing to come in for coffee tantamount to consenting to sex, should a woman sleep with you if you've paid for her dinner, *etc.* Out of interest, he distributed the same questionnaire amongst 'normal' men. The results were exactly the same.

Perhaps beyond asking how to 'love your enemy' therefore, the Christian community should be working out how men can get rid of their 'enemy-status' so that women can be free from the fear and reality of male violence, and men can escape being labelled 'potential rapists'.

Practical changes

On a practical level, men can be sensitive to women's fear of assault by offering female friends lifts home and other such measures. They can examine their own behaviour to make sure it isn't threatening to women, for example not walking too close behind a woman at night so as not to cause her unnecessary fear. It would surely be a positive step for

Christian men to get involved in caring for rape victims, obviously in a very sensitive and carefully thought-out manner, so as to offer love and reconciliation to women from the 'opposite sex' and help prevent potentially deep fear or hatred of men by those women in the future.

This kind of practical commitment by men in the church would provide a valuable and much-needed ministry to women generally, and be a particularly powerful statement to many feminists who feel totally aliented from a patriarchal church which perpetuates the unequal power relations between the sexes. 'For them the church itself signifies oppression. The church is beyond redemption. It is that institution which has in the past contributed most soundly to subduing women and providing the divine justification for doing it.'[15]

For men to adopt this new role of service, involving tenderness, love and patience, rather than qualities of leadership, assertiveness, and detachment so often associated with their more traditional roles in the church, would simply mean imitating Jesus, who offered physical comfort and healing to many women in his earthly ministry.

Due to the emotive nature of rape, and its complex consequences, it could potentially be a fairly disturbing experience for the men and women who committed themselves to this kind of work. It would most likely provoke different issues for the men, than for the women, and perhaps force the men to analyse male sexuality and their own attitudes to a greater depth than they had previously done. Therefore such an initiative would not only require men to imitate Jesus's practical compassion, but also his honesty and vulnerabilty, all of which are costly to put into practice.

It is encouraging if a rape victim even feels able to approach the church for help, given the 'taboo' that still surrounds the issue and the apparent under-reporting of the crime. But what a marvellous demonstration of the reconciling work of Christ it would be if that woman, having been cruelly abused by a *man*, could then be comforted and supported by a man, perhaps alongside women, who could lovingly reaffirm her dignity as a human being.

Values and power

On a wider level, if rape is more an act of power than sex, then it is many of the values in society that bolster men's power whilst demeaning women that need to be challenged. The feminist slogan 'Porn is the theory; rape is the practice' may well be simplistic, but as comedians and certain newspapers continue to confuse sex, soft porn and rape, the idea that women's bodies are for men to use is sold to us again and again.

Certain Tory MPs demonstrated such confused and contradictory attitudes in expressing outrage at the vicarage rape, and calling for the castration of the rapists or at least longer sentences for them on the one hand, whilst having openly supported Page 3 soft-porn as 'light entertainment' and acceptable, 'normal' portrayal of women, when opposing Clare Short's *Indecent Displays (Newspapers) Bill* in 1986.

These contradictions are most clearly exposed when rape and porn are placed side by side on the same page in a newspaper, and the reader is subtly led to relate the two and receive some kind of titillation from their association.

The nature and extent of sexual violence against women is a sad indictment of male culture, and of how women are perceived by men both psychologically and sexually. The pervasive attitude, reinforced especially in advertisements, that women are primarily for male consumption, ideally offered 'free', but if not then to be 'taken' by force, needs to be met by a Christian alternative of mutual care and respect between women and men. In the meantime while 'enmity' between the sexes still exists, we need to remember not only to 'love our enemy', but also to 'pray for those who persecute us'.

Rape/abuse crisis counselling

An estimated one in seven women are potential victims for rape/sexual abuse. In spite of this, the Church remains often unaware and ill-equipped to help women who are either potential or actual victims.

It is vital that you know what you are doing when counselling the abused, and that you have had counselling training. It is not a job for the inexperienced. These notes will *not* teach you how to do it and should not be taken as such but are guidelines that may be helpful when coming into contact with rape and abuse victims.

Rape/abuse victims can or may be:

1. Frightened – of people, places, situations.
2. Angry – at themselves, at the world, at their assailant.
3. Confused – was it their fault? Why did it happen?
4. Hurt – in physical pain and in emotional pain.

You must *never:*

—Say 'I know just how you feel' – you don't, even if you are a rape survivor; the victim will feel differently from you in many ways.

—Imply that it is the victim's fault – this can cripple people emotionally.

—Look shocked or horrified – if you can't help it, explain. Say 'I'm sorry, I find this very upsetting', and pause to recover.

—Pry into what happened – if they want to tell you, they will.

—Say 'God loves you', or other similar platitudes – the chances are that they know that, but it is not necessarily helpful at that moment.

—Just pray with someone and assume that it will be alright – the roots will be deep-seated and will probably need a lot of counselling.

—Divulge names or details to *anyone* without permission. To break trust is about the worst thing you can do. Don't even tell anyone by asking them to pray for 'so-and-so'. The most you can say is 'Can you pray for me and a person I am counselling'. There is no need to say more; God already knows the details.

Please be aware that to be abused is a terrible experience. To be a Christian and be abused can make things more complicated. Common responses include: 'Why did God let this happen?' and 'I called out to God, but He didn't stop it'. I can't answer these questions, and I don't know anyone who can. But being a Christian *does* have advantages. We have God's love and healing power with us, to help us and the victim. Pray constantly, not only for guidance, but for the victim.

It is our duty as Christians, and as members of one family, to care for each other. 'So that there should be no division in the body, but that its parts should have equal concern for each other' (1 Cor 12:25 NIV).

We have a part in helping to rebuild people, and enabling them to become whole and fulfilled within God's family. Victims can become survivors.

Reactions to rape and help for the victims

Shame, guilt helplessness and physical repulsion are just some of the common feelings of rape victims.

Nightmares, sleeplessness, shock, depression and damaged relationships are some of the emotional ways in which they can suffer, too.

In addition to any medical care that may be needed, women who have been assaulted also need special emotional support to come to terms with their experience. The experience of psychiatrists and crisis centre counsellors who have worked with rape victims is that the sooner a woman can start to talk about her experience, the quicker she will be able to come to terms with it.

But for some women it is a long time before they feel able to admit to what happened; they may be prompted to finally speak out by reports of other assaults. Many never tell – and live with a secret hurt for the rest of their lives.

If you know someone who is the victim of a sex attack they can turn for advice and support to:

London Rape Crisis Centre – tel: 01–837 1600
Birmingham Rape Crisis Centre – tel: 021–233 2122
Manchester Rape Crisis Centre – tel: 061–228 3602
Edinburgh Rape Crisis Centre – tel: 031–556 9437

Your local library or Citizens' Advice Bureau may be able to give you further local information.

Questions for discussion

1. In what ways should legal provision for the prevention and punishment of sexual abuse and violence be strengthened?

(These could include: stricter definitions of offences; making criminal previously ignored acts, eg marital rape; heavier sentencing; new rulings on police and court procedure.)

2. How should Christians respond to calls for such severe penalties as the death sentence or castration?
3. Are men who abuse women themselves victims too? If so, what should be done to protect *men* from becoming violent or offending sexually, and what can be done to help those who already have?
4. Is sexual abuse is, as feminists suggest, as much a matter of exerting power as of satisfying sexual urges? If so, why is it that sex gets confused with power? Do we need to rethink our view of sexuality? (For instance, some Christians argue that the nature of the sexual act demonstrates the 'naturalness' of male initiative and female submission. Is this really what the Bible tells us sex is about?)
5. In what ways might a Chrisian style of counselling the sexually abused differ from a secular one? (for instance, in the attitudes encouraged towards men).

References

1. *Women in the World*, Joni Seager and Ann Olson (Pan 1986).
2. Kate Millet, *Sexual Politics*.
3. *Women in the World*, op. cit.
4. *Sexual Violence – The Reality for Women* (Women's Press Ltd 1984).
5. Susan Brownmiller, *Against Our Will: Men, Women and Rape* (Simon and Shuster 1975).
6. Germaine Greer, *The Female Eunich* (Bantam 1972).
7. Mary Stott, *Before I go . . .* (Virago 1985).
8. Elaine Storkey, 'Blind Justice', *Third Way*, March 1987.
9. *The Times*, 3 February, 1987.
10. *The Times*, 5 February, 1987.
11. *The Times*, 4 February, 1987.
12. *The Times*, 5 February, 1987.
13. Lynne Segal, *Is the Future Female?* (Virago 1987).

14. Ray Wyre, *Women, Men and Rape* (Perry Publications 1986).
15. Elaine Storkey, *What's right with feminism* (SPCK/Third Way Books 1985).

This chapter first appeared as an article in the September 1987 edition of *Third Way* and has been slightly revised and used with permission.

Third Way is a monthly magazine providing a biblical Christian perspective on social ethics, political issues and cultural affairs. Subscription rates available from: *Third Way*, PO Box 16, Guildford, Surrey GU2 6FW.

Elaine Ambrose

Elaine Ambrose studied Theology at London Bible College, where she gained a BA in 1986. She attends the Community Church in Romford, Essex, and is personally acquainted with the lesbian and homosexual struggle.

16. Lesbianism – A Christian Option?

Elaine Ambrose

With the increasing growth and visibility of lesbianism today, Christians cannot afford to retain an attitude of fearful condemnation or sublime ignorance. Present concerns about homosexuality in general and AIDS (Acquired Immunity Deficiency Syndrome) cannot be ignored, but will not be covered in detail here. This chapter aims simply to inform readers of some of the ideas and attitudes currently held about lesbianism and to encourage an appropriate response.

Definitions

Lesbianism is the sexual and intense emotional attraction of one woman to another; it may or may not result in full-blown lesbian behaviour. Ask why it is an issue, and several common reasons emerge. These range from presuppositions concerning who and what normality is, to where we draw the line between acceptable and unacceptable religious and/or moral behaviour. Central to this is what the Bible has to say on the matter, and how different interpretations held by Christians present us with one of the most controversial issues facing the Church at this time. In the light of this, we must unashamedly try to discern what God has revealed in his Word, recognising our own orientation, prejudices and fears.

It it easy to generalise about lesbianism and assume certain things which are not necessarily true. For example, a woman who makes a deliberate choice to adopt a lesbian lifestyle is not to be mistaken for a woman who, to all intents and purposes, has never consciously sought after lesbian-centred emotions. Similarly, to be a lesbian does not necessarily imply the practice of lesbianism, any more than to be a single heterosexual automatically implies fornication. In fact, many women who experience lesbian desires do not actually take part in any lesbian activity. Rather, such feelings are often suppressed out of guilt and fear. And whilst lesbianism may be projected by some feminist groups as a valid and desirable alternative lifestyle, this does not mean that all feminists are lesbians, as we shall see, nor indeed that all lesbians are feminists.

The Church's attitude

In the Church as a whole lesbians and homosexuals are usually regarded as heterosexuals 'gone wrong', and are therefore either treated solely as sinners (if they can help it) or as sick (if they cannot). However, most of these women and men are not 'heterosexual deviants' needing a convicting sermon or some kind of medical cure. It is perhaps far more real and helpful to speak simply of people dealing with homosexuality rather than of homosexual people. Why? Because according to biblical teaching God did not, and does not, create anyone lesbian or homosexual. Rather, people are individuals made male and female in his image (Genesis chapter 1). The image of God reveals a unique and perfect blending of both male and female, neither being dominant over the other or independent of the other.

Sadly, often out of prejudice and fear, people label people, and labels push people into ruts where there is no room for growth or development. They 'inform' us, 'I'm straight, he's gay; you're straight, she's gay. And there's an end to it!' However, such an adage need not be the case. Careful consideration of an individual's circumstances is needed, as well as an understanding and application of basic biblical teaching on human sexuality; on how it has been affected in every aspect through sin, and how the gospel brings hope and the promise of wholeness to those who wish to embrace it. This is essential and provides a reliable basis for ministering to people concerned about and involved in lesbianism.

God's view of sin, his limitless power and his unconditional love in and through Jesus Christ are crucial, then, for meeting the needs and questions of women who are either living a lesbian lifestyle or struggling in fear of who and what they are. Where this is an integral part of our gospel there is hope and a way forward. Where this is not so, we are left with an inability to understand and failure to present a relevant Christ-centred lifestyle to those who are already Christian or who might become Christian.

Male and female homosexuality

While male and female homosexuality both concern same-sex attraction and today homosexuals and lesbians are both fighting for 'gay rights', there the similarities generally end. Homosexuals and lesbians tend to keep apart in their own groups and clubs. Culturally, the West has tended to allow affection to be displayed between women. However, affection between men, at least in public, has usually been questioned, unless they are of Latin origins. Even in law, lesbianism has never really been acknowledged until recent years. Queen Victoria refused to believe in its existence!

One of the dominant themes in the nineteenth century (and until more recently) was the sexual passivity of all women. Male homosexuality was rigorously dealt with in 1855 Criminal Law Amendment Act and the 1861 Offences Against the Person Act. Although lesbianism was not put on the statute book on those occasions it was recognised by the medical profession of the time, who understood it to be a 'chromosomatic or psychological dysfunction'. Indecency between females was discussed in the House for the first time in 1921 when a Mr Maacquisten MP introduced a clause in a debate on the Criminal Law Amendment Bill. Many MPs expressed disbelief and disgust. Sir Ernest Wild stated that 'lesbianism saps the fundamental institutions of society, stops childbirth, debauches young girls, produces insanity and causes our race to decline'.

No legislation was passed in the early twentieth century directly prohibiting lesbianism, although the law continued to show strong signs of disapproval indirectly through several court cases in charges of criminal libel and as evidence of cruelty to husbands in divorce actions. In 1956 sexual activity between women was made a criminal offence in Sections 14 and 15 of the Sexual Offences Act. Although no such case has been brought before the courts, over the last thirty years it has been possible to prosecute a woman for the indecent assault of another woman. In practice lesbians, especially amongst the working class, have been prosecuted and imprisoned for their relationships on other charges, notably the laws relating to prostitution.

However, more recently we have seen homosexuality in legislation advance from being a criminal act to being legally acceptable where it occurs between two consenting adults.

Sexually, lesbians appear to be less promiscuous than male homosexuals on the whole. They seek a greater emotional fulfilment and companionship, while for their male counterparts the visual plays an important part, which then stimulates their sexual drive and demands gratification. Even in the lesbian 'scene' many women – perhaps most – are looking for the ideal monogamous relationship rather than an endless supply of lovers or an increased sexual repertoire. There are always exceptions, of course, but on the whole I have found this to be the case.

AIDS

AIDS, and its increasing threat to homosexuals and heterosexuals alike, has raised serious questions about its physical and moral implications which no one can afford to ignore. Speculations as to how and why the disease has arisen include a wide range of ideas. However, the theological debate immediately associated with AIDS focuses on the judgement of God. We shall look at three views on AIDS which are helpful in discussing the subject in relation to lesbian and homosexual behaviour.

1. AIDS as a personal curse

Judgement here means punishment. The gay community are seen to deserve punishment because their behaviour is regarded as especially abhorrent to God, although promiscuous heterosexuals and drug users are also condemned. However, the fact that innocent people have contracted AIDS (e.g. haemophiliacs, wives of unfaithful husbands and babies of infected mothers) raises questions. Is God's judgement arbitrary? Also, not only are innocent people suffering, but some would say that the guilty are not. Those who are suffering are not necessarily the most promiscuous. Following 'safer sex' guidelines does not eliminate promiscuity. The fact that lesbians are a very low-risk group has caused others to presume that God must be female or feminist because he is discriminating against male homosexuality! This 'God-of-the-gaps' argument needs to be seen in the light of more overall biblical teaching. To make AIDS the criterion of whether a person is under the specific judgement of God (i.e. a curse) is to use the Bible simply to support personal prejudice.

2. AIDS is nothing to do with judgement

This is often a reaction to the view expressed above. Some speak with compassion, others out of solidarity with the condemned groups. The argument here stresses that a wide range of practices once condemned (e.g. divorce) are now more widely acceptable, so why should the gay community come under particular judgement? After all, 'Jesus came to save sinners, not to threaten them with appalling diseases.'

3. AIDS is part of God's judgement on society

This view states that any society which rejects God's norms will end up reaping its own harvest, as described in Romans chapter 1. Few can adequately dispute that our society both allows and encourages behaviour which could lead to the spread of AIDS on an epidemic scale. Victims are not only suffering as a result of individual choices but because of a society which promotes unhealthy behaviour patterns as normal.

4. A wider judgement

AIDS presents a series of extremely pertinent questions to Christians. First, it is true that the world in which we live is sick; it is a world under judgement. Christians and non-Christians alike share in its weaknesses, and apart from God's grace would be part of that judgement. Our calling is not to condemn but to be as Christ to those around us in both our attitudes and actions.

Sin and suffering

The relationship between sin and suffering is to most of us as much of a mystery today as it was to Job. Suffering is by no means always the result of and proportionate to a person's sin. In the Gospels Jesus clearly makes this point a number of times. In Luke chapter 13, after he is questioned about the Galileans who had been slaughtered by Pilate, he says, 'Do you think they were worse sinners than all the others just because they suffered in this way? I tell you no' (13:2). In context, then, as far as God is concerned there is no difference between those who have AIDS and those who do not, although in most cases there is a direct link between individual behaviour and being infected.

Whilst in a very real sense most of us reap what we sow, there is also a strong indication in Scripture that our personal conduct before long becomes governed precisely by what we desire (Rom 1:18). The practices in which people indulge and the confusion into which lives are thrown as a result represent at one level the judgement of God in human history. However, this is not the final judgement of which the Bible also speaks. God's judgement in history is never the last word on individual lives, but rather a starting point from which to talk about personal restoration to God.

Churches have an added responsibility at this time to present clear biblical teaching which will help set people free from unnecessary fears and prevent them from drawing simplistic conclusions about people and society at large in the face of this threatening disease. Far from using the AIDS issue as ammunition with which to verbally attack homosexuals, the Church would do well to pray seriously for a cure and to take more initiative in providing medical help and pastoral care for victims and their families and friends.

Lesbianism and its relationship with feminism

Promises in the 1960s that candid sex education and a frank presentation of all aspects of sexuality would result in better adjusted adults have been sadly misleading. The glib assumption that teenagers could be safely sexually active from puberty has produced an increasing number of women with deep sexual problems, including frigidity and infertility. Clinics dealing with sex-related problems and diseases are far from going out of business, and many emotional problems are surfacing, following earlier promiscuity and the trivialisation of sexual relationships. Mistrust is common, and few women can appreciate their full sexual identity in such circumstances. In some respects we are only just beginning to realise the desperate legacy those years have left us.

Politically, women did not really find any more light than with the sexual revolution. It was time to forge a greater solidarity between women for the benefit of women. The Women's Liberation Movement came into its own, replacing political and legal lobbying with marches and demonstrations. Protests against sexism, the devaluation of women and the presentation of them as sex objects have become a well documented feature of the movement. The cry for equal rights has gained a stronger voice over the last decade, with a new and powerful sisterhood rising up to 'expose' the situation. Here women can relate sharing common frustrations and finding the means by which they can be nurtured and supported. It foresees a world in which male dominance will be extinct and female autonomy will be the norm.

The increase in rape and other crimes against women have understandably added fuel and determination to the cause of radical feminists. Wife battering and the struggles of many one-parent families also add momentum to the growing number of groups run by and for women. Perhaps not surprisingly, amongst radical feminists lesbianism is seen not only as a matter of sexual preference. It is a strong political statement, being the final refusal to collude with a heterosexual, male-centred norm. Lesbianism challenges women's dependency on men (sexually, emotionally and economically) and attacks the tradition of heterosexual marriage being the only valid family-based partnership. The message of radical feminism is very clear: patriarchal society does not have the last word; men are irrelevant; women can live and work together successfully in every way.

However while the feminist cause is a real one, and greater equality and dignity for women needs to be gained and maintained, it must also be said that this can never be truly possible outside of a fully Christ-centred world-view.

Did God say?

Many mainline denominational churches today struggle with the issue of male and female homosexuality. A large number within these denominations are promoting the idea that God is actually silent on the subject. The past twenty years have seen the development of a 'gay theology'. If the question, 'Did God say?' has a familiar ring about it, it is not surprising – the serpent was the first to use it, as recorded in Genesis chapter 3, where he encouraged Eve to doubt God's original command (3:1). Today, gay theology questions God's Word in its most immediate and simplistic form. No longer is the Word accepted as revealed and authoritative. Truth is hidden, it is claimed, and needs to be discovered and applied to life as it is today. It is easy to read into the Word what we want it to say – a danger for fundamentalists as much as for others. However, where lesbianism and homosexuality are concerned, different interpretations have had the effect of polarising the Church, with total condemnation at one end and total acceptance at the other. So, what *has* God said?

Almost everything written in the Bible on homosexuality has to do with men. Only one reference, Romans 1:24–27, is written with women clearly in mind, where both men and women are shown as forsaking God's Creation ordinance regarding sexuality. This in itself is seen as symptomatic of turning away from God. However, this is written in the context of the universal sinfulness of humankind, which is summed up in Romans 3:23, '*All* have fallen short of the glory of God.' This must be the starting point for all who wish to debate whether or not lesbianism is a Christian option.

There are various other passages in the Bible which refer directly to homosexuality (see Appendix). I will approach four of these and also comment on the Genesis passage referring to the ordinance of marriage.

1. The Sodom story (Genesis 18:16—19:29)

Assuming the Sodom story is solely about homosexuality and its consequences, is like assuming Jesus is made of wood, because he says 'I am the gate' (Jn 10:7). If this appears shocking, I say it simply to make the point. It is easy to take the story totally out of context and use it to declare anyone with homosexual tendencies to be a corrupt monster just waiting to pounce! I have met many Christians with exactly this attitude. As a city, Sodom was socially, economically and morally corrupt, homosexuality being only *one* symptom of this. The passage emphasises the degeneracy of the men by referring to their apparent hunger for homosexual gang rape. However, a search through the prophets shows that Sodom was condemned for arrogance, greed and social misjustice (e.g. Ezek 16:49), with not a mention of homosexuality. Also in the prophets, the Lord often compares Jerusalem to Sodom and Gomorrah (Is 1:9;3:9; Jer 23:14; Amos 4:11–12 and elsewhere). One might wonder why, if homosexuality was the worst of Sodom's sins, it is not mentioned by the prophets. Also, it needs to be asked whether homosexual gang rape is in the same moral category as a faithful, loving relationship between two men or two women.

2. The Levitical holiness code (Leviticus chapters 18 and 19)

To regard these laws as having absolutely no bearing on Christian living because they are irrelevant today is to misinterpret their place in the Scriptures. Christ came to fulfil them – he did not abolish them, as we know from his own lips (Mt 5:17–20). Consequently, there is much to learn from them about our attitudes as Christians today and about the Exodus people. And whilst it is important to place them in their cultural setting, we must beware of proof texting – that is, sorting through verses such as these and agreeing with what appeals to us and discarding the rest. Scripture must be seen in the light of Scripture as the progressive and complete revelation of God, Old and New Testaments alike. It is our task, therefore, to see how the coming of Christ was the fulfilment of the Law, with particular reference to Old Testament teaching on homosexual behaviour.

Leviticus 18:22 strongly condemned homosexual intercourse at a time when the Hebrews were surrounded by the cults and practices of the Ancient Near East. These included male and female temple prostitution, abominable to the God of Israel. It is too simplistic to suppose, on the strength of this, that God only condemned homosexual practice when linked to temple prostitution and cultic idolatry. The Levitical laws on sexuality are based upon the sanctity of family relationships and in particular upon the one-flesh relationship of marriage. They are not simply polemic against another culture's practices.

3. The Creation ordinance of marriage (Genesis 2:22–25)

Marriage was ordained before the Fall, encompassing both procreation and sex as intimacies to be cherished and thoroughly enjoyed by one man and one woman together for life. Blunt as it may be, God created Adam and Eve, not Adam and Steve, nor Helen and Eve for that matter. Sadly, the beauty of pre-Fall days was not to last. Humankind's turning away from the Creator, Father God and being 'bent' towards the creature in many different ways, was the result of the Fall, which has become embedded into every characteristic of our make-up. At best, therefore, a homosexual or lesbian relationship is a concession, and at worst it is blatant rebellion against the one who created us, loves us and sent Christ to die for us. However we view it, homosexuality was not ordained by God. We do still live in a fallen world, but now we live in the light and grace of Jesus Christ and not in the darkness of the Fall. This should be the means by which we understand and deal with homosexuality and lesbianism, but not the licence accept it and view it as a valid lifestyle.

4. The 'natural' and 'unnatural' (Romans 1:18– 32)

Traditionally it has been thought that God's natural order of things included the heterosexuality of humankind (see Mt 19:4–6; Gen 1:27; 2:24). Today this idea of the order of things is being discounted in favour of the condition existing at birth being seen as the natural condition. Consequently a gay theology considers that men and women can be born homosexual and lesbian, and so have been created in their natural state; Romans 1:18–32 cannot therefore apply here. A second argument suggests that what is natural is determined by the number of people involved. Therefore, since the number of homosexuals and lesbians is growing, how can it be viewed as unnatural?

The main thrust of the text is to show how, despite knowledge of the Creator, men and women choose to follow their own desires, rejecting worship of God in favour of the created, including themselves. God consequently allows them to see just how far they can go without him: he 'gave them over' (1:24, 26, 28). A sympton of this turning from God was an exchange of the Creation ordinance regarding sexual intercourse for homosexual and lesbian practice. What Paul is speaking of, therefore, is not what is and is not natural since the Fall, but what was so *before* the Fall, when any sex outside of marriage was unnatural. The argument for a difference between deliberate choice and apparently 'natural' orientation concerning homosexual and lesbian practice, therefore, is irrelevant here. Paul's train of thought covers both. It should also be noted that Paul lists homosexuality and lesbianism alongside other sins, including gossip, greed, envy and murder. He does not see any one sin as greater than another and does not 'pedestal' sin which is homosexual or lesbian in nature.

5. 'And that is what some of you were' (1 Corinthians 6:9–11)

This passage lists, among other things, sex outside of marriage. Fornicators engaging in sexual relations while unmarried, adulterers sexually involved with someone other than their marriage partner, and those engaged in homosexual practices are among those who will not 'inherit the kingdom of God'. There is a debate over the words Paul uses here – *malakoi* and *arsenokoitai* – traditionally associated with homosexual activity. Gay theology oscillates between saying that these words have nothing to do with homosexual relationships and are to do with male prostitution only, and saying that the true meaning of the words has been lost in time, so that no one really knows to what Paul is referring anyway. However, there are Greek scholars today who remain in agreement with the traditional view. Unfortunately they are not vocal on the subject.

The concluding verse of this passage is, I believe, of real importance and encouragement to anyone questioning homosexuality and lesbianism, especially in regard to his or her own life. It implies not only possible change but a definite process in which Christ himself enables change through the Holy Spirit. This involves the breaking of those labels mentioned earlier and the receiving of sanctification through Christ, which is an ongoing healing and cleansing process. Of course, not all will agree with this, but I am convinced that this is an uncomplicated passage which speaks for itself.

6. A conclusion from Scripture

On the whole the scriptural passages referring to homosexuality and lesbianism appear negative. Active homosexuality and lesbianism are condemned; a person involved is called to repent and seek change; where change seems too hard, painful or impossible the homosexual or lesbian faces either the choice of singleness and chastity in the will of God or of continuing in a lesbian or homosexual relationship while attempting to remain in God's and society's will. In most cases this is far from an easy decision.

Taking the Bible as a whole, we have a picture before us of God's wrath and unconditional love, appropriated in the lives of people of all kinds through the person and work of Jesus. The exact state of the human condition (Romans chapter 5) and a vision of what we can be and grow into in our relationship with God is revealed. Whilst neither homosexual or lesbian behaviour is acceptable before him, in most cases change is possible if the individual wants it. However, it must be stressed that a person involved with homosexual or lesbian sin is no less accepted by God than anyone else involved in sin, whatever form it takes.

'For the kingdom of God is not a matter of talk but of power' (1 Cor 4:20). This is true for those who are finding a transformation taking place in their thought patterns and emotions, as they actively involve themselves in allowing the Lord to crucify their old natures while 'putting on' their new nature – that is, Christ. Where a Christian woman or man is actively involved in lesbianism or homosexuality and says that they find the Lord blessing them richly, even in their relationship, I would suggest that it reveals something of the goodness of God and not that their relationship is good before him.

For people to change how they think, feel and respond sexually, there is the need to offer both support and a new lifestyle in Christ. The Church should be the place where such care and nurturing is given and maintained. How effective is the body of Christ in responding to the needs of someone struggling with homosexuality – and, more appropriately here, a woman struggling with lesbianism?

Church attitude and support

Where the Church has recognised lesbianism as an issue at all, it has basically condemned its practice, as with male homosexuality. It is easy, as we have seen, to preach without listening, and to quote texts without being sensitive either to Scripture or to the person concerned. It is often with no thanks to the Church that a Christian woman struggling with lesbian inclinations discovers that she is still a Christian, loved unconditionally by Christ despite her emotional and psychological disposition. There can be no real compassion for the lesbian without cost to the Church, and that means the Church's sacrifice of all that stands in the way of her wholeness in Christ. The Church needs as much to repent of its homophobia as any lesbian of her acts.

To a large extent it was the hostility of heterosexual people which initially forced lesbians to form their own subculture, as an escape from the isolation they experienced. Similarly, it is the hostility of the Church (due to ignorance and fear) which has produced the rise of the Gay Christian Movement. Originally taking root in the USA and now established in the UK, the movement has drawn together those who believe that Christianity and homosexual/lesbian lifestyles are compatible. When the Church is polarised on this issue it is not surprising that Christians following a gay lifestyle, or gays drawn to Christ but mistreated by the Church, have come together in support and fellowship. The G.C.M.'s existence simply emphasises the Church's inability to cope with the homosexual and lesbian phenomena, yet it is precisely this kind of situation which challenges the already divided Church to exercise a positive ministry, offering real hope to struggling people. As the letter of James reminds us, there is no point in saying what ought to be done if no one actually does anything: 'faith by itself, if not accompanied by action, is dead' (Jas 2:17).

1. Sin and sinner

Concerning Scripture, the choice is not simply between accepting the Bible's hard words or ignoring them. Biblical interpretation and application, as we have seen, calls for the utmost care. Even amongst the most conservative circles of evangelicalism a consistent scriptural interpretation is rare. For example, the Scriptures clearly distinguish between sin and the sinner, continually affirming not only God's loathing of sin, but also his unconditional love for sinners. At present the Church is more adept at condemning the sinner, and many fellowships are guilty of throwing the sinner out with the sin. Where this happens the end result is unbiblical and un-Christlike.

Many Christian women who experience feelings of intense attraction for another woman do not actually take part in lesbian behaviour. Despite this the Church all too easily blurs the distinction between one who 'feels' (orientation) and one who 'acts' (practising). There is good cause for questioning why a Christian fellowship may throw its hands up in horror at someone's sexual temptations and not so much as blink at someone's tendency towards gossip, hatred, anger or pride. It was for no small reason that Jesus said that prostitutes and tax collectors were entering the kingdom of God ahead of the religious leaders (Mt 21:28–32). A self-righteous church-going bigot may well be closer to hell than a repentant prostitute. However, it works both ways, and no one should criticise another's self-righteousness whilst whitewashing their own sexual sin or temptations.

2. The challenge to the Church

The Church is not always willing to face hard facts. There are many who would rather preserve a head-in-the-sand mentality. Generally, the Church is failing to guide new Christians along the paths of moral and ethical discipline at this time. How can young Christians be shown how to grow up with Christlike ethics and morality when 'adults' do not really know how to teach them, or are too embarrassed to try? Consequently, when problems surface or erupt, they tend to be mishandled, given to the pastor (who often may not know how to deal with them), or swept under the carpet. Alternatively, they are passed on to a professional counsellor or psychologist. Undeniably, the help needed may eventually be found, but often the person feels let down or passed about because those around have no idea how to cope. Why is this? Partly because counselling and nurturing someone through often crippling circumstances calls for a great deal of time, patience and vulnerability on the part of the counsellor, which most people are simply not prepared to give. I sense, too, that the difficulty so many Christians have in striking a balance between condemning an active lesbian lifestyle and showing compassionate care for the lesbian may well be due to the lack of conviction of sin in their own lives. However, once a point of honesty *is* reached and we consider what can be done, lesbianism and the Church's response can be seen in perspective. We cannot sit on the fence – either we have the answers or we do not. I believe we do, and the Church's application of these towards many hurting, silent women is long overdue.

3. Counsel

In giving counsel to a woman with lesbian inclinations and/or involved in lesbian activity, her age and depth of experience in lesbianism need to be taken into consideration. Counselling a confused teenager with a crush is not the same as dealing with a mature woman involved in a steady relationship of some years. Nor is dealing with a brief affair, which perhaps began out of curiosity, like dealing with apparently life-long thought patterns and emotions. The more established behavioural patterns and habits become, the greater the difficulty in changing them. However, behaviour which has been learned can be unlearned and, for the Christian, there is the encouragement of reliance on Christ rather than on self alone. It is my conviction that any woman with lesbian behaviour can, if she so desires, be changed through the healing power of Jesus.

The battle with loneliness can be bitter and desperately frustrating. A Christian woman dealing with her lesbianism in the light and grace of God may well sense her predicament acutely. It is the frustration of being able to have what should not be pursued, and longing for what cannot be received: the desire for a husband, but not a man. As I mentioned earlier, what distinguishes the lesbian from her male counterpart is her predominant need for an emotionally fulfilling, stable relationship, rather than a mainly sexual one. Consequently, for a woman coming out of a lesbian lifestyle, the giving up of sexual activity is not as difficult a prospect as losing the intimacy and emotional stability known with her partner.

On the other hand, those who have discovered *agapé* love and affirmation in their church fellowship tend to say how they are able to leave much of the past and its hurts behind.

Instead, they find themselves concentrating on serving Christ and their fellowship through the gifts he has given them. This is probably the most crucial part the Church has to play: surrounding the woman struggling with lesbian tendencies with affirming, accepting love and supportive prayer, enabling her to recognise her worth and value in Christ, showing that there is a positive, lasting alternative to a gay lifestyle, if she wants it, and an alternative which may lead to complete healing and the possibility of marriage.

Severence from the gay scene is necessary for the woman wanting to leave an active lesbian lifestyle. However, the remaining gap needs to be thoroughly filled with the positive alternative of considerate, prayerful fellowship and social life. Without it, and its natural development, she may drift back, if only out of loneliness. Such a responsibility is one which the Church has yet fully to realise. It is not enough to accept glib phrases like 'The Lord will take it from here . . .' We need to respond both with a loving acceptance and a watchful eye.

A mistake made in counselling lesbians focuses on the assumption, 'All you need is the right man'. At best this is a mere half-truth, at worst it is a tragic misconception of what a lesbian woman may be struggling with. To accept that there is a need for a change in attitude towards men is true enough, but this is only one side of the story. There is a greater importance in the healing of attitudes towards oneself and other women. Once these responses are recognised, questioned and changed, only then can the emotional, mental and sexual attitude towards men begin to change. By this I mean that a lesbian attitude is the recognition of legitimate but unfulfilled needs which have then been misinterpreted. These tend to be linked to past bad experiences or love-starvation from one or both parents, and later aggravated in some way, perhaps by rape or by seduction by another woman.[2] What is needed is the introduction of stable, nonthreatening and nonsexual relationships with both sexes. In this way a woman can begin to understand herself and gain a deeper understanding of how loving relationships should be built up between women – and where better a place than in a Christ-centred, loving church fellowship?

For an overview of some of the causes of lesbianism I would thoroughly recommend Elizabeth R Moberly's *Homosexuality: A New Christian Ethic* and Leanne Payne's *The Broken Image.* Two very different approaches, they each reveal a unique understanding of lesbianism, reasons for its development in women and encouragement in dealing with it.

Is change possible?

I have found a great problem with women who believe they cannot change. Where the mind is set, little progress can be made. Women wanting to get out of a lesbian lifestyle meet their breakthrough usually only when their 'label' is broken. For the Christian, this can of course be brought into perspective through her relationship with God. No one's identity should be seen in terms of their sexuality alone, but rather in terms of being a complete son or daughter of the living God. When this can become the focal point, a marked difference in attitude emerges. 'If I am a child of God, how can I be gay? It isn't possible. I may still have problems to be dealt with, but I refuse to believe the lie that I am gay. I am a new creation', one Christian woman prayed simply. Beginning with Christ and self, rather than with self and sexuality, is the difference between standing in a dark room with a candle and opening the shutters to the sunlight, *even though the process may take time.*

We sometimes refer to the Church as 'God with skin on'. We also often speak of the Church as being female, betrothed to Christ (Jn 3:29; Rev 21:2,9). For the lesbian, the Church needs to place a maternal arm around her in comfort and protection, offering a shoulder to cry on and guidance which speaks of the holiness but also of the compassion of Father God. This is an area which holds fear and misunderstanding for many women, especially because 'maleness' has traditionally engulfed our understanding of God to the detriment of knowing both his masculinity and his femininity. The depth of women's rage and fear about sexuality and its relation to power and pain is real, even when with reference to lesbians' simplistic or self-righteous discussions. It is the loving tenderness and strength of a parental Church which is called for in order to bring healing, without giving licence for patronisation or over-protection.

Appendix

God's attitude to homosexual practice	*God's offer of grace to the homosexually tempted*
Gen 19, especially verse 5	Jn 6:37
Judg 19, especially verse 22	Jn 8:32
Lev 18:22	1 Jn 1:7–9
Lev 20:13	Pet 5:6–10
Deut 22:13	1 Cor 6:9–11
Rom 1:26–27	1Cor 10:13
1 Tim 1:8–10	2 Cor 5:14–21
Jude verse 7	Jude verses 24–25

Questions for discussion

1. How do I respond if my spouse shares that he/she has homosexual tendancies or is in fact leading an active 'double life'?
2. How do I respond to a friend or family member in the circumstances of Question 1?
3. Given that a lesbian has committed herself to a church's care, how far should we go before loving–watchfulness turns into mistrusting patronisation?
4. How do I respond to someone who believes God created them to be gay?
5. If someone declares themselves gay is it their right to be sexually expressive in that lifestyle?
6. Jesus does not speak directly for or against homosexuality or lesbianism. What can we draw, indirectly, from how he responds to relationships and how can we apply it?
7. Do you think there will be gays in heaven?
8. Should lesbians be treated differently from male homosexuals?
9. Is the 'Gay Christian Movement' Christian?
10. Should 'cutting off from the fellowship' be brought into

use for a non-repentant lesbian or homosexual in the church?

11. What are the practical implications for a church fellowship caring for a lesbian or homosexual in the church? (One who seeks change, that is).

Bibliography

Alex Davidson, *The Return of Love* (IVP 1970).
Lovelace, Richard, *Homosexuality and the Church* (The Lamp Press 1979).
McClung, Floyd, *The Father Heart of God* (Kingsway Eastbourne).
Moberly, Elizabeth R, *Homosexuality: A New Christian Ethic* (James Clarke 1983).
Payne, Leanne, *The Broken Image* (Crossway Books 1981); *Crisis In Masculinity* (Crossway Books 1985).
Philpott, Kent, *The Third Sex?* (Logos International 1977); *The Gay Theology* (Logos International 1977).
Storkey, Elaine, *What's Right With Feminism?* (SPCK 1985).
Worthen, Frank, *Steps Out Of Homosexuality* (Love In Action 1984).

Roger Hurding

Roger Hurding is well known to thousands for his Christian counselling ministry. He is Author of *Restoring the Image; As Trees Walking* and *Roots and Shoots*. For many years he has battled with diabetes, which forced him to give up his career as a family doctor and later blinded him in both eyes. Although he is partially recovered, Undulant Fever has kept him familiar with the problems of suffering. It is both appropriate and a privilege therefore that he writes the concluding chapter.

17. Restoring the Image – Is Wholeness Possible?

Roger F Hurding

Recently I attended a major conference on pastoral theology, where I was part of a workshop on 'Feminism and Spirituality'. There had clearly been some difficulty in grouping the participants, for the group I joined comprised twelve women and myself – the 'statutory' male! The General Synod of the Church of England had just voted its disapproval of allowing ordained women from overseas to celebrate Communion in this country – and we shared a feeling of acute frustration. For the first third of the session I listened while my sisters in Christ expressed anger, disappointment and hopeful reflection. A Methodist minister present described her sadness over a recent service during which the cup she offered at the Communion rail was refused; one young Anglican felt she wanted to 'take an axe to the establishment'; a third, from a Presbyterian background, declared that 52% of her felt like staying in the Church and 48% was for leaving. The threads of commitment to corporate Christianity were wearing thin.

In the time one of the group looked across at me and asked, 'What do you think of what we've been saying?' I felt like a privileged 'fly on the wall' suddenly asked to explain itself. I said that I too was experiencing anger at the Church's sexist attitudes, but that that anger was mixed with concern at the polarisation which exists within the debate on feminism. I conceded the appropriateness of righteous anger against centuries of intransigence, but expressed a longing to move beyond the in-fighting to recapture our collective calling as men and women serving as God's image-bearers. I recalled the statement of Genesis 1:27, 'So God created humankind in his own image, in the image of God he created him; *male and female he created them*', and voiced our need to rediscover that we belong to one another in our maleness and femaleness as we seek wholeness and the restoring of the divine image.

Is that wholeness possible? Before looking at some key aspects of wholeness in relation to our common humanity, let us consider what it means to be created in God's image.

The image of God

Throughout Church history, biblical scholars and theologians have wrestled with the meaning of the phrase, *imago Dei*. Many have seen certain facets of our createdness as the hallmark of image-bearing: the soul; our power of reasoning; our righteous state before the Fall; the reality of personality; stewardship over the created order.[1] In recent years, though, theological reflection has tended to argue that 'the image' relates to the whole of human existence: spiritual, psychological, emotional, rational, volitional, aesthetic, physical, social.[2] David Clines picks up this emphasis when he quotes W D Stacey: 'The Hebrew did not see man as a combination of contrasted elements, but as a unity that might be seen under a number of different aspects. Behind each aspect was the whole personality'.[3]

We can view our creation as image-bearers under three headings:

1. We are God's representatives

It can be argued that the phrase, '*in* the image of God' is best understood by the words, '*as* the image of God'[4]: women and men have been made *as* his image, as his representatives to rule over the rest of Creation.[5] Perhaps the clearest comparison to this call for humanity 'to act on behalf of' the Creator is found within the dated concept of colonialism, where a viceroy would be appointed to govern a people for a king or queen. Modern life abounds in less exalted examples of representation: an ambassador who seeks to further a nation's interests in a foreign capital; an MP who is voted to carry a constituency's views into Parliament; an archbishop's envoy who acts on behalf of the Church in errands of mercy. Each represents another person or body in his or her respective sphere of service. We are designated to the loftier task of representing the Lord of glory amidst his created order.

2. We are God's representations

However, we are not solely representatives made in an arbitrary fashion by an Absentee Landlord simply to look after the premises while he is away. Who we are is as important as what we do: our essence, as well as our function, is integral to our image-bearing. This twin perspective is suggested in Genesis 1:26: 'Then God said, "Let us make humankind in our image, in our likeness . . . " ' Any distinction between 'image' and 'likeness' is, so Henri Blocher suggests, a matter of emphasis. The word 'image' (*selem*) is frequently used of a statue or an idol made 'according to' the original, whereas 'likeness' (*demut*) points to the similarity of that original.[6]

These closely connected concepts indicate that we are 'representations' of God as well as representatives. We can draw analogies from a number of aspects of human existence. The ancient Greeks, in particular, believed that a piece of sculpture shared in the reality of what it figured: it was a representation, carrying something of the essence of whatever, or whomever, it portrayed. At a simpler level, we see this representational element in the effigy of a head on a coin or stamp, bearing a likeness to the monarch or head of state. More elaborately, we have the same principle in many works of art where, for instance, a painting by Rembrandt of Christ and the moneylenders seeks some representation of the original scene. Likewise in modern technology, where, for example, the image on the television screen evokes, say, some glorious bird of paradise in an Indonesian rain forest or the spectacle of a colourful opera.

As Clines has written: 'A representative may have little or nothing in common with the one he represents, but a representation resembles the original, and re-presents its original.'[7] We may fail in our duty as faithful stewards of the created order but we cannot sidestep the fact that we 'resemble the original', that we are created after the 'likeness' of the Godhead.

3. We are God's relations

Since we are not only representatives but representations, made in God's likeness, we are also called into relationship with him and, thereby, with one another. The theologian H D McDonald declares that, in fact, all facets of God's image are summed up in this personal relatedness, in which we are sons and daughters of the Creator. He points out that Adam is called 'son of God' in Luke 3:38 and then seeks to show the links between our image-bearing and Christ the true Son of the father. He writes: 'When therefore it is said that God created humankind in his own image we must, in the light of the New Testament, see this as the image of his Son. Even at the Creation, Christ as eternal Son with whom the Father was well-pleased was the image in which God created man'.[8]

Being made as the image of God – the trinitarian God whose love is ever reaching out, both within the Godhead and towards his Creation – we too are bidden to love and relate. As sons and daughters, our call is both Godward and towards one another.[9] This twofold dimension is encapsulated in the phrase already quoted from Genesis 1:27: 'in the image of God he created him; male and female he created them'. Here is something vital for us all. Our 'being in the image of God' incorporates our capacity, and need, to be in relationship with others – and this relating both acknowledges and is drawn by sexual differentiation. In this verse we see implied the distinction between maleness and femaleness and, at the same time, the common humanity of women and men: 'he created *them*'.[10]

Trouble with the image

It is as we consider Christ as the image of God and McDonald's contention that we have been created after *his* likeness that we are reminded forcibly of our 'trouble with the image'.

Mark Twain, in his inimitable way, points to that 'trouble' when he writes: 'Man is the creature made at the end of a week's work when God was tired.' The biblical view on the distorted image is not, of course, that the production of humankind was a botch job carried out by an exhausted Creator! It is rather that the making of men and women as the very peak of Creation (described in Genesis 1:31 as 'very good') has been marred by humanity's bid for independence. Our filial relationships with the Lord God have been abused and forfeited, and our sense of oneness with the Father has been fragmented.

This loss of wholeness is seen in every human relationship – not only with God, but with one another, within the self and with the created order. In terms of the theme of this book we note the corrupting influence of disintegration in the relating of women and men. The birth of sexism can be observed in the Lord God's declaration to Eve: 'Your desire will be for your husband, and he will rule over you' (Gen 3:16). Here we find the seeds of female servility and male dominance: bondage and bullying are the ugly by-products of life without God. There are many variations on this 'battle of the sexes'. Sometimes the harmony and equality between men and women is disrupted by an opposite power struggle, marked by female aggression and male passivity. Picasso, for example, reflecting on his own turbulent love-life, depicts this conflict in writhing female forms whose sharp teeth pose a threat to any would-be male conqueror.

We see another aspect of the undoing of God's original plan for men and women, in their sexual behaviour. The patterns of homosexuality that mark many of our lives mar the heterosexual companionship which God intended. Most of us experience a blend of attraction towards both the sexes – and this may be viewed, at its best, as a mirror of the God-given need we all have for friendship with women and men alike. However, as with the sinful misdirections of the hetero-sexual drive, leanings towards closeness with the same sex can become a consuming passion where, in this case, the forbidden fruit of homosexual 'genital sex' is yielded to.[11] The agonising dilemma of sexual frustration with which many non-practising homosexuals battle does, in two important respects, exceed the parallel conflicts for the Christian single person who is primarily heterosexual: the homosexually inclined is both socially ostracised and never has the prospect, within God's Law, of marital union with the object of his or her desire. The tragedy here, of course, is that whether the orientation is primarily towards the same sex or the opposite sex, many have narrowed down their view of sexuality so as to encompass solely their genitality. The God-given perspective that genital sex is not fundamental to wholeness has often been lost.

Restoring the image

Camus once wrote: 'He who despairs over an event is a coward, but he who holds hope for the human condition is a fool.' The Bible, of course, runs counter to this existential nihilism: there *is* hope for the human condition, and that hope is in Christ. The filial, brotherly and sisterly relationships, lost through human rebellion, can be recovered. The New Testament is rich with illustrations, analogies and symbols which depict this restitution. The choice of text is bewildering, but one of the clearest statements is found in Ephesians 2:8–10: '. . . it is by grace that you have been saved, through faith; not by anything of your own, but by a gift from God; not by anything that you have done, so that nobody can claim the credit. *We are God's work of art*, created in Christ Jesus to live the good life as from the beginning he had meant us to live it.' This translation in the Jerusalem Bible is particularly graphic. Through faith in Christ and his finished work of redemption we receive the precious gift of restoration. Once more we can rejoice as sons and daughters of the Father, living 'the good life as from the beginning he had meant us to live it'. Here there is a new creation in which you and I are described as 'God's work of art'.[12] The expression is evocative. God makes of his people, as it were, a masterpiece of sculpture or painting. The original glory is restored by painstaking attention to detail. The grime of misuse and neglect is washed away; the overlay of shabbier attempts at improvement is removed; cracked paint is renewed and the full splendour of tone, colour and movement recovered.

This 'restoring of the image' is modelled on Christ who is 'the image of the invisible God' (Col 1:15). God fashions the Church, his 'work of art', in the likeness of his Son, who sits for the picture. As Dick Keyes has written of Jesus: 'He is the image of God in perfect focus.'[13] We see God himself in clearest definition as we centre our attention on Christ. In our analogy of the painting, God is both artist and subject!

This imaging of God by Christ has many layers of significance. As we have seen, in ancient Greek usage an *eikon* (translated in the New Testament as 'image', 'likeness', 'form' or 'appearance') was a statue, painting or figure on a coin which was not only an image but included the essence of the god or person portrayed. For Christ, though, this point is taken to its extreme: he is both the 'image of God' and God himself. This truth is stated boldly in Hebrews 1:3: 'The Son is the radiance of God's glory and the exact representation of his being.' As Otto Flender writes: 'There is no difference here between the image and the essence of the invisible God. In Christ we see God.'[14]

You and I, God's 'work of art', are, in turn, destined 'to be conformed to the likeness of his Son' (Rom 8:29). This transformation has a step-by-step quality in that we are 'changed into his likeness from one degree of glory to another' (2 Cor 3:18, RSV). The progress of the painting is painstaking – and yet the masterpiece *will* be finished. God's new family, sons and daughters linked with one another in fellowship with Jesus Christ, our 'elder brother', will be complete in him since 'we shall be like him, for we shall see him as he is' (1 Jn 3:2).

In the meantime, with this glorious perspective in view, we are being restored in our image-bearing, made more faithful as representatives and representations – all within reconciled relationships with God and others. As Berkouwer has stated: 'It is precisely with the restoration of his communion, his community, with God, that man comes once more to his true self, and no longer threatens either his own humanity or that of his neighbour.[15]

Let us explore now what the humanising influence of the

'restored image' means in terms of our quest for wholeness in Christ, as women and men who belong to God. 'Wholeness' is one of those all-inclusive concepts that is always too big for our minds to grasp. I therefore propose to look at just three aspects of the subject: *wholeness and health*, *wholeness and maturity* and *wholeness and weakness*.

Wholeness and health

Today we might say there is an almost unhealthy preoccupation with health! This century has seen an explosion of interest in wholeness and healing – through the achievements of Western medicine, the rise of psychologies for the 'whole person', the founding of the World Health Organisation following the Second World War, the dialogue between the Church and the medical profession, the increasing interest in holistic forms of alternative medicine and the emergence of the charismatic movement with its later emphases on renewal, 'power evangelism' and 'power healing'. Health is 'an idea whose time has come'.[16]

The word 'health' is from the Old English, giving us 'hale' in northern dialects and 'whole' in the Midlands and south of England. Although we often use the word 'health' as equivalent to 'soundness of body', its original usage indicated well-being in every part of life. This notion fits well with the idea of wholeness that is fundamental to Judaism and Christianity. Bishop Morris Maddocks makes the point in *The Christian Healing Ministry:*

> Man is . . . always in the process of health: he can never cease his effort to obtain that wholeness, even if that attempt is a cessation from activity and a learning from silence and solitude. For man must be still for his health from time to time, as the Psalmist saw. He must be still to know his God and the things that belong to his peace. Otherwise he will never see his health for what it is – a foretaste of that wholeness to come, when the Kingdom is established and creation healed.[17]

What does this large vision of health have to say about women and men living out their lives before God? To begin to answer this, we need an understanding of both our *common humanity* and *distinctiveness*.

1. Common humanity

As we have already noted, being made in God's image has a 'both/and' quality for women and men. Paul Jewett, in his *Man as male and female*, emphasises the linking 'and' in Genesis 1:27: 'male *and* female he created them'.[18] If Genesis chapter 1 had declared 'male *or* female' we would have to conclude the primacy of difference (or even division) between the sexes; whereas, in fact, we learn here that we are bonded by our common humanity – we are *together* called to be God's representatives and representations. And this perspective of our shared humanness and the mutuality of our image-bearing speaks eloquently of the fundamental equality of the sexes.

It is at this point that many feminists have done us all a service by stressing the 'raw material' common to humankind. Simone de Beauvoir, for example, in *The Second Sex* bemoans the way male-dominated society forces women away from this broad view: 'Now, what peculiarly signalises the situation of woman is that she – a free and autonomous being like all human creatures – nevertheless finds herself living in a world where men compel her to assume the state of the Other.'[19] Roger Scruton, in his monumental book, *Sexual Desire*, shows that de Beauvoir's emphasis has its origins in Kantian feminism – a philosophy which sees who we are *as persons* as establishing 'completely and exclusively all [our] claims to be treated with consideration'.[20]

It is where this viewpoint challenges sexism and affirms the essential humanity and thereby equality of women and men that it is nearest to biblical insight. It is when we remind ourselves that human identity is rooted in our Creator God that we can have confidence to allow Christ to break down the walls of suspicion and aggression which often mar relationships between the sexes. This, surely, is the significance of Galatians 3:28: 'There is neither Jew nor Greek, slave nor free, male or female, for you are all one in Christ

Jesus.' Jewett refers to this manifesto of restoration as the 'Magna Carta of Humanity'. He shows how, in this Pauline 'great charter' of liberty, it is not who we are as sexual beings that is erased in Christ but the barrier of prejudice and hostility between men and women:

> It is not sexuality but the immemorial antagonism between the sexes, perhaps the deepest and most subtle of all enmities, that is done away in him. In Christ the man and the woman are redeemed from false stereotypes, stereotypes which inhibit their true relationship. Thus redeemed, they are enabled to become what God intended them to be when he created Man in his image – a fellowship of male and female.[21]

2. Distinctiveness

Just as the phrase, 'male and female he created them' stresses the common bond of our humanity, it also highlights the distinctiveness of the sexes. Henri Blocher underlines the point when he speaks of the Creation accounts in Genesis:

> [They], like the consequences drawn elsewhere by the Bible, show that the neighbour, 'flesh of his flesh', whom God gives to the man *is* a woman; she does not merely add a few feminine attributes to a 'neutral' humanity. As the hormones permeate the body, so femininity permeates the entire person, intelligence, feeling and will.[22]

Similar statements that emphasise differences between women and men have been unpopular amongst many feminists – not least because such differentiation has often been part and parcel of patriarchal attitudes. We see these over-polarised views in dismissive comments like, 'the woman's place is in the home' and, 'trust a woman not to think things through'. Sexist remarks such as these are a travesty of any distinctiveness between men and women that the Bible might indicate, and go way beyond Blocher's discerning remarks.

Yet there are still real difficulties in knowing how to think about this distinctiveness. Those who insist that the essential difference between the sexes is biological – in terms of hormone balance and reproductive capability – are on safe ground. The dilemma comes when there is any attempt to evaluate 'gender' (the concept of maleness and femaleness) which, inevitably, is full of assumptions that depend on social setting and cultural background. Many of us readily question Western presuppositions that lead to stereotypical views of men as aggressive, go-getting, up-front, decisive and logical and women as passive, unambitious, retiring, uncertain and irrational. Such notions bristle with 'exceptions to the rule' and male prejudice. An extensive survey of American attitudes carried out in the early 1970s confirmed the dominance of sex stereotypes, with a bias in favour of 'masculine' traits. Three-quarters of the sample said that men and women differ in over forty aspects of behaviour, and both sexes expressed a preference for ways of acting that were deemed male.[23]

John Nicholson, in his book, *Men and Women: How Different Are They?* explores a wide range of research which seeks to clarify matters of sex and gender. The book makes fascinating reading, as Nicholson unpicks many of the tangled skeins of assumption and bias on the subject of male and female characteristics. He tackles, for instance, the commonly held views that women are weaker, moodier and less intelligent than men, and shows clearly that these generalisations are either false or need heavy qualification.

There is, of course, in any such evaluation the methodological difficulty of unravelling the influence of upbringing and society's expectations from any intrinsic similarities and distinctions between the sexes. With respect to physicality, the obvious biological differences between men and women are supplemented by dissimilarities in size and stature: men are on average 7% taller and 20% heavier than women. Incidentally, there is evidence that taller people are (if you will forgive the pun) more highly regarded. Nicholson points out that Jimmy Carter is the only American president this century who has won his way to the White House against a taller opponent![24]

In spite of the apparent advantage that men have due to their greater physical bulk, it is undeniable that women last longer! An intriguing piece of research carried out on 40,000 monks and nuns – all tee-total non-smokers, free from the stresses of business and family life – established that, by the age of forty-five, the nuns could anticipate living five-and-a-half years longer than the monks.[25]

Those who have observed non-Western cultures see work patterns which raise further questions about physical strength and the sexes. There is evidence that, whereas men are adapted for shorter, intenser bouts of activity, women have greater stamina for regular and more protracted work. Margaret Mead points to this division of labour, for example, amongst the Iatmul people of New Guinea, where men are 'capable of strong output of effort, but demanding long periods of recuperation,' and women are 'better fitted by nature for the routine tasks of everyday life'.[26] However, this contrast is by no means universal and she concludes that 'a survey of five societies shows how arbitrarily the work-rhythms of men and women can be arranged.'[27]

With respect to variations in patterns of labour between the sexes and the longevity of women, the bland statement that men are stronger than women needs to be carefully modified.

Similarly, Nicholson demonstrates that in mood and intellect there is no straightforward male supremacy. The cyclical nature of women's emotions is matched to some extent by the less recognised influence of the male hormone on men's feelings. Further, a woman's tendency to verbalise more readily how she feels can be regarded as advantageous compared with the man's inclination to react to stress by silence – and heart disease![26] With respect to overall intelligence, there is no difference between the sexes, although it could be said that men tend to be better at visual-spatial tasks and women at verbal challenges. However, there is some evidence that these distinctions are culturally conditioned and that the gap between them is being narrowed.[27]

It is here that we might say a little more about homosexuality, for there is a certain inevitability that, where the idea of gender differences is most dismissed, there is a tendency for heterosexual and homosexual genital sex to be seen in a similar light. If all that matters is the personal, as in Kantian feminism, then physical union between the same sexes has an identical validity to love-making between a man and woman. Scruton indicates the importance of dissimilarity between the genders when he writes, albeit tentatively:

> Is there anything in the homosexual act which is the *proper* object of obscene perception? A positive answer to that question must rely, I believe, on the strangeness of the other gender – on the fact that heterosexual arousal is arousal by something through and through other than oneself, and other as *flesh*. In the heterosexual act, it might be said, I move out *from* my body *towards* the other, whose flesh is unknown to me; while in the homosexual act I remain locked within my body, narcissistically contemplating in the other an excitement that is the mirror of my own.[28]

In the long run, we do not help the conflicts of many who have homosexual leanings by explaining away the residual core of male and female attributes. In our search for wholeness and health we all need, I suggest, to hold to both the common humanity that binds women and men together in their image-bearing and the distinctiveness – pared of the overlay of prejudice and generalisation – that makes our mutual enterprise rich in variety.

Wholeness and maturity

There is a scene in Oscar Wilde's *The Importance of Being Earnest* where Jack Worthing announces the death of his brother, Ernest. The governess, Miss Prism, responds judgementally when she hears he died of a 'severe chill'; she exclaims, 'As a man sows, so shall he reap.' The Reverend Canon Chasuble rebukes her with the words, 'Charity, dear Miss Prism, charity! None of us are perfect. I myself am peculiarly susceptible to draughts . . .'[29] One suspects that Chasuble felt he was near-perfect, according to his own way of seeing things. Be his a mistaken view, the quest for perfection seems deeply rooted in human nature. The idea of growth leading to fulfilment, completeness, maturity or wholeness is part of this yearning for perfection.

One of the key New Testament words in this area is *teleios* and its variants meaning 'complete' or 'perfect'. In Paul's writings the word occurs five times and has the sense of 'adult' or 'mature'. The context is usually one of achieving wholeness and maturity in a relationship with Christ. Sometimes the emphasis is on corporate growth, as in Ephesians 4:13: 'until we all reach unity in the faith and in the knowledge of the Son of God and *become mature*, attaining to the whole measure of the fulness of Christ'. Sometimes the stress is on building up the individual, as in Colossians 1:28: 'We proclaim [Christ], admonishing and teaching everyone with all wisdom, so that we may present everyone *perfect* in Christ.'

Studies of emotional maturity have revealed that the higher a person scores on indexes of emotional maturity, the less they tend to emphasise differences between the sexes.

As we consider the practical outworking of our common humanity and distinctiveness as women and men in our growth towards maturity, we can take these same two perspectives: *togetherness* and *separateness*.

1. Togetherness

In the account of the Creation in Genesis chapter 2 we read that the Lord God said: 'It is not good for the man to be alone. I will make a helper suitable for him' (verse 18); or, as the Good News Bible has it: 'I will make a suitable companion to help him.' The Hebrew word translated 'helper' or 'companion' never implies subordination; it indicates, rather, the distinctiveness and equality of a partnership. Indeed, God himself is sometimes described as the 'helper' of those in need.[30]

So, at the heart of the Creation of man and woman we find a call for 'togetherness', a mutual relationship which brings the qualities and characteristics of the one to the other. This companionship is fundamental to the image-bearing of *all* men and women and is not unique to marriage. The more general declarations in Genesis 1:27, 'male and female he created them', and in Genesis 2:18, 'I will make a helper suitable for him', are statements within the Creation accounts that form a background to and preface for the more specific proclamation of marital union in Genesis 2:24, 'and they will become one flesh'.[31]

In our journey towards wholeness, then, we should emphasise the need we have for one another. Friendship and fellowship between men and women, whether single, married, divorced or widowed, are integral to mature living. There are, of course, potential distortions of the enriching nature of such relationships. Married Christians, in particular, have often been nervous about keeping or starting friendships with single people for fear of the 'eternal triangle'. This apprehension is frequently a measure of marital insecurity and needs to be understood. However, both married and single people miss out when the marriage has a 'fortress' mentality. James H Olthuis, in distinguishing between friendship ('a God-given way to be intimate which does not involve physical intercourse') and marriage, makes the same point:

> Once we have distinguished the different structures for marriage and friendship, we no longer need to see the one as a competitor of the other. Relieved of the impossible burden of being forced to fulfil all human desires and needs by itself, each relationship in fact can help and support the other. A married man can be friends with another woman, married or unmarried, provided that they both know that the relationship is friendship and not marriage. Enriched through their friendship, each has more to give to their other relationships.[32]

One of the hallmarks of such friendships is their openness to others. Unlike the excluding nature of the 'in-love' relationship – with, in the context of marriage, its expression in sexual union – friendship enjoys the company of the other in open-endedness and without possessiveness.

Many find a parallel dilemma in their friendships with the same sex. The richness of being with a good companion, whether in some common enterprise or in sharing a flat, can be tainted by the innuendoes of those who suspect genital involvement whenever they see human closeness. C S Lewis pricks the balloon of this poisonous frame of mind when he writes:

> The fact that no positive evidence of homosexuality can be discovered in the behaviour of two friends does not disconcert the wiseacres at all: 'That', they say gravely, 'is just what we should expect'. The very lack of evidence is thus treated as evidence; the absence of smoke proves that the fire is very carefully hidden. Yes – if it exists at all. But we must first prove its existence. Otherwise we are arguing like a man who should say 'If there were an invisible cat in that chair, the chair would look empty; but the chair does look empty; therefore there is an invisible cat in it'.[33]

Let us never be ashamed of our 'togetherness', whether in friendship, family or fellowship. Others may misconstrue, but let us be faithful to the one who calls us his friends, has set us within a wider community and commands us to 'bear one another's burdens'.[34]

2. Separateness

Maturity is being able to be separate and distinct from others as well as to contribute to the interdependence of relationships. The Hebrew word translated 'helper' in Genesis 2:18 means literally 'as opposite him'. This dispels any notion of a mutual cosiness that incorporates a loss of individuality. Women and men need each other and are drawn into companionship, but it is their distinctiveness that provides the magnetism. The title of Robin Skynner's book on family and marital therapy, *One Flesh: Separate Persons*, captures the balance well – at least in the context of marriage.[35] More generally, men and women are called to both togetherness and separateness: there is a mandate for both co-operative and individual growth.

It is here, as always, that we should seek a balance. There are many who so major on the 'separateness' that they move into isolationism. A patient of mine, a postgraduate student in her mid-twenties, told me one day in the surgery that she and her husband had decided to split up after two years of marriage. 'Why?' I asked. 'I thought you were both happy!' 'We were,' she replied, 'but *that* was our problem. Our individuality felt threatened by our being together – and so we decided to go our separate ways.' A year later she was a sad and depressed figure: her husband had found someone else and, as I understand it, the marriage finally broke up. This couple had not been able to resolve the tension within 'one flesh: separate persons'. In opting for separateness they lost their life together.

More fundamentally, there is a stance which cuts off from the opposite sex in an aggressive form of independence. The implication that there is no mutual need is summed up in the feminist axiom: 'A woman without a man is like a fish without a bicycle.'

The true value of separateness is found within the experience of solitude. Here there is a capacity to be alone without feeling lonely. Those who have discovered inner resources of peace and a sense of destiny at the hand of God will be able to ride the storms of misunderstanding, rejection and loss. Even when contact with others is at its most meagre, our identity as a man or a woman is intact – because, to quote Dick Keyes, 'our identity is an identity derived':

> God is not a theological means to a higher psychological end. God is not a means to any other end. God is the Alpha and the Omega, the beginning and the end. Our true identity is found in accepting our status as creatures of this infinite Creator God and in rooting our sense of identity in his. Our identity is an identity derived.[36]

Wholeness and weakness

Throughout our consideration of wholeness and health and wholeness and maturity we have been reminded of a third perspective: wholeness and weakness. We live in 'in-between' times: in times of promise and anticipation of glory ahead, but also times of disappointment and frustration at present realities. Our destiny of completeness – when God's image is fully restored in Christ – can feel elusive within the exigencies of our daily lives. Things are not as we would wish. Many battle with circumstances which are hard to bear, such as acute or chronic illness; long-standing physical or mental handicap; a loss of faculties with ageing; the birth of a deformed child; a persistent tendency to depression or anxiety; thwarted sexual desire; the break-up of a close friendship or marriage; the death of a loved one. The disintegrating influence of sin can further undermine our relationships: friendships that promised well may be betrayed; family life is often more about scoring points off one another than mutual acceptance and care; marriages may break themselves on the rocks of frustrated idealism or selfishness; Christian fellowship may be riven by personality cults and gossip.

Amidst life's stresses of circumstance and folly many become isolated and lonely. Henri Nouwen in his *Reaching Out* echoes the heartache of those who thus face hard questions:

> But what then can we do with our essential aloneness which so often breaks into our consciousness as the experience of a desperate sense of loneliness? What does it mean to say that neither friendship nor love, neither marriage nor community can take that loneliness away? Sometimes illusions are more livable than realities, and why not follow our desire to cry out in loneliness and search for someone whom we can embrace and in whose arms our tense body and mind can find a moment of deep rest and enjoy the momentary experience of being understood and accepted?[37]

Nouwen does not sidestep the anguish but points to a way forward: 'the conversion from loneliness to solitude' – and it is in Christ that you and I can find the wholeness of solitude invading the weakness of our loneliness. Jesus, in facing his coming trials, anticipated extreme isolation. He said to his friends, 'a time is coming, and has come, when you will be scattered, each to his own home. You will leave me all alone' (Jn 16:32). And yet, at that stage, that aloneness was solitude rather than loneliness for he added, 'Yet I am not alone, for my Father is with me.' It was later, on the

Cross, that ultimate desertion was experienced when even the Father turned away, while the Son carried the darkness of our sin. We can truly say that Christ knew the extremity of dereliction in order that you and I, women and men on the road home to glory, might never journey alone.

Questions for discussion

1. If being 'in God's image' is primarily about relating to God and others, what does 'restoring the image' mean for you in your daily relationships?
2. List what you consider to be male and female characteristics. Which do you see as culturally conditioned and which as intrinsic? Pool lists.
3. What does our call to 'togetherness' and 'separateness' mean for you, as a group and individually? You may like to share your thinking in the contexts of friendship, family and Christian fellowship.
4. What differences do you see between the ideas of loneliness and solitude? Some, within the group, might like to share an experience of either loneliness or solitude. How can we progress from loneliness to solitude?

References

1. See, for example, H D McDonald, *The Christian View of Man* (London, Marshall Morgan & Scott, 1981), pp. 34–41.
2. As in David Clines' 'A Biblical View of Man', *The Christian Brethren Research Fellowship Journal* 28 (1976), pp. 9–38; see also G C Berkouwer, *Man: the Image of God* (Grand Rapids, Eerdmans, 1962), p. 77.
3. Clines, p. 10.
4. Henri Blocher, *In the Beginning: the opening chapters of Genesis* (Leicester, IVP, 1984), p. 85.
5. See Genesis 1:26; Psalm 8:4–8.
6. Blocher, pp. 84–85.
7. Clines, p. 24.
8. McDonald, p. 41; see also Blocher, pp. 89–90.

9. This twofold call to love is seen in Jesus' summary of the Law in Luke 10:27.
10 Karl Barth was the first major theologian to argue that our fellowship as male and female is the essence of being in God's image. See the discussion on Barthian theology in Paul K Jewett, *Man as male and female: a study in sexual relationships from a theological point of view* (Grand Rapids, Eerdmans, 1975), pp. 43–48, 69–86. See also the criticism of Barth in Blocher, p. 81.
11. See the prohibitions of homosexual *practice* in Genesis 19:7; Leviticus 18:22, 20:13; Judges 19:23; Romans 1:26,27; 1 Corinthians 6:9,10; 1 Timothy 1:8–11; Jude 7. For a discussion of these verses, see Richard Winter, 'Homosexuality' in Bernard Palmer (ed.), *Medicine and the Bible* (Exeter, The Paternoster Press/CMF, 1986), pp. 152–157.
12. Here the Greek word is *poiema*, meaning 'what is made, a work or creation'. I am grateful to Sheila Stevens of Lee Abbey for first drawing my attention to the Jerusalem Bible's translation 'God's work of art' and its rich imagery.
13. Dick Keyes, *Beyond Identity: finding yourself in the image and character of God* (London, Hodder & Stoughton, 1986), p. 109.
14. Otto Flender in Colin Brown (ed.), *Dictionary of New Testament Theology*, Vol. 2 (Exeter, Paternoster, 1976), p. 288.
15. Berkouwer, p. 100.
16. For a fuller treatment of 'Wholeness and Health' see Roger F Hurding, 'Healing' in Palmer (ed.), pp. 191–216.
17. Morris Maddocks, *The Christian Healing Ministry* (London, SPCK, 1981), p. 7.
18. Jewett, pp. 37–38.
19. Simone de Beauvoir, *The Second Sex* (Harmondsworth, Penguin, 1953), p. 29, quoted in Roger Scruton, *Sexual Desire: a philosophical investigation* (London, Weidenfeld & Nicolson, 1986), p. 408.
20. Scruton, p. 258.
21. Jewett, p. 143.

22. Blocher, pp. 100–101.
23. John Nicholson, *Men and Women: how different are they?* (Oxford, Oxford University Press, 1984), p. 7.
24. Ibid., p. 44.
25. Ibid., p. 47.
26. Margaret Mead, *Male and Female* (Harmondsworth, Penguin, 1962), p. 168.
27. Ibid., p. 169.
28. Nicholson, pp. 66–71.
29. Ibid., pp. 75–79.
30. Scruton, p. 310.
31. Oscar Wilde, 'The Importance of Being Earnest' in *Plays: Oscar Wilde* (Harmondsworth, Penguin, 1954), p. 280.
32. See, for example, Exodus 18:4; Deuteronomy 33:29; Psalm 33:20; 146:5.
33. Humanity is seen as made in God's image even after the Fall; see Genesis 9:6 and James 3:9. For a discussion of this point, see Roger F Hurding, *Roots and Shoots: a guide to counselling and psychotherapy* (London, Hodder & Stoughton, 1986), p. 251.
34. James H Olthuis, *I Pledge You My Troth: a Christian view of marriage, family, friendship* (New York, Harper & Row, 1975), pp. 114–115.
35. C S Lewis, *The Four Loves* (London, Collins/Fontana, 1963), p. 58.
36. See, for example, John 15:15; Ephesians 3:15; Galatians 6:2.
37. Robin Skynner, *One Flesh: Separate Persons: principles of family and marital psychotherapy* (London, Constable, 1976).
38. Keyes, p. 76.
39. Henri J M Nouwen, *Reaching Out: the three movements of the spiritual life* (London, Collins/Fount, 1980), p. 35.

Bibliography

Atkinson, D J, *Homosexuals in the Christian Fellowship* (Latimer House, Oxford, 1979).

Baker Miller, Jean, *Toward a New Psychology of Women* (Penguin, Harmondsworth, 1978).
Berkouwer, G C, *Man: the Image of God* (Eerdmans, Grand Rapids, 1962).
Blocher, Henri, *In the Beginning: the opening chapters of Genesis* (IVP, Leicester, 1984).
Clines, David, 'A Biblical View of Man', *The Christian Brethren Research Fellowship Journal* 28 (1976), pp. 9–38.
Eichenbaum, Luise and Orbach, Susie, *Understanding Women* (Penguin, Harmondsworth, 1983).
Hurding, Roger F, *Restoring the Image: an introduction to Christian caring and counselling* (The Paternoster Press, Exeter, 1980).
Hurding, Roger F, *Roots and Shoots: a guide to counselling and psychotherapy* (Hodder & Stoughton, London, 1986).
Jewett, Paul K, *Man as male and female: a study in sexual relationships from a theological point of view* (Eerdmans, Grand Rapids, 1975).
Keyes, Dick, *Beyond Identity: finding yourself in the image and character of God* (Hodder & Stoughton, London, 1986).
Kraft, William F, *Sexual Dimensions of the Celibate Life* (Gill & MacMillan, Dublin, 1979).
Lewis, C S, *The Four Loves* (Collins/Fontana, London, 1963).
McDonald, H D, *The Christian View of Man* (Marshall Morgan & Scott, London, 1981).
Mead, Margaret, *Male and Female* (Penguin, Harmondsworth, 1962).
Nicholson, John, *Men and Women: how different are they?* (Oxford University Press, Oxford, 1984).
Nouwen, Henri J M, *Reaching Out: the three movements of the spiritual life* (Collins/Fount, London, 1980).
Olthuis, James H, *I Pledge You My Troth: a Christian view of marriage, family, friendship* (Harper & Row, New York, 1975).
Scruton, Roger, *Sexual Desire: a philosophical investigation* (Weidenfeld & Nicolson, London, 1986).
Smedes, Lewis, *Sex in the Real World* (Lion, Tring, 1979).
Storkey, Elaine, *What's Right with Feminism* (SPCK/Third Way, London, 1985).

Tournier, Paul, *The Gift of Feeling* (SCM Press, London, 1981).
Vanier, Jean, *Man and Woman He Made Them* (Darton, Longman & Todd, London, 1985).